"Liberty is an acknowledgment of faith in God and His works."

~ Frederic Bastiat ~

IN CONGRESS, July 4, 1776.

The unanimous Declaration of the thirteen united States of America:
When in the Course of human events, it becomes necessary for one people to dissolve the political bands which have connected them with another, and to assume among the powers of the earth, the separate and equal station to which the Laws of Nature and of Nature's God entitle them, a decent respect to the opinions of mankind requires that they should declare the causes which impel them to the separation.

We hold these truths to be self-evident, that all men are created equal,

that they are endowed by their Creator with certain unalienable Rights,

that among these are Life, Liberty and the pursuit of Happiness.--That to

secure these rights, Governments are instituted among Men, deriving their

just powers from the consent of the governed, --That whenever any Form of

Government becomes destructive of these ends, it is the Right of the

People to alter or to abolish it, and to institute new Government, laying

its foundation on such principles and organizing its powers in such form,

as to them shall seem most likely to affect their Safety and Happiness.

Prudence, indeed, will dictate that Governments long established should

not be changed for light and transient causes; and accordingly all

experience hath shewn, that mankind are more disposed to suffer, while

evils are sufferable, than to right themselves by abolishing the forms to

which they are accustomed. But when a long train of abuses and

usurpations, pursuing invariably the same Object evinces a design to

reduce them under absolute Despotism, it is their right, it is their duty,

to throw off such Government, and to provide new Guards for their future

security…

…And thus was placed the keystone of a bridge from old to new,
from tyranny to autonomy and from oppression to opportunity. A
bridge leading to, not simply a new country, but a new social

compact, unique in the history of mankind. Rarely have so few words initiated a reformation of such import…words brilliant in their simplicity, blinding in their clarity, and radical in their Conservatism. Coupled with the Constitution, a roadmap had been created to navigate towards a form of government that instilled in 'we, the people' the power to seek the destiny of our natural longings for freedom and self-determination. For the first time in human history, order and liberty had conceived a synergetic balance. The wisdom contained in 'The Declaration of Independence,' a simple proclamation of definitive truths, proved to be the critical element designing the formation and maintaining the growth of this new social structure, a structure to be supported by the appropriate cultural, governmental and economic pillars that hold up every society. What of the structure's foundation, then? Without the proper foundation, this new tower of freedom would crumble under its own weight, no matter how well it was engineered. The edifice that is America was constructed with a foundation that is essential for the underpinning of any human endeavor - God, the Creator. As a fledgling country, we did not just acknowledge the Creator, nor did we simply grant Him a supporting role, but we knew absolutely that He is the sole reason for our existence and the sole origin of our unalienable rights that cannot, by definition, be granted or revoked by any earthly being or institution. The integration of the Divine into every aspect of our new government was, for its founding, by design; and, for its success, by necessity. "Freedom requires virtue, which requires faith, which requires freedom" (Os Guinness; *The Golden Triangle of Freedom*).

The ensuing years in our nation's early history were marked, for the most part, by a strict adherence to the founding principles of our nation. A faithful reliance on Providence and an enduring consecration of our country to God became the beacons that guided our course as a young nation. George Washington acknowledged as much in observing, "…it is the duty of all nations to acknowledge the providence of Almighty God, to obey His will, to be grateful for His benefits, and humbly to implore His protection and favor." (Thanksgiving Proclamation; Massachusetts Centinal; Oct 14, 1789). Benjamin Rush, a signer of the Declaration of Independence, concurred with virtually all of his contemporaries when stating, "The only foundation for a republic is to be laid in Religion. Without this there can be no virtue, and without virtue there can be no liberty and liberty is the object and life of all republican governments" (On the Mode of Education Proper in a Republic, 1806). There are numerous other quotes attributable to our founding fathers, and others in government from the early years of our nation's existence, that subscribe to the idea of an America imbued with Judeo-Christian convictions affecting virtually every aspect of the cultural, political and economic order. In 1782, the Congress of the United States approved the Bible for use in all schools. 'In God We Trust' was added to all coinage in 1864. From the halls of Congress, to the halls of Justice, to the town halls, county seats, state capitols, schools and businesses of all kinds - religion, no, God Himself, was intrinsically woven into the fabric of America. While decrying the obvious dangers of a state sanctioned religion, our founders were nonetheless staunch advocates of a government and society girded by religious morality…not by force, not by law, but by a rational, reasoned understanding of absolute truths. They knew that 'unalienable rights,' divorced from God, were hollow and devoid of persistence. The founders were under no misconception that reliance on all things Providential would be some type of magic elixir that would preclude any failure, defeat, or mistake, whether by the individual or by the state. They were assured, however, by faith, that placing our future in the hands of God, and consecrating that future with a commitment to steadfast virtue, would create and maintain a people of long endurance in freedom and liberty. Considering the inherent flaws of human nature, the success of the American experiment became nothing short of extraordinary.

The declarative consecration of America to God and the embrace of Judeo-Christian ethics would produce results over the next decades unimagined by any other nation in the history of mankind. Law and order, personal responsibility, self-reliance, and limited government became the engines of extraordinary growth. A deep-seated morality was the modulator that kept the engines working in proper order and with a focused outcome: the ascension of the individual to new heights by optimizing humanity's best nature. As the individual progressed, so did the whole of society, and America quickly became a trove of hope and a shore of opportunity for many who yearned to improve themselves: their lives, their material comforts, and their standard of living, yes; but also the virtuous and moral nature within.

To any rational mind, then, it would be pure folly to remove, or trivialize the importance of, the clearly defined foundation of our country. At our own peril do we excise the Creator from what He has created. Yet, that is actually the course of action we have undertaken. We have not just forgotten God, nor merely diminished Him, nor even simply denied Him. We have despised Him. We have forsaken His perfect mercy, and in so doing, tempted His perfect justice. We have exiled Him from virtually every aspect of our society: schools, military, places of business, government buildings, and courthouses. We have rebelled against Him even in our churches, where His laws and commandments are often rewritten or ignored as the expansive disease of moral relativism has infected all things religious with the poison of secularism. Just as with the nation of Judah, as depicted in the Book of Chronicles of the Old Testament, we have made an enemy of our own God.

Why? Why would a people, any people, turn their backs on their own God, the bedrock of their nation and the origin of their fundamental rights, the Being who created them, loved them, and redeemed them? Such irrational behavior can only be traced to one of two origins. Either we, as a society, have gone collectively insane, or we have made a choice, albeit subconsciously, to embrace the opposite of goodness, the opposite of truth, the opposite of God: the devil himself - Satan - an actual being. Just as all things good and sacred find their being in God, all things evil and profane find their being in the devil. He has done a marvelous and thorough job in convincing most of us that he does not really exist. We no longer mention him in our 'intellectual' society for fear of scoff and ridicule from the enlightened elite. Our churches rarely mention him, out of the same fear. One can assume that many of those who yet profess a belief in God would, in the same breath, pass off the devil as a myth, a fabrication of our religious heritage. The devil is just fine with this perceived non-existence as he finds it much easier to pierce our defenses to evil and reside anonymously within our souls. As confounding as it is to sanity, we have replaced our allegiance to God with an abhorrent alliance with the devil, whom we have convinced ourselves does not really exist.

Yet, we affect astonishment as we survey the cultural landscape and see that our country is falling apart. By virtually every conceivable measurement, from every angle, and through even the most optimistic lens, the main pillars of our society are corroding from within. Culturally, politically and economically, our ethos is infested with evil. Incrementally, especially over the past half-century, the decay has been spreading. The columns and beams of civic virtue, principled government and economic convention are swaying and buckling under the immense weight of humanity's worst nature. The endless quest for temporal pleasures has replaced our desire for heaven while the hedonism of modern vices preclude our fear of hell. We have willfully banished God from our culture. Evil has emphatically filled the void.

American culture has changed so drastically in such a short period of time that we really are, compared to just fifty short years ago, a country with a completely different value system. In many instances, today's values are the polar opposite of what they were just two generations ago. Hard work and self-determination have been replaced by entitlement and 'village' dictate. The institution of marriage and the traditional family, having been the cornerstone of society for thousands of years, have been attacked, dismantled, and redefined. The entertainment industry, advertising and music, once wholesome and rich in values, are now nothing more than outlets for pornography and violence, all under the banner of 'freedom of speech.' When a culture values and defends the free expression of pornography and violence over the free expression of religion, the end is nigh. To many, animal rights (not to mention 'personhood rights' being projected upon inanimate objects such as rivers, oceans, and plants) are more sacred than the rights of the unborn. We demand the demolition of memorials to the 'Ten Commandments' while defending the erection of satanic statues. The education system, previously the envy of the world, now produces mostly dreadful results and is nothing but Marxist, social engineering via propaganda and behavior control…merely a seminary for the Progressive religion. Substance has been defeated by style; character, by victimization; responsibilities, by rights; and work, by welfare. Though examples of decency do exist throughout our culture, they have now become anachronistic. We have gradually morphed into a depraved and offensive people, turning our society, as a whole, into a cesspool of Sodom and Gomorrah proportions. "Remember upon the conduct of each depends the fate of all" (Alexander the Great).

The debasement of governance in America began much earlier than that of our culture, and, having accumulated over time, there is now a litany of aberrations that are in direct opposition to the intent of our founding. The primary duties of any legitimate government are to secure, for every part and member of society, a defense from outside aggressors; to maintain the integrity of its borders; to legislate remedies, laws, and rules that prevent the dominion of one over another; and to safeguard the individual's natural rights. We have managed to warp that simple intention into the grotesque distortion of a bureaucratic behemoth, which has turned against the people whose welfare it was commissioned to protect. The original governing concept of 'citizen servants' has been replaced by wave after wave of narcissistic politicians with sociopathic tendencies; and a federal government formed solely to defend our liberties, within the parameters of extremely limited and counter-balanced powers, has become nothing more than a leviathan oligarchy that has grossly violated its original charter. The entrenched two-party political system was never intended by the founding fathers, and has become, over time, a cancer on the body politic. The oath taken by every public servant in defense of the Constitution has been slowly dissipated until it has become, at best, meaningless and, at worst, a treasonous lie. Individual rights, as enumerated, have been raped repeatedly with impunity. The same 'long train of abuses' that sparked a revolution two centuries ago has become commonplace once again. Unelected 'czars' and regulatory agencies formulate government policy. The executive branch illegally crafts legislation and ignores other laws that it alone deems inconvenient to its pursuits. The judicial branch legislates from the bench while ignoring the will of the people. Property rights are nullified at the whim of politicians, and enforced by an ever-expanding police state. Warrantless searches are carried out regularly as the government spies on its own citizens. Domestic government agencies, not just homeland security, but also the departments of education and agriculture, among others, now possess a military-capable arsenal of weapons. Notwithstanding some pockets of resistance, the majority of Americans are woefully ignorant of the interior dismantling of the greatest nation on earth. "Single acts of tyranny may be ascribed to the accidental opinion of the day; but a series of oppressions, begun at a distinguished period, and pursued unalterably through every change of ministers (administrators) too plainly proves a deliberate, systemic plan of reducing us to slavery" (Thomas Jefferson; *A Summary View of the Rights of British America*).

From an international perspective, America has unfortunately lost the moral high ground that it rightly possessed during most of its early history. Once a righteous nation, fighting for liberty and promoting good over evil at great personal and national expense, we are now involved in countless, and mostly unworthy, military adventures around the globe that have done little but to perpetuate cycles of violence. War games that serve only the designs and profits of the military-industrial complex; regime change operations that punish those who we tag as 'unfriendly'; fomenting unrest to secure an uninterrupted flow of oil; nation building to install a government favorable to the political establishment - not to mention the secret prisons, the practice of torture, and extra-judicial killings - all are morally reprehensible and have stained this once great nation with the blood of millions of innocent people. We define our excursions into other sovereign nations with such altruistic slogans as 'Operation Enduring Freedom,' 'Operation Bright Star,' and 'Operation New Dawn,' or bring to a boil the patriotic, super-power juices with 'Desert Storm,' 'Operation Urgent Fury,' and 'Operation Infinite Justice,' but our war-faring has recently been more about world control and less about the defense of freedom. American exceptionalism has died as America has become unexceptional.

Cultural and political infection can fester for decades, if not centuries, but both can also self-heal if the majority retains the will and the moral capacity to do so. Political decay can be reversed at the turning of an election cycle; cultural decay, at the turning of a generation. Economic rot, on the other hand, has the capacity to violently decimate any country once it has reached the point of no return. The United States, by any number of measures, has passed that tipping point. We stand at the cliff's edge where the majority of Americans no longer espouses the ideals of sacrifice and hard work, instead relying on the government for nearly every need. The qualities of personal responsibility, accountability and resilience have atrophied from lack of use. Once touted as the land of opportunity, America is now the land of lotteries, lawsuits, entitlements and fraudulent insurance claims. From the perspective of commerce, free market principles, the pistons of our economic engine, are being thwarted by mostly asinine government regulation, strangled by mega-corporations, and held hostage by self-serving unions. Financial institutions, insurance companies, and other monolithic enterprises are now too-big-to-fail, having contracted politically transmitted diseases from bedding down with the government. Their union is one major reason behind the recent 'great' recession, yet the perpetrators emerged from the rubble unscathed, while the individual paid the price for their master's stupidity.

On a macro-economic level, the astronomical debt that we have been gorging ourselves on for decades cannot possibly be repaid. Creating money out of thin air, currency devaluation, government manipulation of financial markets and measurements, the annihilation of the middle class, the hubris of central planning control, and the bastardization of free enterprise, all have set the stage for what will soon become the most catastrophic economic collapse the world has ever known. All of the actors in this epic tragedy are contributing to the economic strangulation of America, each blaming the other for their suicidal recklessness: the greed of the rich versus the sloth of the poor; the mercenary capitalist versus the utopian socialist; the degenerate regulator versus the corrupt banker; and corporate welfare versus social welfare. All parties make the 'entitlement' claim for their piece of the pie. Unfortunately, we do not have the wisdom to see that the entire pie was consumed long ago. 'Payment due' will come soon enough and, when it does, the pain and suffering that ensues will be on a scale that is unfathomable, will bleed across international boundaries, affecting the entire globe, and the likely tangential reactions by governments worldwide will only exacerbate the misery as wars will be waged for the right to stand on top of the ash heap that remains.

We can blame many of our country's woes on our government, and we would be right in that summary judgment. However, what is the government other than the people who have formed it, endured it, and allowed it to contort into the self-serving, maniacal slave master that it has become? Ultimately, it is 'we, the people' who shape the national conscience, and that conscience has been dysfunctional for some time now. We are finding that democratic concepts can be counterproductive when the righteousness of the majority has all but disappeared. The problem is not in the sin, for sin has existed in every age and time, under every form of government, and across all classes of people. The distinction that mars the current age is the concept of sin as enlightenment, as progress. Throughout the history of mankind, sin, whether venial or mortal, whether individual or social, was typically carried out under the cover of darkness. Sin was almost always followed by shame, usually inward remorse for sin that remained unknown to others, or, most definitely, public shame for those sins that became known communally. Shame was once a most productive motivator in preempting sin, as well as an effective vehicle for redemption subsequent to sin. In the current climate of moral relativism, both personal and public contrition are now much maligned, in spite of their innate power to remedy destructive behavior. In our post-religious culture, repentance is neither necessary, productive, nor even possible. Shame has died while sin has been elevated to celebratory levels. There has never been a time when sin has been as enthusiastically honored as it is today by a majority of the populace. When a society reaches into the shadows to embrace sin, and when that sin is welcomed into the light, becomes accepted, then legislated and protected, then declared 'good,' the demise of that society is imminent. "Woe to those who call evil good and good evil, who put darkness for light and light for darkness" (Isaiah 5:20). The pride we carry in our national sins will lead to an equally scaled penance. The fruit of Eden is ripe once again, and as we continue our ravenous consumption from the tree of good and evil, despising God, and befriending Satan, we will find ourselves, once again, naked.

As the pillars of culture, government, and economy continue to erode, where does one find the hope to persevere amid these pessimistic realities? We find hope in the same place it has always been - in the foundation of this great country; in the honor of individual and, therefore, societal, morality; in the respect for the natural order that has always defined mankind's existence; in the humble awareness that there is a God, and, yes, that there is a devil. We have so degraded ourselves on every conceivable level that the national body may be damaged beyond repair. Just as the root of our problems, obviously, is moral in nature, so must the solutions, intuitively, be moral, as well. It will, however, take a purging of historic proportions to cleanse our collective anthropology. The outcome of that purification will be entirely up to us. Either we will acknowledge our sin, repent, and rebuild on our original foundation, or our nation, in its current state of self-destruction, will cease to exist. False patriotism aside, even the latter is a desirable alternative to the current unraveling. Nothing in life remains static…it either improves, or degrades. Economies rise, then fall; cultures ascend, then retreat; governments prosper, then implode under their own weight; and nations appear, then vanish. Thus, it has always been, and America is no different. Nationalism, based on the status quo of a people drowning in their own evil, only adds weight and speed to our inevitable demise. It is not the nation of America that needs to be grieved, but the notion of America, grounded in her morality and allegiance to Providence. That notion can only be resurrected in conjunction with a complete re-creation of our first principles and a national repudiation of our disordered culture, our imperious government, and our wanton economy: the prodigal country returning to God.

On American Culture

"The propitious smiles of Heaven can never be expected on a nation that disregards the eternal rules of order and right, which Heaven itself has ordained."

George Washington
Inaugural Address, 1789

Of Wisdom and Knowledge

*Wisdom and knowledge are as the sea and the rock
Both have achieved unparalleled heights of strength and experience
One being fluent, far-reaching and forever renewing
The other, hardened, steadfast and resolute
Pauline or Petrine, singularly infertile
Yet United...*In the Beginning…

Civilization: A Prologue

What are considered to be the greatest civilizations in the history of humanity each took decades, if not centuries, to build. They often borrowed essential and proven elements from preceding civilizations, such as political, educational, economic and legal models, among others. Such models, however, were not the antecedent of reaching their plenary summit. What propelled continual advancement was, first and foremost, their culture. A civilization's culture is what animates its progress or regress, what defines the shape and scope of its polities, and, ultimately, what determines its success or failure. Great civilizations are only limited by the desire to attain new heights, a desire generally fueled by the consummation of wisdom and knowledge, the parentage of morality - the relentless quest for that which is good, for that which is God. Venerable societies fervently seek God at the apex of human existence – our individual consciousness. For one to find 'evidence' of God, one must look no further than within one's own human consciousness. Our ability to reason, to think, to ponder our own existence, to know right from wrong…where does it come from? That which is our soul. It is not the work of physiological processes. It is neither psychological, chemical, nor anthropological. It is our transcendental ability to seek God that so substantiates God's existence. Reason is the voice of God; truth is God's discourse with us; and virtue is our response. The fruit of this symbiotic exchange is the birth of eminent civilization. "But what is liberty without wisdom, and without virtue? It is the greatest of all possible evils; for it is folly, vice, and madness, without tuition or restraint" (Edmund Burke).

There is no greater testament to the benedictions of a God-centered civilization than the total desolation manifested by its outright rejection, or the obvious detriment caused by the progression of its forfeit. Communistic societies, by cultural doctrine, fully deny God, and the sinister aftermath is felt to this day. Many other civilizations developed cultures on a fullness of morality, but as that sense and practice waned, the retreat from the summit was relatively swift. As morality passed, so did the state. History is replete with such repetition, but the warning signs are largely ignored. Immorality has a tendency to feed upon itself, so the regression typically begins slowly, expands exponentially, and, without a reversal, soon turns into a freefall, a plummeting into oblivion. "A general dissolution of principles and manners will more surely overthrow the liberties of America than the whole force of the common enemy. While the people are virtuous they cannot be subdued; but when once they lose their virtue then will be ready to surrender their liberties to the first external or internal invader" (Samuel Adams).

Common Sense

The first sacrifice of a declining culture is common sense. The symmetry of logic and moral certitude is a hallmark of any healthy society. When one is compromised, the other is likewise diminished. When both are undermined, human actions and thought processes, once resolute and automatic, become uncertain and incredulous, to the point of becoming absurd. Without common sense, the concepts of self-reliance, self-control, and individual responsibility are discarded in favor of victimization, social engineering, and a collectivist mentality. Rules and regulations replace natural cognitive reasoning. Words are stripped of their meaning and definitions are forcibly changed, all while common sense becomes uncommon. Warning labels are endemic to modernity, alerting us to obvious consequences otherwise fully comprehended by any five-year old, and directing a hyper-cautious people to mental atrophy. We now require a manual to perform the simplest of tasks. Throughout American culture, common sense is currently confused and lightheaded, no longer sure of itself. In generations past, we could be assured of exactly how common sense would respond to idiocy, when…

…the State of New York is doing away with literacy tests for evaluating the competency of prospective teachers because Black and Latino teachers are scoring too poorly, due to "factors like poverty and the legacy of racism" (Kate Walsh, President, National Council on Teacher Quality).

…amidst nightly riots in Portland, Oregon, the chief prosecutor has declared that he will not pursue charges of disorderly conduct, criminal trespassing, interfering with law enforcement officers, escape in the third degree, harassment, and rioting. He also mandated that a deputy district attorney must review any referred charges of resisting arrest or assaulting a public safety officer, with consideration for the "chaos of a protesting environment." District Attorney Mike Schmidt ironically claimed the unusual move "would lead to a safer community"…

…we need direction to consume a hot cup of coffee, a tutorial on how to properly wash our hands, or a label warning not to put a person into a washing machine…

…a statue of Christopher Columbus in Elizabeth, New Jersey will be replaced by a monument for Marsha P. Johnson (born Malcolm Michaels, Jr.), a drag queen and schizophrenic prostitute who was an instigator of the Stonewall Riots in 1969, and who apparently committed suicide in 1992...

...an advertisement by a state-sponsored lottery promoting gambling is followed by a state department of health advertisement for gambling addiction...

...Female sports programs have been neutered, and the accomplishments of female athletes denied, and in some cases erased, by a warped reimagining of Title IX protections, which now include men who believe they are women competing against women who really are women...

...the simple and straightforward concept of separate bathrooms for men and women incites a culture war...

...during the COVID19 pandemic, individuals were forbidden from getting married, visiting a dying relative in the hospital, attending school, and going to religious services, but abortion mills, marijuana dispensaries, strip clubs and casinos, were all considered essential businesses; and, 'Black Lives Matter' rioters were exempted from any restrictions, even implicitly encouraged to gather in groups of thousands...

...a federal judge has ruled that the city of Laguna Beach, California, must pay Edgar Torres Gutierrez, an illegal immigrant protected under the DACA program (Deferred Action for Childhood Arrivals) and charged with a DUI, a monetary award of nearly $20,000 after he was held in local custody for being in the country illegally...

…a young woman commits suicide while in jail, and her family receives a two million-dollar settlement from the taxpayer, even after the courts found no criminal or civil wrongdoing whatsoever on the part of law enforcement…

…the University of Arizona, through the office of its Vice-Provost of Inclusive Excellence, has released a student guide entitled *Diversity and Inclusiveness in the Classroom* on its college campus, turned day-care center, in which appears the following: "Oops/Ouch: If a student feels hurt or offended by another student's comment, the hurt student can say 'Ouch.' In acknowledgement, the student who made the hurtful comment says 'Oops'"…

…Jesse Jackson, Jr. receives a six-figure income from a workers' compensation claim (paid for by taxpayers) while incarcerated for stealing campaign money, because "the stresses of his job as a US representative" were responsible for his diagnosis of a bi-polar disorder…

…Those who never borrowed huge sums of money to go to college must now pay the debts of those who did…

…The purpose of the decennial census is to count how many American citizens live in the country. Somehow, it is 'racist' and 'Un-American' not to include non-Americans in the count of Americans…

…the raising of children is replaced with behavioral drugs in schools and households across the nation…

…under the *Earned Income Tax Credit* program, many low-income workers receive a 'refund' for taxes never paid on income never earned, averaging $3,000 per household, totaling approximately $75 billion annually…

…gun control advocates completely ignore the fact that nearly all mass shootings occur in 'gun free' zones…

…Roughly 120,000 US citizens each and every year remain on Medicaid after winning millions in the lottery, costing taxpayers $47.5 million per year (Congressional Budget Office, Cost Estimate, March 24, 2016)…

…Carleton University has removed weight scales from their campus gym because the scales are instruments of fat shaming, and may 'trigger' unpleasant feelings…

…'Black Lives Matter' was responsible for much of the domestic terrorism across the country during 2020-2021, yet was nominated for the Nobel Peace Prize…

…the Transortation Security Administration, a law enforcement arm of the Department of Homeland Security, accepts illegal alien arrest warrants as a form of ID to board domestic flights…

Moral Relativism

The demise of common sense is evident throughout our culture, yet has been passed off as simply a humorous, societal oddity. Historically, however, it has often been the harbinger of a nascent crack in the foundation of many past cultures, as it is usually attributed to one of three phenomena. It is either an actual deterioration of the collective intellect, or the machinations of the leader-elite class in order to change behavior, or, worse yet, a precursor to the deliberate reversal of the natural juxtaposition between good and evil. Often, it is all phenomena, in cooperation with each other. Whatever the case, it requires a gullible and vacuous populace possessing a certain amount of moral ambivalence. As the people become more exploitable and less prone to sound reasoning, their moral ambiguities increase by a greater magnitude. As their level of moral uncertainty increases, their ability to distinguish between virtue and iniquity obviously becomes severely limited until it reaches the point where good and evil are interchangeable, and then, reversible. This is the definition of what has become known as moral relativism, a blasphemy slowly suffocating our culture with utter insanity, beginning with the inane, and then methodically progressing to the wicked. As we succumb, we no longer simply shake our head at cultural foolishness – no, we begin to pay homage to profligacy, when:

...free speech is framed as violence when practiced by Conservatives; violence is framed as free speech when practiced by Progressives...

...we have made sodomy legally and socially acceptable yet criminalize the defense of traditional marriage...

...'artistic' impressions such as a cross floating in urine is lauded, but a manger scene in the village square is outlawed...

…Medical research performed on animals is considered atrocious abuse yet the same performed on the human fetus is entirely appropriate…

…Parents in Ohio lose custody of their 17-year old daughter because they do not support her male transition…

…Gender Reveal Parties for unborn babies are categorized as 'violent,' yet the mutilation of those same unborn babies by abortion is considered 'choice'…

…The city of Seattle promotes and provides, at taxpayers' expense, heroin pipes and kits for the rectal injection of meth to drug addicts…

…In some states, 'bridge cards' (used as a vehicle for the disbursement of welfare benefits) can be used at strip clubs and casinos…

…People for the Ethical Treatment of Animals (PETA) has exposed the criminality of the backyard cookout, equating the barbecuing of chicken with the Holocaust…

…a Muslim truck driver refuses to deliver beer, and successfully sues his employer for religious discrimination, but a Christian florist is forced to service a gay wedding...

…a home invader injures himself during the commission of a felony burglary and wins a lawsuit against the homeowner…

…Joseph Matthew Smith, a 23-year-old convicted of molesting two children and accused of the sexual abuse of thirteen others, was released from prison after conveniently 'changing' his gender from male to female (at taxpayer expense). The Iowa Attorney General assured the public that he is no longer a threat because "they now have different hormones." (Des Moines Register; *Convicted of sex crimes as a man, felon no longer deemed threat because of gender change*; January 16, 2020)…

…the State of Maryland, two days after the alleged brutal rape of a 14-year old high school student by two illegal immigrants, introduces legislation to make Maryland a 'sanctuary' state to protect law breaking illegal immigrants from legal action and deportation…

…feminism decries the objectification of women, yet remains silent regarding admitted sibling molestation by feminist icon Lena Dunham, and the sexual gyrations of Miley Cyrus…

…officials with the Delaware Department of Education attempt to pass a regulation that would allow students to determine their own gender and race without parental knowledge…

…the government has the ability to levy fines of up to $250,000 for using the wrong pronoun when addressing the transgender population, a group that constitutes less than 0.3% of the population…

…the cost of transgender sex-reassignment surgery is covered by Medicare and Medicaid in some states but most dental work and eye exams are not…

…the city of Scottsdale, Arizona welcomes the Satanic Temple to offer the invocation prior to a city council meeting…

…the Brooklyn Public Library invites drag queens to children's story time to read from books that embrace gender nonconformity and promote homosexuality…

…a seven-year-old boy can be reprimanded for saying his teacher is "cute," but holding a sexual exploration class in grade school is perfectly fine…

…'free speech' is used as an excuse for vile and pornographic content, but the owner of a private company is forced to resign, and a Fire Chief from Atlanta is fired, simply for expressing their personal disagreement with gay marriage…

…a 15-year old girl is gang raped on *Facebook Live* and forty people actually watched in real time, and not one of them reported it to the police…

…a peaceful protest defending traditional marriage is considered 'hate' speech, but a Black Lives Matter riot, calling for violence against all Conservatives, is protected as a first amendment privilege…

…Tim Tebow is chastised for passionately vocalizing his faith while Bruce Jenner is showered with adulation for denying the indisputable reality of his gender…

… Airbnb, Coca-Cola, PricewaterhouseCoopers, and Procter & Gamble have all demonized the state of Georgia's 2021 election reforms as being persecutory of minorities, yet they are each corporate sponsors of China's 2022 Olympic Games. Yes, that China…the one practicing genocide and live organ harvesting; the one enslaving ethnic minorities in forced-labor camps; and the one murdering approximately one-hundred million of its own citizens over the past seventy years…

Our culture has purged common sense and exalted moral relativism. In so doing, we have begun to mock truth, making each of us the arbiter of right and wrong…hundreds of millions of disparate truths and a horde of individual gods. We have similarly attempted to banish any concept of sin by favoring this more malleable truth, yet the only sin that remains – the violation of individual will, the denial of '*my* truth' – is, ironically, the one sin, the original sin, that leads us back to all the others. Throughout history, it has been this one sin that has plagued the human condition. Nevertheless, we have quietly convinced ourselves that *my* truth is the only truth that matters, and that *absolute* truth has been slain, not even realizing that the argument is self-refuting. If there is no such thing as 'absolute truth,' then we cannot claim, as a coherent argument, that 'there is no absolute truth' is an 'absolute truth.'

Absolute truth has not, and never will be, vanquished. "Truth does not become more true by virtue of the fact that the entire world agrees with it, nor less so even if the whole world disagrees with it" (Maimonides, Jewish philosopher and Rabbinic scholar). Truth is universal, timeless, and can never be modernized, nor can it be subjugated to the shifting winds of our popular culture. We have not slain truth; we have simply abandoned it. Within our denial of truth, evil becomes more agile, infecting thoughts of the human and

cultural psyche previously immune to its twisted arguments.
Rational thought, based on thousands of years of human
experience and an inherent understanding of natural law, has been
replaced with warped reasoning, mass confusion, and a caricatured
redefinition of all that is good. We no longer reside in a rational
world, but in an unconscious asylum. Truth is now synonymous
with hate, and morality with evil. Confusion is the devil's seed, and
he has sown these distractions throughout our culture. Across the
entire spectrum of our human endeavors, behaviors and institutions,
anomalies abound: our concept of rights and responsibilities; the
function of our families; our understanding of human sexuality; the
education of our children; entertainment, media and advertising; our
concept of work and welfare; our personal health; and our respect
for life itself. These distortions are being driven by moral relativism,
as it is swiftly becoming the approved doctrine of an increasingly
secular society. A culture writes its own obituary as it willfully, and
without regret, redefines morality by trading the absolute for the
relative. The relative moralities become so numerous and so
opposing as to be worthless, and from them are conceived the
rationalized immoralities that will undoubtedly mature into the
complete chaos of amorality…the absence of God.

The tragedy of moral relativism in America is perfectly illustrated
by the storied history and the current dissolution of the Boy Scouts
of America. For generations an American icon of all things
absolute, the Boy Scouts have recently been sacrificed on the altar
of incremental secularism. As a microcosm of American culture, the
Boy Scouts epitomized the values of wholesome masculine
character, self-reliance and patriotism, as well as faithfulness to

God, family, and community. Piece by piece, the integrity of the BSA has been splintered by external siege and disowned by internal dereliction. In feckless vanity, the organization has abandoned its identity, its very nature: its masculine nature by allowing female members; its moral nature by allowing homosexual, then transgender, members; and ultimately, it will, in time, yield its godly nature by welcoming self-professed agnostics and atheists…the ultimate objective. The entire charade has never been about gender identity or even gender equality, but about the revolution of a 'theophobic' secularism.   At that point, the transition will be complete and the heritage dismantled. What moral relativism has wrought on the Boy Scouts of America is merely a sampling of the designs that are likewise transforming the entire culture…the legacy undone.

Progressivism vs Conservatism

For nearly two centuries now, but primarily since the social revolution of the 1960's, a major cultural clash has been ongoing between Progressivism and Conservatism, with common sense and moral certitude being the major casualties. Progressivism is the ideological framework that achieved critical mass as a reformist movement in the late 19th / early 20th century and sought to promote social justice, check the power of large corporations, thwart political corruption and incompetence, and advance conservationism. Modern Progressivism then morphed into a parody of itself, however, as it traded social justice for social control; replaced its disdain for large, centralized corporations with allegiance to large, centralized governments; camouflaged political corruption and incompetence under layers and layers of bureaucratic corruption and incompetence; and bartered conservation for militant environmentalism. The neo-Progressivism that began in the 1960's added new chapters to the cultural jaundice of Progressivism, including an outright contempt for conventional morality, a repression of individual sovereignty, and, most telling, the expulsion of God from society. Within that endeavor lies a breathtaking level of foolish conceit, and the results of this absurd vainglory have laid at our feet the culture we now deserve.

When our increasingly Progressive culture formulated the drug 'if it makes you feel good, do it,' we began what has become a regimen of cathartic prescriptions whose sole purpose is to induce a disordered mental state, and whose side effects leave us susceptible to Progressive manipulation. The potion was enhanced with a second drug, a heavy dose of victimization, as a vaccine against any obligation to personal accountability. The third and final drug, 'there is no right or wrong,' that we are each a god unto ourselves, proved the most psychotropic. Alone, the drugs could be counteracted with a decisive, though often painful, injection of maturity. The interaction of all three drugs together, however, has left our culture in a state of catatonic adolescence, from which there appears to be no remedy.

To comprehend the disorder of Progressivism, one must begin with an understanding of the distinctions of Liberalism - both *Classical Liberalism*, whose philosophies have defined the constitution of Western Civilization, and *Modern Liberalism*, whose philosophies are intent on destroying the same. While both are related in some ways, the chasm between the two ideologies is immense. Many historians and political scientists suggest that generic Liberalism, over time, will inevitably collapse upon itself because its vertex of consummate personal freedom simultaneously spawns the elements of its own demise. In other words, unrestricted freedoms, divorced from order, responsibility and morality, will inevitably self-destruct when left to their own devices. As the liberal order disintegrates, it begins to feed upon the very structures and institutions from which it arose, and without a correction, implodes with devastating effect. Thus, the 'liberalism equation': Classical Liberalism minus self-restraint equals Modern Liberalism, and Modern Liberalism minus objective virtue equals Progressivism, or, in essence, individual illiberalism.

Even with a minimal level of introspection, does Progressivism not perceive the folly of its own limitations or the eventual catastrophic results of its own succession? Progressivism has become the antagonist of Classical Liberalism, which advocates for the deism of natural law, unalienable rights and their concomitant responsibilities, and a substantially limited government, while unapologetically defending individual freedoms and self-determination, all of which can only endure within a covenant of moral conviction. Furthermore, paradoxically, Progressivism has trademarked and dogmatized the tenets of Modern Liberalism, which espouses the egoism of unrestrained freedoms, unbridled passions, and man-made rights, each realized through government coercion, and all thriving only under the caprice of moral ambiguity, the philosophical poison of existentialism, and even the outright denial of reality. "Men are qualified for civil liberty in exact proportion to their disposition to put moral chains upon their own appetites" (Edmond Burke). The chains have been abandoned and the appetites have become insatiable. As such, Progressivism implies that the individual can be or do anything that he or she can contrive, not within the boundaries of virtue, but through illusions that can only be validated by the impression of government mandate. The results of this poisoned philosophy only serve to disqualify civil liberty for us all.

The dichotomy is telling. If one can break through the confusion, one comes to the realization that there are two Progressive constants amidst these opposing leftist beliefs: a repulsion of absolute truth, and a veneration of government control, or, when blended, simply a profound denial of God. These constants are not unprecedented, as they have, in one form or another, appeared throughout history, always with disastrous results. The 'good intentions' often referred to when discussing Progressive policies, as they are scrutinized over time, only serve to give cover to the movement's obvious malignancy. As such, one can no longer give the benefit of the doubt to the disingenuous means, masquerading as solicitous aspiration, when the ends are morally destitute and culturally catastrophic. "The road to hell is paved with good intentions" (Henry G. Bohn: *A Hand-book of Proverbs*; 1855). Progressivism is nothing, if not a second bite of Eden's apple.

The writings of Jean Paul Sartre, the 20th century French existentialist, atheist and avowed Marxist, as well as those of Friedrich Nietzsche, the 19th century philosopher, and proponent of nihilism, as well as atheism, reflect the conflicting thought patterns that have evolved into modern day Progressivism. According to Sartre and Nietzsche, every individual is fully free simply by the essence of his or her existence. The concepts of God and objective truth deny this 'evidence' of freedom because they attempt to constrain the individual with moral and religious prohibitions. If, in fact, man is truly free merely because he exists, then God cannot exist (or, per Nietzsche, "God is dead"). What Sartre and Nietzsche, as well as all students of atheism and nihilism, fully understand with corresponding intention, yet will never admit, is that if every individual is free, and each person is essentially his own 'god' and lives by his own 'truth,' then society devolves into nothing but an array of diametric wills that sow unrestrained civil discord, followed by anarchy, and eventually terminate in the fracture of civilization...the penultimate goal of Communism, second only to their postdated lust for ultimate control. If there is no God and no objective truth, then the only recourse to cultural order lies in the hands of those with power. Consequently, this fatal experiment ironically leaves the 'inherently free' individual a mere slave to an oligarchy of temporal gods, and a prisoner of his own human nature.

Progressivism has ingested the worst of its related philosophies and expropriated their most damaging attributes, albeit surreptitiously. Progressivism is Modern Liberalism's ugly fraternal twin, Socialism's brother by incest, and the first seed of Communism's progeny. Communism, even under its more eurythmic redefinition as 'progressive,' is nothing if not the manifestation of cultural, political and economic Satanism…it is pure evil. "When we get ready to take the United States, we will not take it under the label of socialism….We will take the United States under labels we have made very lovable; we will take it under liberalism, under progressivism, under democracy. But take it we will" (Alexander Trachtenburg, Communist Party USA). Progressivism is neither new, nor is it progress; it is simply incremental Communism. Progressivism is the rehashing of consistently failed ideas, infested with mold and reeking of spoilage…propaganda, intimidation, parasitical governance, racial quotas, political censorship, covert persecution, exploitation of tragedy, and a perverted appraisal of evil. Progressivism has risen once again behind the curtains of newly fabricated, illogical definitions of freedom, equity, inclusiveness, diversity and tolerance. A constant rebranding is required to hide its true intent. The labels by which it is known may change, but the ideology remains with the same common denominators: an unintelligible loathing of the nation's founding beliefs, a full embrace of godlessness, and a belittling disdain for the individual – all brought together under an umbrella of unparalleled hypocrisy and contradiction, and recently intensified with the rancor of mob mentality.

In unequivocal hypocrisy, why is it acceptable for a restaurant, or its patrons, to deny service to someone based solely on that person's stated conservative opinions, yet it is the epitome of intolerance and bigotry for a florist shop to decline participation in a gay union? The restaurant, in the act of serving the customer, offers neither approval nor rejection of the person's opinions. The florist, in the mandated act of specifically crafted artistry, is forced to approve. The former is the general denial of a basic commodity that has nothing to do with the beliefs of the customer. The latter is the specific denial of a distinct commodity that expressly affirms agreement with an activity that is contrary to a commonly and deeply held religious conviction. The former is typically accepted by the injured party with civility, the latter with protests, lawsuits and demands of confirmation.

Why are Conservative speakers at college campuses across the country heckled and harassed, yet Progressive speakers widely respected and embraced? The former are regularly met with riots, property damage, and physical threats, the latter with first amendment privilege, inclusivity and appeasement.

Why was Mitt Romney nearly tarred and feathered by the media for stating that 47% of Americans are wholly dependent on the government, while that same media was noticeably silent when Hillary Clinton called all Trump supporters 'deplorable,' 'bigoted,' and 'irredeemable?' The former is true, the latter a prejudiced slander of personalities.

No one demanded that the Watford Football Club rename its 'Sir Elton John' stand after the musician referred to religious people as "hateful lemmings." The vehement backlash against Margaret Court, one of the most successful tennis players in the history of the sport, for stating that "tennis is full of lesbians," however, immediately led to an invective outcry and vitriolic insistence that her name be removed from a tennis stadium in Australia.

Mammoth corporations that are faithful to Progressive dogma can, 'in good conscience,' threaten to abandon an entire community, city, or state, yet a small bed and breakfast is fined out of business for refusing to host (also, 'in good conscience') a gay wedding.

In irrational contradiction, Progressivism has created the depravity that is ravaging the health of our culture, and, simultaneously, desires and proposes to destroy the traditions, social structures and institutions essential to its healing. As our culture smolders in ruin, Progressivism's response is to napalm its dying embers. The Progressive movement despises religion, the concept of religious liberty, and the moral code that it sustains, yet will bend over backwards to defend Islam, in spite of its blatant misogyny and actual persecution of homosexuals. Latter day liberals sanctify the diverse traditions and beliefs of illegal immigrants while scorning the same of lawful citizens. The pacifist loathes the military, yet warrants that transgender individuals be able to serve. The feminist equates the institution of marriage with slavery while vehemently demanding marriage equality for gays and lesbians. The fact is, many contradictory Progressives only defend the women, minorities, immigrants, and alphabet-gendered who share their philosophy. No quarter is given to the 'civil rights' of any member of these groups if those members happen to wear the label 'Conservative.'

The duplicities and incongruities of Progressivism are obvious and, when scrutinized, the reasons behind them are just as apparent. The leftist agenda opportunistically creates, and then commandeers, the divisive cultural issues of the day. "The left wants power because that is essentially their state of grace in their secular religion. They want to run people's lives so they can design utopia for all of us. That's what turns them on—it's the lust for power" (US Attorney General, William Barr). Often, in order to lend an air of moral authority to its designs, and to appeal to those of the Christian tradition, Progressivism will appropriate the otherwise religious virtues of tolerance, freedom, justice, equality and rights, not in deference to their ultimate source and summit, God, but to a more secular superiority, as a means to an end, that ultimately serves its power lust and advances its temporal, cultural and political philosophies. If the essence of God is removed from any virtue, then that virtue is without foundation, and is simply an abstract mimicking of morality, soon to be washed away when it becomes expedient to do so. Furthermore, by infiltrating legitimate social movements, sensationalizing their causes and effects, and then propagating a cult-like psychology among their followers, Progressives achieve the cultural turmoil that furthers their subversive ideology. Progressivism holds no real affinity for Islam, minorities, the LGBT community, feminists or illegal immigrants (other than an appreciation for, and emulation of, their militant tactics used to incite cultural change), but uses them as pawns, the 'useful idiots,' in its quest to marginalize, and eventually vanquish, its true archenemy – America, and the Conservative, Judeo-Christian principles upon which she was founded.

Recognizing and resisting the germination of evil, especially when hidden amongst the synthetic flowering of enlightenment and moral relativism, is the most consequential calling of every great civilization, and is the grade by which its succession is measured. *"Little progress can be made by merely attempting to repress what is evil. Our great hope lies in developing what is good"*…President

Calvin Coolidge. Progressivism holds an asymmetric and distorted vision of what constitutes existent evil, and in some cases, *"represses what is good while developing what is evil."* Many leftist elites have outrageously attempted to equate America's blemishes with the unspeakable abominations of Nazi Germany, which to any rational mind is peak stupidity. Additionally, Communism is never repudiated despite clear evidence of its menace to humanity, yet the free enterprise system, which has improved the lives of an untold number of human beings throughout recent history, is endlessly maligned as wicked. Having a large family is selfish and irresponsible but sacrificing your unborn child is not. Teaching young adults the virtues of purity and self-control is sex shaming while access to pornography is liberating. Guns and other inanimate objects are evil but the people who abuse them are not. ISIS is the new Nazism, and it is widely regarded with the same appeasement and silent conciliation. Carbon emissions, as a metaphysical plague on the earth, are demonized, whereas unbounded human genetic engineering is ignored as an exigent threat to the integrity of every human being. The *Family Research Council,* which has never engaged in any form of violence, is labelled a hate group for its ardent support of traditional marriage, yet *Antifa,* a fascist, 'anti-fascist' group which unapologetically resorts to physical violence and property damage, is saved from any such label. "Violence is not a requirement for being listed as a hate group," at least as so defined by the Southern Poverty Law Center, the self-appointed marshal of a latter-day, secularized scarlet letter. Why are peaceful gatherings by conservatives labelled as hateful, while riotous gatherings by Progressives defended as 'protest'?

The Progressive movement's perverted concept of evil makes one legitimately question its capacity for moral reasoning.

Progressivism, at first, will offer sanctuary to error and then, patiently and without apology, nourish and encourage that error until it becomes accepted, defended and embraced...the normalization of iniquity. Progressivism has thus become the devil's ally - as unwitting dupes for some and willing accomplices for others - and the creed of an alternative, secular religion, and a brand new, populist divinity. The Progressive version of god, assuming a belief that one even exists, is reduced to a deity that is merely a social worker or community organizer; a god of greeting card sentiments; a god of forgiveness without the requisite repentance; a god, not of redemption, but of unconditional acceptance; a god of mercy but not a god of justice. Mercy without truth, without contrition, without penitence, without justice, is nothing but a contrived Progressive placebo, and, yet another tool of cultural subterfuge to undermine the spiritual foundation of America.

Those who advocate for modern Progressivism are little more than useful puppets performing a well-choreographed dance at the behest of those who vehemently disavow the capacity of the individual. The marionettes are controlled by many Progressive strings – suppression of speech, moral relativism, political correctness, sexual license, victimization, wealth redistribution, and smothering bureaucratic control, among many others. The lead wire, however, is divisiveness – and it serves the Progressive agenda well. With head askew, limp on its side, and flaccid limbs performing rote movements, the protagonist of forward progress will always seek to create dissension – child against parent; race against race; age against age; labor against capital; citizen against police; women against men; poor against rich; gay against straight; vaccinated against unvaccinated…endless, fabricated flashpoints with each movement meticulously engineered to maximize upheaval, as though they were plagiarized from the pages of the Marx's *Communist Manifesto,* or *Das Kapital.* If one can convince another that he or she is a victim, a soldier of conviction has been created. If many can be convinced of the same, an entire army has been commissioned to wage a war against a perceived enemy. Organize one group, and then antagonize another. Exploit emotions, foster resentment, foment envy…and the simple-minded will follow in lock step, all while tripping over each other in an intersectional race to the bottom. The consummate objective for the Progressive movement, currently playing out on the ground of the cultural wars, is to merge all disparate leftist agendas into one ultimate offensive to eradicate the current order. By cross-fertilizing various singular ideologies, each relatively impotent on their own, into one organized and vast final solution, the Progressive end game is in sight. Thus, the formerly detached crusades of ascendant group identity - radical feminism, socialism, racism, sexual liberation, communal property, abolition of police, militant environmentalism, and class struggle - all converge, and, interspersed with the adhesive of varied crises, emerge as one…no longer individual quixotic movements, but a leviathan revolution whose obvious ambition is the embrace of chaos, the destabilization of American culture and the destruction of western civilization.

American Conservatism, unlike Progressivism, has never needed a reason for deceptive change, and has never faltered in, or apologized for, its core belief in the God-given power of the moral individual as the requisite element of a truly free society. Pure Conservatism, unshackled by the chains of a mutable and transitory ideology, is the genesis of liberty, the remedy to millennia of individual servility and oppression, and the pabulum of the malnourished human spirit. Conservatism is eternally ancient and perpetually new - an intergenerational compact that holds supreme confidence in the timeless and cherished virtues that have been proven to be the heralds of cultural ascent. Conservatism is a mirror that reflects reverent honor for the values that were created and protected by previous generations, while projecting that same distinction forward for the benefit of generations to come. Conservatism is also mature and self-aware, acknowledging when it has fallen short of its own ideals, and taking seriously the responsibility of correcting course when the need arises. Respect for law and order, personal responsibility and individual accountability, property rights, fiscal prudence, the right to life and liberty, absolute morality, and all other tenets of Conservatism, passed down in whole from the Founding Fathers, have been the driving force behind the individual character traits that have made America the greatest nation in the history of mankind.

By acknowledging and seeking God, Conservatism rejoices in the highest potential of the individual. By banishing or redefining God, Progressivism despairs in the worst potential of the individual. Conservatism builds, while Progressivism destroys. Conservatism is boundless, optimistic, and uplifting. Progressivism is offensive, patronizing, and limiting. Both are self-fulfilling ideologies. As Progressivism has continued its advance into every sphere of our cultural identity, the results, far from realizing progress, have been a slow but evident social decline.

Words

One obvious criterion of an advancing civilization is found in its language, in its ability to communicate clearly and effectively. The building blocks of that language are, of course, found in its words. More than any other diagnostic, the spoken and written word become primary components of ascent in all functions of a given society, including its legal, educational, political and economic systems, but primarily in the maturation of its culture. When speech is unencumbered by restrictions, unimpeded by institutions, and untrammeled by legislation, a cultural renaissance is boundless. Conversely, when a society's speech is chained by popular acceptance, policed by the marketplace, or, at its most damaging, fettered by the political class, cultural progress is not merely hindered, but halted. Worse yet, individuals themselves become regulated by those who govern speech. They who control the language control the people.

The manipulation of language is an essential prop of all totalitarian philosophies, most notably Hitler's Germany and Lenin's Russia, and is in widespread use in America today. "The worst thing one can do with words is to surrender them" (George Orwell; *Politics and the English Language; 1946).* We no longer use words to inform and enlighten, but to deceive and indoctrinate. Whether by euphemism, hyperbole or outright redefinition, nearly every facet of American culture peddles in this specious word engineering. Politicians, liberal elites, and the legacy media, however, seem to have an outsized, unique affinity for the exploitation of words precisely because of its ability to delude, control thought, and transform cultures. Euphemisms magically convert the murder of unborn babies into 'women's reproductive health,' illegal immigrants into 'refugees,' genital mutilation into 'gender reaffirming care,' discrimination into 'affirmative action,' and sodomy into 'same sex marriage.' Hyperbole inflates disagreement to hate speech; freedom of association to racism; and desires to rights. When hyperbole and euphemism do not suffice, words are often redefined by semantic contortion….transposing patriot to terrorist, morality to extremism, and, in turn, good to evil. Tolerance has become intolerant; anti-racism has become racist; equality has become equity; and liberalism has become illiberal. Truth is no longer truth at all but, instead, a meandering inconsistency that mollifies an immature conscience. Justice is now fairness, without the constraints of facts and personal accountability. Mercy is now nothing but amnesty for the permanence of poor decisions and unrepentant transgressions. Love is now simply the all-encompassing rationalization of nihilism.

Nowhere is the butchering of the 'Queen's English' more evident, and absurd, than in the recent fabrication of new pronouns. There are now dozens of personal pronouns, including the likes of (f)aerself, eir, per, ve, xyrs, zie, and xem. Per the newly commissioned grammatical gestapo, the list of new pronouns is infinite, as each individual can continually create their own. 'They,' normally a plural pronoun, can now refer to one person, which, prior to modern linguistic torturing, was indicative of schizophrenia. The sentences created with these words are pure babel, and laughably nonsensical. For example, "She went with her friend to their favorite restaurant, then she went home by herself," excruciatingly becomes, "(F)ae went with xyr friend to eirs favorite restaurant, then ze went home by perself," or any number of other, unintelligible variations. Not only is society expected to conform to this idiocy, but individuals can also be charged with a criminal offense (in government, academia and other politically correct arenas) if they do not honor these faux pronouns and made up words.

The massive conglomerates of the social media world have gradually become co-conspirators in the control of words. The 'fourth Reich' of information whores, Facebook/Instagram, Google, YouTube and Twitter, are now the self-appointed cultural speech police, and their platforms exist primarily to replace reality with orchestrated fantasies. 'Big Tech,' whose very business models are predicated on the worldwide trafficking of personal information, claims to be guardian of all 'truth,' and will actively shame, nullify, and otherwise 'cancel' all who stray from political correctness….the Progressive Inquisition. They are not to be trifled with, lest you be banished to oblivion by enforcement of their 'community standards.' Patently false remarks, such as "antifa violence is a myth," are amplified by the powers that be, and programmed to spread like wildfire, while obviously true statements, such as "there are only two genders," are flagged as hate speech and relegated to the trash bin of 'offensive language.' "The truth is what we say it is"…or so it seems is the diktat imposed by the 15,000 members of Facebook's 'content review team,' which is simply 'newspeak' for the 'ministry of censored speech.' As the integrity of words is forsaken, subjugation renders freedom deaf and self-determination mute. Despotism takes root and, word by silenced word, smothers liberty with disdain.

Emotions are the only constant in the cultural 'war on words,' intentionally so. If words and their meanings can be so capriciously changed and controlled, then so can thoughts, and ultimately, behavior. Obviously, passions and sentiments are more easily tamed when precision and clarity are abandoned. As such, 'male' and 'female' are now interchangeable because they are suddenly based strictly on 'feelings.' Words have been abducted, and held for the ransom of cultural change. The psychological conditioning is so palpably transparent, yet our puerile culture either does not comprehend the chicanery, or willfully chooses ignorance. "It is easier to fool people than to convince them that they have been fooled" (Mark Twain). When words are definite and their meanings uniform and consistent, deception becomes exposed and is rendered harmless. Furthermore, the free exchange of speech, and the thoughts, ideas and actions that speech engenders, are paramount for the vitality of a sovereign people…without them, we become culturally illiterate and susceptible to tyranny.

Political Correctness et al.

Political correctness, possibly the most glaring example of the incapacitation of common sense, commandeered words, and our society's embrace of moral relativism, is a term directly appropriated from classical Marxist ideology, and was introduced in America by aspiring communists during the 1960's social revolution. Initially, PC was masked as a harmless, even virtuous attempt to promote social 'fairness' and the elimination of anything deemed offensive. The mask was slowly and methodically removed, however, as political correctness became a militant attempt to impose restrictions on speech and behavior that did not comply with Progressive ideals, as evidenced by relentless tirades of compelled diversity, an irrational obsession with race and multi-culturalism, and an endless parade of simulated discrimination and bigotry; by a celebration of mediocrity through participation trophies and scoreless games of competition; by a confounding defense of sexual perversions cloaked in bathroom wars, gay marriage and an entirely new alphabet of genders; by a litany of excuses for destructive behavior, from drug abuse to criminal acts to terrorism; and, most vehemently, by unbridled anti-Christian and anti-Conservative propaganda...just a small sampling of political correctness gone mad and a precursor to today's version of George Orwell's prophetic 'doublethink':

- According to the Equal Employment Opportunity Commission, it is illegal for employers to discriminate against criminals because it has a disproportionate impact on minorities...also, a federal court ruled that illegal immigrants can sue American employers that refuse to hire them because they require workers to be U.S. citizens or legal residents (Corruption Chronicles; *Court Rules Illegal Aliens Can Sue over "Discriminatory Employment Policy" Requiring Green Cards*; April 11, 2018) .

- All U.S. government agencies are banned from producing any training materials that link Islam with terrorism. In fact, the FBI has gone back and purged references to Islam and terrorism from hundreds of old documents.
- American public schools in California and other Western states have prohibited clothing depicting the American flag in order to avoid inflaming students who identify as Mexican nationals.
- A recruiter's job advertisement for 'reliable' and 'hard-working' applicants was rejected by a job center, as it could be offensive to unreliable and lazy people.
- The term 'brainstorming' is banned – and replaced with 'thought showers', as lawmakers thought the term might offend those with mental illness.
- A government-backed booklet reportedly warned nursery teachers that playing 'musical chairs' encouraged aggressive behavior.
- A school renamed its Easter eggs 'spring spheres' to avoid causing offense to people who did not celebrate Easter.
- And the categorization as hate speech of these 'racial microaggressions': "I believe the most qualified person should get the job"; "Everyone can succeed in society, if they work hard enough"; "America is a melting pot" – all condemned for instilling exclusivity and discrimination.

The concepts of 'I'm ok, you're ok,' 'live and let live,' and 'unconditional love' were all borne of the PC movement as well - seemingly very innocent, and, in some ways, positive character traits. The stated goal was merely the acceptance of personal differences, yet the ultimate agenda has served to lay the foundation of today's censorship and cancel culture, then tomorrow's complete suffocation of free speech. As with most attempts at Progressive engineering, there was an ingrained, sinister purpose underlying these outwardly benign phrases. What was set into motion was a *quiet revolt against morality*. Morality, by its very nature, is guilty of discrimination, as it distinctly and unapologetically separates right from wrong. In order to subvert conventional morality, or at least diffuse it, all forms of discrimination must be condemned. Hence, rules become optional and standards of appropriate behavior, since discriminatory, are initially downplayed, then wholly denounced. The ultimate Progressive design realizes that a constant and repetitive censure of discrimination will slowly, but eventually, lead to a full cultural reproach of morality. By socially shaming any sort of unpopular (i.e. religious/Conservative) opinions on behavior, lifestyles, and traditional values, the actual goal was to silence, as much as possible, any cultural discourse that may have shed a negative light on the 'new morality.' Over the ensuing years, opinions became synonymous with disagreements; disagreements, with judgement; and judgement of actions, with condemnation of souls. All are now conflated into this recently concocted composite of exclusivity, hate speech, and thought crimes. Thus, if one holds an unpopular opinion of someone or something favored by the neo-Progressives, it is immediately tantamount to hateful disparagement and damnation, worthy of public excoriation…simply for having an opinion or an allegiance to morality. Only the secularists are permitted to freely opine, disagree, and judge with impunity; and condemnation is, ironically, likewise reserved solely for the same group – all of the acrimony being directed at those who are no longer afforded the prerogative of personal conviction.

'Unconditional love' has, by design, become a cultural talking point, as 'love' now means total acceptance and an embracing of degenerate lifestyles, as well as the defense and celebration of corrupted values. 'Unconditional love,' by its very nature, is amoral. Real love, first and foremost, is compelled to defend truth. Only pseudonyms of love can defend a mockery of truth. No longer, however, can one advocate, even respectfully, for morality, or offer, even compassionately, wise counsel. Such genuine concern for individuals, for our society as a whole, is now defined as hatred. Slowly and purposely, over many decades, these relative moralities, these man-made 'virtues' of the progressively enlightened, have silently transposed the definitions of love and hate, then, of course, good and evil. No longer residing only in the adolescent fatuity of the hippy generation, this mindset has now infiltrated the philosophy of the 'intelligentsia' – the social, political and even religious leaders of the current age, summarized most alarmingly by none other than a Supreme Court Justice. Anthony Kennedy, in his infamous "mystery of life" passage of the 1992 Planned Parenthood of Southeastern Pennsylvania v. Casey decision, declared that, "At the heart of liberty is the right to define one's own concept of existence, of meaning, of the universe, and of the mystery of human life." Moral relativism is most definitely not 'at the heart of liberty.' No, it is liberty's ruin.

Similarly, the movement to quell what is deemed 'offensive' speech has become entrenched in our schools, media, and places of business; yet, equal protection it is not. All manner of speech offending Christians and traditional values are largely ignored, even tacitly encouraged, while society considers any speech that carries negative connotations regarding immoral behavior as blasphemous hate speech in need of immediate repudiation, punishment and 'sensitivity training.' What began as a request for the mere acceptance of personal differences has quickly become a demand for the affirmation of cultural depravity, accompanied by a vengeful policing of thoughts and words. *The quiet revolt is no longer shy and reticent.*

'Diversity' was passed the politically correct baton soon thereafter, a notch up in the incremental attack on an 'outdated' value system. The attack is two-pronged. The concept that diversity, in and of itself, is of any intrinsic worth, makes no sense. Diversity can be culturally beneficial, culturally insignificant, or culturally insidious. If diversity is measured by a positive attribute or honorable trait, then diversity is a worthy goal. If diversity is defined solely in terms of hailing from a different culture, or having a different skin color, then diversity is value-neutral and thus holds no real worth one way or the other. If diversity results in the corruption of a nation's founding principles, or worse yet, the disavowal of transcendent, objective truth, then diversity becomes a societal poison to that culture. The latter is the first prong of attack. The 'diversity' that a majority of Progressive disciples is seeking to advance by making its creed socially acceptable, and its opponents, social outcasts, is wholly due to an outright contempt for the once-honored values of traditional morality. How else can one explain the irrational insurgence of transgenderism? If our Progressive society can convince a preponderance of people that men can be women and women can be men, then virtually any idiocy is immune to reason.

Diversity's second prong of attack is brazenly Marxist in its implementation. By endlessly heralding the attributes of those who are cast as marginalized and an underrepresented minority…the 'oppressed,' and by simultaneously denigrating the characteristics of those cast as traditional and an overrepresented majority…the 'oppressors,' the initial battle lines of cultural revolution are drawn. Notice how diversity was initially celebrated as merely being embracive of customs, ideas and backgrounds outside of the cultural mainstream. Notice now how diversity has, over the years, methodically become a weapon to silence, then punish, those who built and maintained that culture. Diversity is merely the engine of class struggle which intentionally drives the violent overthrow of all social structures. It is neither progressive, nor inclusive, nor constructive. The entire purpose is rot and destruction…the resurgent stench of Marxist halitosis.

The celebration of diversity hides behind race, nationality and gender but in reality has much more to do with a subordination of, and disdain for, the absolute distinctions of our American founding. Deceptively packaged as 'inclusive,' diversity is actually a tool designed specifically to be schismatic. Our current culture is a testament to the fact that nothing divides like diversity. Furthermore, constant obsession with incidental vagaries of diversity intentionally draws attention away from the cultural imperatives of objective truth and moral character. The notion that diversity is necessary to combat the many 'ism's' of our culture (i.e. racism, sexism, etc.) is nothing but a false premise utilized by Progressives to hide their intended dilution, then suffocation, of Conservatism - the only 'ism' that they truly fear - seeking only to sow the anarchy of cultural discord, to eventually achieve a plurality of dissent, and then to realize the culmination of their ultimate goal of destructive revolution. Diversity is the 'Trojan Horse' of our culture war, a concept we have been indoctrinated to worship, and, if we choose otherwise, an edict that we will be compelled to accept. In the obfuscation, we fail to see the entrapment of diversity for what it truly is…a premeditated subterfuge from within to conceal the deliberate destruction of our culture. Progressives have taken to heart the New Testament passage, "a house divided against itself cannot stand" (Mark 3:25), not as a warning against cultural division, but as a methodology that instigates the same.

Progressive diversity is lauded only if the distinctions are exactly the same. If diversity was the panacea that it is claimed to be, then why is there such an automatic and militant contempt for any values, opinions or thoughts that diverge from the decrees of our self-ordained, cultural masters? They do not seek diversity at all, but actually a monotone of speech and a uniformity of thought – a forced cultural conscription into a radical transformation of conscience. Progressives claim "diversity is our strength." Their brand of an ideologically invariant diversity, however, is not a strength, but a cultural undoing of which they are fully aware. They have seized our national motto, *'E Pluribus Unum'* (out of many, one), and claim that diversity is the means of reaching this end. Yet, what they actually espouse is the exact opposite, *'E Unum Pluribus.'* With tireless resolve, they have turned the cohesive 'one' into the dissonant 'many.' Unity is our strength, not diversity. We have been purposely softened over the past few decades with countless sermons on the godliness of diversity, and with a resolute denigration of the consonant tenets of our moral and religious founding. The Progressive obsession with moral diversity has led to the expropriation of our culture's education system, government, media and entertainment, and, in concert with the subversion of family, parental control, and cultural virtue, has willfully corrupted our minds with persistent and complicit intent. At the risk of furthering conspiracy theories, note that there is only one plausible motive for our society's preoccupation with diversity, and that is a blatant attempt to dissipate our founding philosophies to further a cultural revolution. What hath diversity wrought in America? The celebration of sodomy; the elevation of Communist Marxism; the destruction of marriage and the family; the diminution of law and order; the scourge of pornography; the rebirth of racism as anti-racism; culturally weaponized science, health and education; an absurd spectrum of genders; and rampant illegal immigration. *The quiet revolt becomes louder and more confident.*

Most recently, political correctness has continued advancing with unrelenting antagonism. 'Tolerance' and 'extremism' are now the watchwords utilized to perpetuate the same belligerence against all social mores once hailed as decent and desirable, even crucial for the proper functioning of society. The Venerable Archbishop Fulton Sheen wrote in 1931, "Tolerance applies only to persons…never to truth. Tolerance applies to the erring, intolerance to the error…Architects are as intolerant about sand as foundations for skyscrapers as doctors are intolerant about germs in the laboratory. Tolerance does not apply to truth or principles. About these things we must be intolerant, and for this kind of intolerance, so much needed to rouse us from sentimental gush, I make a plea. Intolerance of this kind is the foundation of all stability…America, it is said, is suffering from intolerance. It is not. It is suffering from tolerance: tolerance of right and wrong, truth and error, virtue and evil…" Or, as so presciently summarized by this anonymous quote, "Tolerance will reach such a level that intelligent people will be banned from thinking so as to not offend the imbeciles."

As it is woefully apparent, today's concept of tolerance is designedly disordered and its cultural momentum only moves in one direction. Oddly enough, the primary tenet of the state sponsored edict of tolerance is *intolerance* for those who dare to disagree - those who are now labelled extremists. The intolerant must not be tolerated. That which was once considered culturally wholesome, and absolute good, is now extreme. No longer are ridicule and public shame enough; lives of the intolerant extremists must be ruined – censorship in the name of tolerance and ostracism in the name of inclusion. The unclean can now be banished from public restaurants, and harassed at their own homes. 'Coexist' may trend well as a bumper sticker but it is neither the intention nor the methodology of those who would, if given the chance, forcibly silence all those who disagree with them. Truth is now subjugated by tolerance, and virtue is now defined as radicalism. This brand of 'neo-tolerance,' along with the new-found, tortured congruence between morality and extremism, has already unlocked the gates of hell, and…as time passes…as the gate keepers are silenced…as good and evil continue their transposition…the gates will be breached. *The quiet revolt has become clamorous and contemptuously bold.*

As the outbursts turn to furor and the conceit to enmity, political correctness becomes hostile and its adversaries must be subdued. The Chick-Fil-A restaurant franchise, founded by S. Truett Cathy and now headed by his son, Dan Cathy, has become the nemesis of the PC army due to the Cathy family's support for traditional marriage and their prescriptive opinions on homosexuality. The antipathy became so inflammatory that numerous public servants threatened to deny the franchise a license to open new locations in their jurisdictions, simply because of the Cathy's publicly stated convictions. Dan Cathy personally supported "the Biblical definition of the family unit" and he prayed for "God's mercy on our generation that has such a prideful, arrogant attitude to think that we have the audacity to try to redefine what marriage is about." He and his company financially support organizations that agree with his views. There has never been any evidence, or even a claim, that Dan Cathy, his company, or any of his franchises, have discriminated against homosexuals in hiring or serving, or in any capacity whatsoever. On the contrary, a Chick-Fil-A franchise in Hollywood sponsored a special fundraiser for Campus Pride, in order to raise money to ensure the safety of LGBT students on campus. Another franchise in Orlando offered free food at the scene of the Pulse nightclub mass shooting, where more than fifty gay men and women were massacred. Chick-Fil-A regularly feeds the homeless and members of the military, and donates millions in college scholarships in the localities in which they operate – helping people regardless of their sexual inclinations amid constant and fallacious claims of discrimination. The real discrimination is evident in the 'Chick-Fil-A is not welcome here' diatribe by elected officials who have renounced their sworn oath to uphold Constitutional principles. Politicians and regulatory administrators have unconstitutionally suppressed Mr. Cathy's right to free speech, as well as his right to pursue a legal business opportunity in a location of his own choosing, simply because they disagree with him. That is tyranny.

In light of the current escalation of animosity toward religion, and the heightened, impugning rhetoric against conventional morality, a malevolent ill will has taken hold. "The further a society drifts from truth, the more it will hate those that speak it" (George Orwell). Make no mistake; the castigation of those faithful to an orthodox Judeo-Christian creed, and to the patriotic embrace of American foundational precepts, will lead to the reality of mounting persecution. The siege has begun, and for modernity, is no longer advancing in stealth. The religious freedoms honored by our bill of rights are being methodically annulled – speech stifled, opportunities denied, exclusions multiplied, and shame cast – by the very entity that is commissioned to protect these rights. Persecution is not just coming…it is already here. Watch, as a county clerk in Kentucky is jailed for refusing to issue gay marriage licenses (now the law of the land), while numerous other clerks were left untouched when they unlawfully issued gay marriage licenses (then the law of the land); or, as the Internal Revenue Service illegally targets Conservative/religious groups with no other intent but to silence them and criminalize their beliefs, while granting 501C3 tax exempt status to the 'After School Satan Club' within ten days of its application; or, as the US Army refuses to allow an honor guard to participate in a Flag Day celebration at a Baptist church, yet will allow that same honor guard to celebrate in a parade for gay pride. Listen, as the mayor of Houston demands that Christian pastors turn over their sermons to the government for review, approval, and possible legal action; or, as the city of Lansing, MI bars a small farmer from selling his produce at the local farmers' market because of his religious objections to gay marriage; or, as a public high school football coach in Washington state loses his job for briefly praying after each football game. Beware, as the Attorney General of the United States seeks to punish under law anyone who may disagree with a scientific theory; or, as US Senators employ a constitutionally banned religious test during the confirmation hearings for cabinet posts and judicial appointees; or, as a public college in Michigan has students arrested, simply for handing out copies of our founding documents. Gradually, the assault is becoming more acute, the uneasy discomfort being replaced by a genuine discrimination and a progression of virulence - threats of prosecution more trenchant, Christian doctrine made illegal, churches reproached, financial penalties and tax modifications implemented. No longer is the 'separation of Church and State' a pretense to simply remove Christianity from the public square. No, it is now an obviously strident attempt to remove Christians themselves. Tim Gill, a Progressive donor and activist who has turned his $500 million fortune into the nation's most powerful 'gender alphabet police force,' does not parse words when he exclaims, "We're going into every state in the country and punish the wicked". The burgeoning hatred will likely escalate further, as hatred is wont to do, transmuting into compulsory re-education, physical violence, and even imprisonment, all at the hands of a society and a government that is rewriting the declaration of our 'unalienable' rights. Freedom of speech, freedom of religion, and freedom of association are all being systematically invalidated by a theocracy of secularists.

This demonic rebellion against traditional values originated slowly, purposely, in order not to draw attention to itself. Small increments of evil are a bit more palatable to human sensitivities than a full and immediate onslaught. Likewise, the arenas in which the initial revolt takes place are specifically chosen to appear inconsequential. From there, now rooted and growing, evil spreads quietly, yet efficiently; unnoticed, yet pervasive.

Of Good and Evil

Unbeknownst, Armageddon wages for the nonce
A nemesis weaned on fruits of the same garden
Silently maturing into all that life wants

Slowly passing, the revelation that depicts
An ephemeral battle of good and evil vying
For that which grows and that which constricts

Until that end, the devil's refrain
As God is banished from each thought
Hell is the world that will remain

"...therefore, God gave them over to..." (Romans 1:26)

Intemperate Diversions

Why are we at all interested in whether or not Kim Kardashian has cellulite? That question alone typifies the abysmal depths to which our 'wardrobe malfunction' culture has sunk. In our current age of eternal adolescence, no longer targeted at just the teenage demographic, this is the type of absurdity that is courted by all major media, and regularly legitimized as news. We have become obsessed with countless vapid embarrassments that were once relegated to the trash heap of gossip tabloids, but are now fashioned as a cultural relevance. Until recently, pop-culture had been a small, infantile subset of our culture. Now, it has fully absorbed our consciousness and, in so doing, has become what defines us as a people. We champion the crass and emulate the crude. We only desire to be amused, not educated; soothed, not challenged; noticed, not respected; and popular, not principled. In nearly every facet of our culture, we encourage vanity and indulgence while losing our sense of virtuous comportment. We constantly seek attention. The whole concept of 'selfies' is not as innocent as it seems, but rather, represents the solipsism that has encompassed a large contingent of our culture. We waste so much time 'posting' every emotion, 'following' every celebrity, and yearning for as many 'likes' as we can possibly get. There are seemingly no limits to our extreme intemperance, or to our abandonment of natural restraint. The discipline required for self-control and moderation, especially in regard to our endless desire to be entertained, has devolved in equal share to our desertion of common sense and our adoption of moral relativism. We ridicule the dignified and glorify the indecent. We languish in ignoble spectacle, all the while surrendering our character and forsaking our aspirations to righteousness and decorum. Aristotle once proclaimed, "All men by nature desire to know." In order to know, one must think. Postmodern man has forsaken the natural inclination to think, and then to know, and has fully replaced it with the desire to be…entertained.

Entertainment

In almost every culture that has witnessed the death of common sense and the rise of moral relativism, decay follows in the arena of entertainment. Recall the ridicule that was inflicted upon some adults and social/political leaders of the 1950's as they castigated the lack of morals in rock and roll music and the increasing level of sexuality on display in movies and television, though tame when compared to today's levels. Dismissed as puritanical and old-fashioned, their views were roundly scoffed. Slowly their voices faded from public discourse and the immorality in the entertainment industry reached new heights of depravity with each passing year. If those same ears from the 1950's had heard future lyrics such as 'deny your maker'; or, 'if you're into evil you're a friend of mine'; or were made privy to the outright debauchery of numerous genres of music, especially the sheer pestilence of most rap music, but also of many movies, books, magazines, and even prime-time television shows; or heard news reports of satanic worship and black masses…all of society would have banded together in outright disgust and disbelief, and demanded an immediate end to such social viruses. Ensuing generations, however, slowly and methodically desensitized to an ever-increasing level of entertainment rot, not only enjoy and promote such perverted theater, but also feverishly applaud its actors, shower them with adulation, and even present them with awards.

'For mature audiences only' is an incomplete oxymoron. A truly mature individual would find no value in the level of decadence that infects many forms of modern diversion. Sex and violence punctuated with profanity has become the thesis of all exhibition, ravaging our sense of decency while compromising our moral reason. While the number of entertainment venues has exploded over the past few decades, the quality has fallen to imperceptible levels. We are so consumed with entertaining ourselves that there is little time left to do anything else. With hundreds of television channels, unlimited radio stations, social networking, and especially the internet, the amount of information available to us all is extraordinary. So much knowledge to pursue, so much education from which to satisfy our endless quest for a purposeful life; but no, we choose instead to subject ourselves to tawdry and juvenile tripe that merely insult our intelligence and rationalize our trespasses. Television has become nothing if not glamorized filth…a vending machine for vice and banality. Hundreds of reality shows plague the airwaves, full of scripted, circus-like theater, from polygamy to 'real' psychics, Dr. Pimple Popper, 'RuPaul's Drag Race,' 'my 600 pound life,' teen moms, and 'queer as folk.' Our cult heroes and 'role' models are the likes of the Kardashian/Jenners, Miley Cyrus, Howard Stern, Cardi B and Charlie Sheen…the more deranged they are, the more popular they become. Sports, no longer simply a healthy pastime, have become a cultural spirituality for many. There is little doubt that more people in the US watch Sunday football than attend church. We pay entertainers astronomical sums of money. The economics of it all, while embarrassing, do make sense…societies pay the most for what they value the most. We are more likely to succumb to astrology, horoscopes, and tarot card readings than to utilize the gifts of our past experiences and future goals to direct our present rationality. Violence, across all forms of entertainment, is pervasive and must gradually increase in order to continue to satisfy our calloused perceptions. Cordially, we invite strangers and their vices into our homes, and then, we just watch them, hour after hour. Others' perversions have become our daily amusement. For a generation, voyeurism has been standard fare in virtually every home in America, every night, and the results have been nothing but culturally regressive.

Our heroes are no longer real, but fictitious characters on a screen, and even they are being reshaped by the blurred lines of moral relativism. The use of false moral dilemmas and heroes with very questionable character traits only serve to elevate the 'ends justify the means' storyline portraying what was once thought of as evil to be socially acceptable, such as revenge or promiscuity, while other, more secular sins, such as 'hate speech' and 'thought crimes,' are relegated to the lowest tier of hell. No longer is there a strict code of traditional right and wrong, but instead a preponderance of moral 'grey' areas where heroes and villains are often indistinguishable. From the 'virtuous' heroine who repeatedly prostitutes herself in order to defeat the greedy and chauvinistic corporate magnate, to the maverick law enforcement officer who resorts to unlawful violence to thwart the slightly more violent antagonist - our growing moral immunities are silently shifting our affinity away from a pure, paramount virtue to a more flexible moral code, with the ultimate goal being the death of real conscience. The recent passing of Hugh Hefner, the founder of the 'Playboy' empire, was met with a flourish of accolades approaching reverence. He was eulogized with a level of idolatry and adoration previously reserved only for great men and women of unimpeachable virtue - as a 'cultural icon' who had lived an 'exceptional and impactful' life. A misogynistic, perpetually immature man, the father of mainstream pornography, has been elevated to cultural hero status.

Advertising

Not to be left behind, advertisers have recorded our society's level of degenerative worship and are more than happy to pander to our base instincts. Choice has become a caricature of itself while luxuries are now rebranded as staples. Most products and services are useful and, on occasion, necessary, yet the extent to which advertisers will go, and that the public is willing to be led, is intellectually embarrassing, always exaggerated, and often unabashed lying, We are exploited by a culture drowning in meaningless slogans, mostly for commodities and services of marginal utility. We not only accept inferior quality but now expect it as well. In many instances, we have become the product that is being sold, especially across many social media platforms. We are drawn in to one venue and then our thoughts, preferences, likes and dislikes are being sold for profit to other venues so that they, in turn, can do the same. The consumer, as a person, has become a profit center, and the cost of goods sold is our dignity and human worth. Our lives have been littered with junk mail and entombed within a spam folder. Advertising, deceptive by its very nature, has become nothing but an incessant barrage of tasteless drivel, from all possible media. We are harassed in every waking hour, as marketers compete with each other to sell their wares by attempting to satisfy our hunger for the seven deadly sins: get skinny, become beautiful, eat this, drink that, drive this, have an affair, increase your libido, defy aging, sue them, get rich, take this drug, impress your neighbor. They all come with either illegible fine print or rapid fire wording at the end, with the ubiquitous disclaimers, the 'see store for details,' the 'restrictions and limitations apply,' and 'actual results may vary,' all of which simply deny what was promised in the first place. Are we that gullible?...that devoid of sound reasoning? Obviously, we are, as the marketers would not continue to churn out such insipid directives if we did not blindly abide by them; and that is exactly what we have allowed them to become: self-indulging decrees from a group of people who, pathetically, yet in reality, controls our wants and needs by manipulating our habits, thoughts, and feelings.

Holidays

Another measurement of the cultural health of any people is their celebration of holidays. As with the entertainment and advertising that captures a society's attention, its holidays reflect what it considers worthy of honor and commemoration. Although most holidays in the western world find their origins in Christian feast days, it is obvious that secular society is attempting to strip them all of any religious meaning and expropriate their intended purposes in order to drive a less than spiritual promotion of mass consumerism and self-aggrandizement. When the 'holy'day of All Hallows" Eve, the vigil which honors all saints in their quest for holiness and all things good, becomes the holiday known for its obsession with sex, violence, death, and an affinity for the devil, one can easily measure the moral health of the revelers. Likewise, when a holiday honoring the patron saint of an entire country simply becomes an excuse for drunkenness; or, when the holiest day on the Christian calendar has been replaced with a trite bunny and a basketful of candy; or, when a day of thanksgiving to God for the many blessings of a nation has been usurped by a penchant for gluttony and football; or, when the birth of our Savior is overshadowed by greed and materialism during months of commercial prostitution – it then becomes obvious that virtually every major holiday has been debased by our culture. Granted, many of our current holidays began as pagan festivals prior to their religious counterparts, but the definitive transformation back to paganism, often with the added twist of extolled depravity, offers disturbing insights into our collective moral compass.

The Arts

Art, under all of its disciplines, has produced the profoundly beautiful throughout history. Paintings, literature, sculpture, music, poetry…indeed, all forms of art…have taken small and seemingly insignificant manifestations of our human senses and created the sublime. Disparate sounds masterfully woven into grand concertos, approaching the divine. Simple ink and blank canvas collaborate to rival the grandeur of nature. Clay, stone, wood and metal magically transformed into stunning renditions, and breathtaking moments, of the human condition. Simple words, alone as clutter, then as wreathed, impassioning the soul. The emotions created immediately satiate the senses. The profound splendor is not confined to preference or personal taste, as it is instantly and objectively evident, even to the untrained sense. True art is of a universal quality, a timeless visual and auditory excellence that soars toward perfection.

Unfortunately, awe-inspiring art of this type is substantially absent from the common age, or has at least been relegated to obscurity, replaced by the imposter of 'modern' art. The social construct of relativism has tentacles that reach far into our culture, even into the creative world of art. Real art transcends relativism. There can be no such thing as a 'relative' majesty. Modern art is grounded in the relative, in subjective preference and meandering expression, often embracing the crass, the incomprehensible, the facile, and the pretentious. The ordinary has become praiseworthy, and the profane challenges the sacred. It is much easier, and likely more profitable, to shock than to inspire, to copy than to invent, to debase than to dignify. The noble has been replaced by the flashy and the ostentatious, and the exquisite, by the obnoxious and mediocre. Modern art is reflective of a culture that prefers confusion, vulgarity and flamboyance to order, purity and elegance.

Nowhere is the virtuous more loathsome, and the debased more honored, than in Hollywood. Filmmaking, an art form once championed with a mind toward the highest yearnings of the human soul, toward the quest for the innate goodness found in every person, and toward the celebration of reaching that potential, has, with full awareness, descended to the depths of the exact opposite. Frank Capra, the eternally optimistic movie director from the mid-1900's, attempted to salvage that noble mission with classic films such as *Mr. Smith Goes to Washington'* and *'It's A Wonderful Life,'* but noted realistically toward the end of his career that "practically all the Hollywood filmmaking of today is stooping to cheap salacious pornography in a crazy bastardization of a great art to compete for the 'patronage' of deviates." This observation was from 1971. Imagine the editorial Mr. Capra would pen today.

The Media

The mainstream media, as a Progressive force, has gradually taken control of our culture. Far removed from the critical role of the media envisioned by our founders, the 'fourth estate' has self-transfigured into nothing more than, for the most part, an extension of the government and the socialist/progressive movement. The founders realized that, especially for a republic, the dissemination of truth to the populace was imperative for an educated vote and informed decisions. "Educate and inform the whole mass of the people…They are the only sure reliance for the preservation of our liberty" (Thomas Jefferson). Once heralded for unwavering honesty, unbiased objectivity, and unimpeachable autonomy, the modern media is of late little more than a vendor of propaganda, and a manipulative agent of behavior control. The media once presented facts and allowed the consumers of news to arrive at their own conclusions, to think for themselves. Now, out of laziness, bias, or simple corruption of ideology, the media present their own manipulated version of the facts in order to indoctrinate the consumer to *what* he should think, and *how* he should think it. News is now purposed, not to impart knowledge or distribute information, but to maximize ad-clicks. Additionally, advertisements fashioned as legitimate news stories test our capacity for discernment, and social media as a news source has greatly exacerbated the devaluation of verifiable truth. News reporting has been replaced by 'What's Trending.' No longer reserved to the 'fringe,' the tabloids, or the nonsense peddlers, the legacy media itself has likewise branded its own form of misinformation, half-truths and calumny, if not actual slander and false witness. The media deliberately uses the fanaticism and drama of blatant dishonesty as a tool, and has thus become a traitor to the liberty of intellectual thought. This same media that used to intentionally promulgate its clandestine agenda as a 'conspiracy theory' imagined by those that would dare make the claim, no longer even operates under a pretense of objectivity, as it is demonstrably more vested in partisan politics, covert policy making and social engineering than it is in true journalism. "A new consensus has emerged in the press…that truth isn't a process of collective discovery, but an orthodoxy already known to an enlightened few whose job is to inform everyone else" (Bari Weiss, former New York Times opinion editor).

As advertisers are to business concerns, so the media has become to political concerns. 'Fake news' has become endemic, perpetrated by news anchors, reporters, politicians, and even presidents. Dan Rather, a veteran news reporter and anchor, created a completely new genre of reporting – 'fake but accurate' - that has become commonplace. The regular, and deliberate, acceptance of 'anonymous' sources empowers reporters to fabricate references in order to push an agenda. Fact-checkers are now needed to validate the veracity of news reporting. As testimony to the inveterate corruption, fact checking of the fact-checkers is actually required. While the mainstream media feigns to be the guardian of all truth and the arbiter of factual information, it turns out that the single greatest source of 'disinformation' in our culture is found in the profession that simultaneously controls that information. By both commission and omission, far too often, the media, throughout the political spectrum, is more agenda-driven than fact-driven, more an entertainment venue than an information source, and more beholding to personal bias than to professional standards…yet more ground ceded to the weeds of tyranny. "Wherever despotism abounds the sources of public information are first to be brought under its control" (President Calvin Coolidge).

The art and honor of true journalism has been terminal for decades. With the advent of 'public relations' in the early 20th century, the use of propaganda was born in the arenas of politics and commerce. Once the powers-that-be realized that they could effectively form, control, and direct public opinion, propaganda became a staple of advertising, public policy, and electioneering. The media was initially reluctant to participate in this sham of public persuasion camouflaged as news reporting, yet, prodded on by government and business pressure, gradually adopted a more 'content-free' concept of news reporting while simultaneously employing the principles of group/crowd psychology as an effective means of controlling the populace. Edward Bernays, the 'father of public relations,' and a contractor to numerous businesses and government agencies, was more than forthcoming in his description of the deceptive and controlling methodology of propaganda: *"The conscious and intelligent manipulation of the organized habits and opinions of the masses is an important element in democratic society. Those who manipulate this unseen mechanism of society constitute an invisible government, which is the true ruling power of our country. ...We are governed, our minds are molded, our tastes formed, our ideas suggested, largely by men we have never heard of. This is a logical result of the way in which our democratic society is organized. Vast numbers of human beings must cooperate in this manner if they are to live together as a smoothly functioning society...In almost every act of our daily lives, whether in the sphere of politics or business, in our social conduct or our ethical thinking, we are dominated by the relatively small number of persons...who understand the mental processes and social patterns of the masses. It is they who pull the wires which control the public mind"* (Edward Bernays, *Propaganda*; 1928). Our opinions are formed by our perception, and our perception is distorted by the information we are allowed to receive. Fast forward, nearly a century later, and we can clearly see, through the ebb and flow of the years, how we have arrived at an age of mass delusion. What an unadulterated debasement of a once proud and respected profession.

What was once a small pond of journalists and news reporters - invertebrates all, swimming in the same direction and repeating a continual cycle of ingesting and regurgitating their own Progressive excrement - has now become an ocean of the same, poisoning the entire water supply. Prodded on by a corporate, academic and 'Big Tech' oligarchy, the media has contaminated every drop of our cultural and political seas. Without the aeration of free speech, the septic media are able to peddle not only in 'less than candid' reporting and calculated exaggeration, but in outright and relentless lies. "A lie told once remains a lie, but a lie told a thousand times becomes the truth" (Joseph Goebbels). Truth has become bias, and lies have become objective. Those lies are broadcast and defended while the truth is ridiculed and veiled. "Facts reported by the media may later turn out to be wrong" is an actual, and telling, disclaimer used by National Public Radio in its role as a 'professional' news organization. Transparency has been replaced by algorithms; tolerance, by cancel culture; reality, by nonsense; credibility, by guile; and the free exchange of ideas, by censorship. The media's remains are nothing but noise, an intentionally obstreperous din to distract from the deafening sound of the implosion of our culture.

Human Sexuality

No clearer vision exists of a society's moral philosophy than through the lens of its respect for life and its understanding of human sexuality. The "progressive" sexual revolution of the 1960's has shrouded that very lens with a cloak of hedonism, as it redefined the concept of sexuality from selfless to selfish; from devotion to desire; from love to lust. We have become obsessed with all things sexual. Since that decade, the cultural meaning of 'love' has become so pruriently warped that love is now synonymous with sex. What was once private, respected, even sacred, is now public theater, dishonored, even profane. Universal promiscuity is nothing short of a pandemic, ruining lives, relationships, families and entire cultures. Sexual passions without the boundaries of commitment have often prophesied anthropological descent. Sex as common and vulgar is everywhere, sown into the very soil of our consciousness. We have blemished the true meaning of love, mocked its virtues and confounded its powers, reducing it to nothing more than an animal response to a corporeal desire.

Sex is not love. Sex is an expression of love, but it is not love. God is love. Without God, there can be no love. If our reasons for loving someone are based solely on emotion, our own happiness, or satisfying our own human desires, then true love will forever escape us. To share in the rapture of God's love is to rise above and reach beyond our humanity; is to place the well-being of others above our own; is to capture within our lives a sincerity of self-denial, sacrifice and service. These are the virtues of love. Of these, true love is begotten. Once born, as with a child, love must be nurtured in order to mature. The growth process is fueled by love's own intrinsic powers: the perceptive power of faith, the redemptive power of charity, and the enduring power of hope. These are the powers of love. Of these, true love is perfected. Any love that blatantly contradicts these virtuous elements is not love at all, but an impurity unto love.

Of Love and Impurity

The purity of Love is in essence our Savior
As a soul's creation defines salvation's origin
To mimic its sanctity is to blemish its grace
For impurity assumes an apathetic contempt for life
And so transforms our quest for the Divine
Into the ultimate antithesis of humanity

From Immodesty to Pornography

For some time now, the concept of modesty, the simple yet profound reflection of a pure respect for love, sex, and the human body, has been shunned as prudish and uptight, and written off as outmoded and regressive. Oddly enough, the call to purity is now ridiculed as 'body shaming,' and many forsake common sense by actually stating that modesty contributes to a 'rape culture.' The death of modesty in our culture was the first step in a wanton progression of sexual perversion, for we have eschewed the once prevailing belief that our bodies are not our own. As we demand ownership of our flesh and champion unfettered sexual license, we simultaneously, and ironically, find our sexuality abused by an ever-growing litany of abjections, including abortion, pornography, homosexuality, transgenderism, pedophilia, sex trafficking and prostitution, rape, sexual abuse and the exploitation of women, AIDS and other sexually transmitted diseases, all of which have effected great misery on marriages, families and society itself. While it may appear to be a great distance between immodesty and such social depravities, there nonetheless exists a clear vision, for the youth of our culture especially, between an unhealthy view and immature understanding of sexuality and the resulting projection of its defilement. The American Academy of Pediatrics reports that sexually active adolescents are more likely than their abstinent peers to be depressed and suicidal, to use illicit substances, and, of course, are at significant risk of acquiring one or more sexually transmitted diseases, many of which are incurable (Aleteia: Novemeber 15, 2014).

Modesty simply and beautifully places physical love on a spiritual pedestal and does not taint it with the stains of an obsessively degenerate world. Sex and the human body are not to be ashamed of, yet neither are they to be comic material; not to be feared, yet neither to be conquered; not to be worshipped, yet neither to be exploited. Sex and the human body are to be respected, and modesty is the means by which we portray this respect – by thought, by word, and by the way in which we dress. A triumphant revival of this once honored virtue is necessary to reverse the impurity suffered by the physical, and the irreverence suffered by the spiritual, aspects of love.

The most obvious causal link arising out of immodesty can be found in the cultural psychosis caused by pornography. Pornography is the direct result of festering perversions incited by a momentum of immodesty. A worse social disease there has never been, and likewise, never one as communicable. In a society without sexual morality, the beautiful becomes grotesque, the pure becomes toxic, and sexual love is degraded to nothing but carnal mating. Pornography is a logical step down into this pit of wretched contamination. With instant and anonymous access to all types of media, the use of pornography has reached epidemic proportions. Currently, profits from pornography in the US exceed the revenues of television's three largest broadcasting companies (Kimmel, Michael, *Guyland: The Perilous World Where Boys Become Men*: Harper, New York; 2008). The magnitude of resources wasted is unfathomable: financial resources and the capital of time, to be sure, but more crucially, the bankrupted spirituality and moral stock made worthless. Similar to alcohol and drugs, pornography is addictive by its own nature. Once ensnared by its potent attraction, the escape is emotionally arduous and mentally grueling, not to mention torturous to the soul. Purveyors care not about the misery they have wrought, the relationships ruined, and the families ravaged. Just as the dealer of drugs is culpable for the desecration of the body, so the dealer of pornography is culpable for the desecration of the soul. As a culture, we lament the scourge of human trafficking throughout the world, yet we are unable to identify the 'free speech' of widespread pornography as its sponsor. Although anonymous, pornography *is* human trafficking, initiating in the dark shadows of a polluted mind, and then, when ripened, materializing in the contagion of human indignities. Even under the shroud of privacy and seclusion, pornography's damage to society is debilitating, as the individual resides in an acrid and warped perception of the meaning of human sexuality, which, in no small way, will pathologically infect his every thought and human interaction.

Marriage and Family

Glaringly obvious to any student of human history, to any expert in anthropology, sociology, or theology, even to any advocate for social justice, is the vital cultural impact of the institution of marriage as the bond that substantiates the family as the pillar of creation. Marriage has been culturally and divinely infused with characteristics and expressions of love unique unto itself. Marriage is the only human relationship consecrated by all types of love – physical, emotional and spiritual. The power of a marital union is immense, not only for the man and woman sacredly joined, but also for society as a whole, for it is from this union that life is rightly formed and society is perpetuated. Marriage initiates the self-sustaining cultural circle: a healthy marriage begets a healthy family, a healthy family - a healthy community, a healthy community - a healthy culture, and, in full circle, a healthy culture begets a healthy marriage. Possibly the most pitiful waste of our current society's cultural resources lies in the ignorance and, in many cases, outright desecration, of the blessed marital bond. Divorce is rampant. Single-parent households are the norm. Marriage has been bastardized to include other relationships that, by simple definition, could never be a true marriage. How tragic it is that an institution of such magnificent power and purpose, truly a wellspring of virtues, has been spiritually gutted, societally marginalized and, in turn, made culturally impotent. As marriage can now mean anything, it will soon, in turn, mean nothing.

Every aspiration to a holy life finds sanctuary within marriage. Unlike any other vocation, marriage has as its sole purpose a complete commingling of two persons – a unity that leads kindred spirits to the revelation of love's aforementioned intrinsic powers: one faith, one charity, and one hope. Over time, these unique powers become self-fulfilling. Faith, charity and hope are necessary for any successful marriage and, reciprocally, are a by-product of that marriage. This symbiotic relationship continually regenerates itself, effecting an endlessly powerful force that protects and enriches itself in spiritually exponential proportions, and, in so doing, emits this power concentrically to further and further expanses of the human condition. An inestimable cultural treasure, one marriage such as this creates a thriving and healthy family. Many marriages such as this create a thriving and healthy society and are the genesis of human flourishing.

The single most debilitating cultural crisis in our current age lies in the manner in which we have come to view the institution of marriage. Marriage is not simply a civil contract, but a covenant, and not a mere conditional promise, but a lifelong commitment. When a man and women join themselves before God, they become irreversibly one – not two at 50%, but one at 100%. Just as two fires that join forces become one fire, rendering it impossible to separate or distinguish one from the other, so it is with marriage. This is not simply poetic imagery, but truth, and the truth becomes evident through the miracle of procreation, a blessing not afforded to any other human relationship.

Children are the visible proof of a marriage's commingling union. As such, they also become the primary victims of the spiritual and emotional carnage left in the wake of divorce. Divorce is familial dysfunction, and that dysfunction will likely remain with a child throughout his or her life, often manifested in self-loathing, substance abuse, depression and further discordant relationships. While a husband and wife may physically separate themselves through divorce, while they may be able to dispose of their troubles and eventually escape their perceived pain, their children have no such recourse. A child's nature as being created one from two becomes a curse in the shadow of divorce. For them, separation and escape is not an option. Worse yet, divorce can cause serious spiritual decay in a child's soul, even as its instigation was in no way the fault of the child, for it will inevitably play a negative role in the child's perception of morality. For the sake of the children, the family, and even society, marriage was never designed to be disposable. Marriage cannot be cast aside because it ceases to provide worldly dividends. No matter how hard one tries to nullify its existence, the power of marriage yet remains - it may be dormant but can never be diffused. Married couples must never ignore the source of their power. No matter how distressing their worldly troubles may be, they have within themselves the resolution. With God, the first person of every blessed union, no difference is irreconcilable. Granted, separation may be unavoidable in those instances where abuse or neglect has created a situation unsafe for one spouse or the other. Pragmatically, as none of us can claim perfection, relationships can and do become poisoned. One or the other spouse may try to extinguish the fire once ignited in unison. In a society that honors morality and the marital vow, however, these unfortunate cases would be the rare exception and not the rule.

A flourishing marriage creates a flourishing family. Those blessed with children have been called by God to share in the glory of creation. Through the conception of physical life, they likewise play a magnificent role in the formation of souls and the population of heaven. Culturally, this was once the predominant view, and in honoring this belief, parenthood became a vocation of the highest order, and the nuclear family clearly identified as the centerpiece of a thriving culture. The whole of society depends on the viability and wellness of the family. As with any large group, whether in the military, or business, or government, the health of the collective is only as vigorous as the sum vitality of its parts. One would think that society, in its own self-interest, would always seek to maintain this vision in defense of the wholesome family. "If you want to change the world, go home and love your family" (Blessed Mother Teresa of Calcutta). Quite the contrary is the current appraisal of the quintessential family. It appears that every aspect of our culture is intent on the destruction of the family. From economic policies that often result in the forced removal of both parents from the home in order to financially sustain the family; to a consumerist mentality that leads to the willful escape of both parents from the home to satisfy their lust for materialism; to the advent of no-fault divorce which de-emphasizes permanence within marriage; to the practice of contraception which forsakes fertility within marriage; to cultural movements such as radical feminism that demean motherhood and childcare; to the social acceptance, and even staunch defense, of single-parent homes; to an education system which often ridicules and undermines parental authority; and, perhaps most sadistically, to the cultural redefinition of marriage – these and many other evil forces incomprehensibly portray a society determined to sabotage the integrity of its own foundation. Thus, it becomes obvious that the incessant Progressive defense of changing gender roles, feminism, gender fluidity, pornography, homosexuality, transsexualism, gay marriage, contraception and abortion, is ultimately an intentional effort to destroy the cradle of humanity – marriage and the family – with the void to be filled, of course, by the totalitarianism of state control. This is an evil that no man could conjure up on his own. Such a diabolical design can only spew forth from the mind of the devil in the deepest recesses of hell.

Men and Women

For thousands of years, the roles of men and women have always been a constant - fertile ground upon which the family has thrived, a stabilizing force that has held society together, and a spiritual fixture that has served as a conduit to God. The recent attempts to reconstruct these roles have initiated or compounded many of the cultural failures of our age, especially those that relate to the raising of children. As a direct result of manipulating these roles, many children in effect grow up parentless and, amid confounding irony, without the proper role models – generations of children needlessly succumbing to an epidemic of diseased families. The traditional roles of men and women have been created by God for a clear and specific purpose which is not for the direct benefit of man and woman, but, instead, for the functional health of the family and the welfare of children. When these roles are jettisoned from society for purely self-serving reasons, the fallout has a deleterious effect on children, decomposes the family, and contaminates the whole of society. These results are painfully apparent in our times, yet society seems so perfectly apathetic to this, one of the major causes of its self-destruction.

Specifically, it is the changing role of women in today's world that has exhorted the masses to accept familial upheaval and decay all in the name of perceived liberation. Granted, many social, political, and even religious changes concerning the equality of men and women have been needed for generations. The role of women, however, was never in need of change. The role of women, just as with men, has been divinely predetermined, and, therefore, is not ours to change. Instead, it is our attitude toward, and appraisal of, the role of women that needs to be radically transformed.

Looking back through history, the prevailing attitude toward women was founded on a two dimensional feminine model with each dimension being totally at odds with the other. On the one hand, women were generally held in high regard, respected, and even revered. On the other hand, in the social, political, religious, and business arenas, women were largely excluded, ignored and suppressed. In effect, women were viewed as little more than a prized possession, a valuable to be admired and regarded with great devotion, but also a kind of sub-species of humanity. While this latter view of women was, in the least, inhumane, the former view was imbued with a great wisdom and insight. In an attempt to rectify these inequalities of the past, modern man has taken steps that would rightfully abolish the discrimination and manipulation of women. We have gone about the task with the most admirable intentions, yet we have attacked the wrong foe. Instead of challenging man made attitudes regarding the worth and respect of women, we have challenged God-given attributes of the role itself, all in an attempt to 'empower' women. Society has not empowered women. Instead, society has quietly brainwashed women into perceiving themselves as useless, unproductive and unfulfilled, lest they take on the questionable qualities that once beleaguered only men. No longer is it in vogue for a woman to be gentle, nurturing and selfless – and at home. Now she must be cunning, power hungry, and self-absorbed - and away from the home - in order to wrench success and personal fulfillment out of the hands of a modern world, which, in turn, is strangling her true identity.

An objective cause and effect evaluation of women's changing roles leads to obvious conclusions, yet we seem to lack the courage to address them in the face of prevailing social misconceptions. As women have left the home in droves, the home has been irreparably damaged. It is that simple. The absence of women in the home has directly lent itself to the decay of the family; to psychological and emotional damage to children of all ages; to child abuse; to teen violence, promiscuity and suicide; and, most damaging, to a dearth of spirituality within the family. Furthermore, our culture's obsession with sexual license has tarnished the concept of women in the workplace by naively promulgating infidelity and divorce, and, in so doing, has granted acquiescence to the cultural philosophies of birth control and abortion. The blame does not lie with either gender, but instead with society as a whole. How can we not see the immense value of the traditional role of women in the family, and in society, when its absence has created such cultural disorder and chaos? We are promoting a pretense of 'liberation' for women at the expense of our children, our families, and our culture.

None of this is to say that women should never work outside the home, or that those who do should not be treated with exacting equality in relation to their male counterparts. What is apparent, however, is that, except in cases of dire and honest financial straits, society should promote and genuinely desire that those women who have both husband and children would rejoice in the work of the home, in the role of raising their children, and in the true fulfillment of being a mother and a wife. The maternal nature must no longer be denigrated, but honored for its unparalleled consequence. We should esteem, not belittle, the women who sacrifice for their children's sake; affirm, not betray, the wisdom of those who appraise the family room over the board room; and exalt, not disparage, the ambition and achievement of motherhood. Any culture that does less only cheats itself by blindly ignoring the course and content of its future.

Undoubtedly, the maternal role is the most demanding, difficult and often the least appreciated of all vocations; yet, it is also, by far, the most momentous - indeed, the most heroic. The role of the woman inside the home easily surpasses in importance any human endeavor, overshadowing heads of companies and even heads of state, for while corporations and nations will shortly pass into oblivion, the ennobled posterity of motherhood will forever be. It has been said that the hand that rocks the cradle rules the world. Let it now be said that the hand the rocks the cradle holds the keys to heaven – true and lasting empowerment.

Feminism, or at least its original intent, has been a worthy cultural movement. Treating women as second-class citizens was, and remains, a repressive and demeaning form of discrimination. Equal rights for women that, to this day, continue to be won are long overdue. Radical/militant feminism, however, has commandeered the cause and, over the past few decades, has accomplished little but to expound on a vitriolic hatred of men and a prejudiced belittling of women who do not blindly submit to the fascist code of a bitter and unhinged membership. Of all the drivers of the Progressive agenda, neo-feminism is, by far, the most hypocritical. Radical feminists despise men even as they simultaneously aspire to be more like them. Feminism scorns the historically low standard of sexual mores for men, but instead of attempting to raise that standard, they debase themselves to the same level. The watchwords and catch phrases that define the feminist movement, 'choice,' 'equality,' 'rights,' etc., apply only to women who are faithful to the Progressive doctrine. If a woman, any woman, defends independence from feminist ideology, that being her 'choice,' she is immediately and viciously chastised. If a woman has achieved 'equality' within a 'male-dominated culture' by succeeding on her own merits and reaching the pinnacle of her vocation, she is yet marginalized and ridiculed if she fails to espouse the acrid tenets of radical feminism. If a woman fulfills her ambition of becoming a wife and mother, which is her 'right,' she will face a condescending derision, nonetheless, by the militant wing of her own gender. The recently organized 'Annual Women's March,' in its duplicitous claims of hyper-inclusivity, embraces women as prostitutes, porn stars and strippers, but excludes women who are pro-life.

Feminists abound in Hollywood and throughout the entertainment industry, and are constantly feigning disgust at the objectification of women, yet the product they create and deliver consistently cheapens their own femininity and reinforces the concept of women as nothing but a sexual commodity. Power brokers in Hollywood have for years engaged in evident, yet largely ignored, sexual abuse of women. As obscene misogyny has recently become public, feminists are disingenuously aghast, as they fail to make the connection between sexual perversions behind the scenes with the bottomless pit of sexual perversions in front of the camera, a psychological defect much like deploring obesity while exalting gluttony. The mindset of a culture that has created the '#metoo' movement in order to fight the evils of sexual abuse is the same mindset that created the need for the movement in the first place – the 'liberation' of sexual promiscuity with neither consequence nor commitment. When individuals are no longer expected to control their sexual passions, a concept wrought by the pronounced contradiction of modern feminism, abuse inevitably follows. Sexual harassment resides throughout the entire spectrum of modern indecency, from immodesty to pornography. Widespread indecency not only leads to sexual harassment, it *is* sexual harassment. When a debased society's 'entertainment' repetitively portrays pornographic activity as normal, even heroic, in many instances, there should be no shock when pervasive sexual exploitation becomes the norm.

Modern feminism has proven itself a cultural farce perpetrated by women who are insecure in their femininity, by a culture that enables the exploitation of women while affecting condemnation, and by a society that is in denial of the genuine worth of the feminine gender. Possibly the most insincere feminist of all time, Hillary Clinton, spitefully intimidated and falsely accused any and all women who brought to light the sexual abuses committed by her husband amidst his numerous extramarital hobbies. The entire feminist movement was noticeably silent regarding the misogyny and predation of the most powerful man in the world. Planned Parenthood claims to be the guardian of women's rights, yet defends the eugenics of sex-selective abortions, which, in overwhelming numbers, are reserved for the inhumane 'cleansing' of unborn females worldwide.

While there has been evidence of true gender inequality throughout our culture, much of the disparity has been eradicated over the past few decades. What remains is minimal, if not non-existent, yet it continues to be strategically orchestrated to fit the Progressive artifice of divisiveness and contention. Women are conditioned to believe that they are forever downtrodden, and that sexism is rampant in every social arena, none more so than in the workplace. The 'wage gap' drama is yet another liberal contraption fabricated to support the need for a governmental solution to a perceived injustice. It is simply a political construct, pandering to the 'victimized' for votes and power, and it is largely a myth. The narrative is relentlessly repeated, however, as it has proven to be an effective ploy in the Progressive playbook of continually pitting one group against another. "Women are paid 77 cents on the dollar *for doing the same work as men*" is a verifiably false statement, yet one often parroted by those simulating patronage for gender equality. The statistic is massaged from annual calculations made by the Census Bureau, and then repackaged into propaganda for those prone to exploitation. The '77 cents' figure is simply a mathematical calculation based on the average annual earnings of all women versus all men across all occupations, with absolutely no differentiation factored in for chosen careers. This is not at all a strict comparison based on the *same work.* An identical illusion could use the same line of deceptive reasoning and, by choosing the income data points of female doctors and male truck drivers, claim that women make four times the amount of men. With all else being equal, especially occupation and hours worked, the pay difference all but disappears. When other personal decisions and preferences are factored in, such as women being typically willing to accept lower pay for higher benefits, maternity leave, and compensation flexibility for child and elder care, the disparity is statistically insignificant (US Department of Labor: CONSAD Research Corporation, *Gender Wage Gap Final Report;* January 12, 2009).

Changes affecting the role of men, especially husbands and fathers, have occurred quietly and virtually unnoticed when compared with the drastic metamorphosis of the female role…quiet and unnoticed, but just as damaging to society. These changes, in some ways, are a direct result of the feminist movement, and in other ways, unique expressions of a male culture indoctrinated with false notions of strength and success. Similar to our present culture's misunderstanding of the nature and role of women, our society is again attacking the wrong enemy when it comes to the nature and role of men - the worth of masculine qualities as proscribed by God versus the distorted attributes of manliness ordained by our culture.

A major change in the composition of the traditional male role as father revolves around the age-old concept of provision. The virtues necessary to succeed in the fatherly role are in direct confrontation with the qualities of life espoused by a materialistic society. Providing for one's family has taken on a meaning and purpose that far exceeds the basic intent of the historical model that has served both societies and families so well for centuries. The fruits of labor that enable a man to provide food, shelter and clothing for his family no longer satisfy his appetite. He feels it is his duty to live amid excess, considers himself successful only when his family is engorged with things, and rationalizes his own selfishness and time away from his family as a sacrifice to attain these ends. The responsibility of provision was fashioned by God for the purpose of life sustenance, not material gluttony. Those men who believe the opposite do themselves and their families a great disservice in two ways. First, this penchant will, in practice, most certainly convey to all members of the family, especially young children who are beset with a constant temptation to submit to no one or nothing but self. Second, the more a man provides in terms of worldly goods, the less his family gains in other essential areas, primarily by virtue of his absence. When provision leads to neglect, better that our children live in material want.

Just as God is the foundation of our nation's origin, so should He be the foundation of the family, and it is incumbent upon every father to build and maintain that foundation in unison with his spouse. If fathers would invest as much time and effort in their children's spiritual welfare as is invested in their physical, material and intellectual development, they would then unlock the real treasures of fatherhood. There is no greater earthly joy for a father than witnessing his child's discovery of God's love, than joining with his child in experiencing the only lifestyle that leads to true peace and happiness, than knowing deep in his heart that he has done everything in his power to protect his child's soul from the ways of the world and prepare his child's soul for the endless promises of heaven. If there was only one possible success in life afforded to each father, it is exactly this for which his whole being should strive.

The covenant of fatherhood is a covenant of two parts. The first is between God and every father: that each man who is granted the purity of a child's soul will discover perfect fulfillment upon the promise that, primarily, he will dedicate his life to the spiritual well-being of that soul entrusted unto him. The second covenant is between a father and his child: a relationship grounded in disciplined love, tempered in patience and forgiveness, and whose sole purpose is mutual salvation, for inasmuch as a father holds the salvation of his children as his most genuine desire in life, so he ensures his own. While the world has relegated such paternal aspirations to nearly imperceptible levels, the family, in turn, has suffered a truly pathetic disintegration. A dissoluble family, as witnessed especially in this country, is yet another precursor of the pervasive moral decay that has led to many of the ills we face as a society. The correlation between a weakening, spiritually passive fatherhood and the functional obsolescence of the family is far from superficial. When time is eroded by absenteeism, wisdom by worldliness, and sacrifice by selfishness, the very roots of the family become exposed and are easily washed away. The shifting bulwark of the family is in desperate need of spiritual reinforcement. Fathers need to look beyond the mere responsibilities of feeding, clothing and sheltering their children. Whether in the finest or most impoverished circumstances, these are but fleeting – it is their souls which last forever.

The demoralization of young boys and adolescent men is perverting society at its very core. Instead of advocating for young men by extolling the prerequisite propriety of healthy masculinity, our culture seems intent on disowning young men by declaring them fallow in their very nature. Modern society has deemed the mere substance of masculinity to be inherently effete and irredeemable, and male youth are inculcated with this prejudice throughout their formative years from every possible medium. The conscious and relentless hyper-sexualization prevalent in our culture, perpetuated by agents of neo-Progressive ideals, has throttled the male psyche from childhood onward. He is mocked by those same agents for falling prey to what he is yet unable to comprehend with maturity, and mocked again if he attempts resistance, as he is dragged back in, time and again. He is told to respect a female's slattern rights but he is not afforded the same respect for his raging hormones. He is prompted to question his sexuality at every turn, to experiment, and to surrender to his malformed passions, to follow them no matter the despairing depths to which they lead. He can neither escape the pervasive exposure nor is he given the guidance to perceive its grievous intentions or the tools to defend against it. The heroic few that do emancipate themselves are subsequently met with derision, yet again, for their conviction to chastity. Similarly, he is subjected to an endless progression of unadulterated scenes of violence, and as his underdeveloped conceptions do not allow him to filter those images with any sense of mature reflection, he will often imitate them. When he does, even in small ways, he is then cast as monstrous and ushered to self-loathing. He is further manacled by a dearth of decent male role models, often by the absence or indifference of his own father, and subsequently turns to mere pseudonyms of caricatured and inimical male personas as depicted in movies, television programs and music videos. We entrap him with stimuli that he is not able to process and then dare him to respond. We set the stage for his descent, and then blame him for acting upon it. This maelstrom of emotions thereupon leads to a further erosion of internal worth, to drug and alcohol abuse, to the dereliction of responsibility, to the mistreatment of women, and to the self-fulfilling prophecy of degenerate masculinity. Pity the boy who is sentenced to wallow in our culture's self-created, vindictive and intentional subversion of manhood - a verdict from which he will likely not recover. We systematically break him in his innocence and borrow astonishment when the broken boy becomes the broken man. "It is easier to build strong children than to repair broken men" (Frederick Douglass).

As a punishing response to male domination in virtually every society since the beginning of time, our current culture appears bent on propagandizing to itself that men are superfluous, that manly qualities are obsolete. The deliberate portrayal of men as Neanderthal, childish buffoons in movies, television shows and many other cultural forums only serves to foster the false perception that the archetypical man is not a requisite element of our culture. In many pockets of society, men are no longer required to play an essential role in providing for a child, or parenting a child, or, outside of the obvious, even fathering a child. The once heralded masculine qualities of sacrifice, self-discipline and constancy have lost their connection to honor, having been widely replaced with selfishness and inconsistency. Courteousness, chivalry, and respect, having been traded for vulgarity and narcissism, are no longer expected, or even desired. These and other character traits that once defined a man have been buried beneath the shadow of cosmetics, layers of ink, and the distraction of jewels. Healthy confidence, rigor, and precision have been overcome by hesitance and coarseness; clarity, by vagary; excellence, by mediocrity; and willpower, by weakness. In short, men have been marginalized, figuratively castrated, and, the worst of it is, we shrugged nonchalantly, simply abetting the incapacitation of our manhood. By design, our culture has abducted the 'man of character' and presided over his demise.

Gender Confusion

Given our culture's deliberate crusade of gender anarchy, there should be no surprise or wonder, then, regarding the new age dilemma of gender confusion. The blurred lines forcibly drawn by a culture that is intent on erasing natural gender distinction have created a great deal of consternation for both men and women – a tragic inner turmoil that cries out for humane and sensitive concern. For some, their psychological tribulations are real – trials that should never be intensified by personal condemnation or callous derision, yet neither should they be placated and affirmed. For others, the frustration and anguish caused by the denial of their God given gender identity is both regrettable and corrigible, being largely driven by our society's perverted concept of sexuality. In a time of healthier sexual logic, a reasonable assumption can be made that a full majority of those presently disoriented would not so be. For others still, there is no confusion at all, just simply the proud, rebellious denial of their sexual nature proscribed at conception. A Montgomery County, Maryland, school district survey reports a 582% increase in the number of students identifying as gender nonconforming over a two-year period (*Daily Caller;* Oct 11, 2022). For these, a plausible rationale can be defended that their self-identified counter-sexuality would not exist but for imitative exhibition – a 'cultural grooming' perpetuated by the perceived societal popularity, vogue acceptance, and present-day, cult-like status of any sexuality that deviates from the norm – far different than the fully debunked LGBT talking point of "born that way.' The more aberrant the behavior, the more iconic it has become. Furthermore, in a society awash in the damnation of 'cultural appropriation,' why is transgenderism not considered 'gender appropriation?'…and, how does removing genitals affirm gender if genitals don't define gender?

The rationalization for gender fluidity has meandered wildly in recent years based on variations of biological, neurological, hormonal and genetic theories (any but psychological). The random and frenetic search for any proof of, or scientific explanation for, the presence of a 'gender spectrum' is indicative of an implicit bias. In other words, the proof was so passionately desired that the science was publicized as settled before the theories could even be tested. Not finding a definitive scientific basis for any such premise, however, the sexual revolutionaries turned to their science of last resort – the social sciences. Subsequently, the definition of the word 'gender' was changed from being a synonym of 'sex' to having a more pliant ambiguity, was then reclassified as a social construct, and voila, gender became 'fluid.' The process, far from being scientific, could be applied to any foolish concept, or any 'social construction,' that desires a predetermined outcome:

> **Sex/Gender**: Sex is a physical reality defined as either male or female. Gender is now a socially constructed feeling…a self-created perception of a range of sexuality. Just because a man 'feels' he is a gendered female does not mean that he is a woman…it simply means that he believes himself to be a woman. He has male sexuality but claims to have female gender, yet he is still a man. He can use institutions to force others to agree that he is a woman; he can use governments to create laws that defend the perception of his femininity; he

can force society to pay for his genital reconstruction – but he remains a man.

Eyesight/Vision: Eyesight is a physical reality defined by the ability to see. Vision is now a socially constructed feeling…a self-created perception of a range of sight. Just because a blind man 'feels' he has vision does not mean that he can see…it simply means that he believes he can see. He has no eyesight but claims to have vision, yet he is still blind. He can use institutions to force others to agree that he has vision; he can use governments to create laws that defend the perception of his vision; he can force society to pay for his glasses – but he remains sightless.

Mobility/Ambulation: Mobility is a physical reality defined by the capacity for movement. Ambulation is now a socially constructed feeling…a self-created perception of a range of movement. Just because a paraplegic man 'feels' ambulatory does not mean that he is mobile…it simply means that he believes himself to be mobile. He has no movement but claims to have ambulation, yet he is still static. He can use institutions to force others to agree that he is ambulatory; he can use governments to create laws that defend the perception of his ambulation; he can force society to pay for his shoes – but he remains immobile.

Assuming that science will yet find a causal connection between a physiologic function of the body and gender dysphoria, whether that be genetic marker, hormonal imbalance, biological anomaly, or any other deviation from normalcy, sound medicine, nonetheless, should never match the treatment to align with the aberration, but with a return to the natural state. For example, if a hormonal abnormality were proven the cause of gender dysphoria, the medically honest response would be to use hormonal treatment to normalize the condition, not resort to genital destruction to validate the abnormality, which is as preposterous as using radiation to relieve depression. Likewise, if a neurological condition were discovered to be the determinant factor of gender confusion, then neurological therapy would be a far more appropriate response than gender reassignment. If a mentally deranged person identifies as Elvis Presley, we do not perform plastic surgery to conform his features to the king of rock 'n roll. Even if his claim is proven psychologically sincere, and is found to be genetically written on a specific chromosome, we still do not affirm that which denies reality.

Outside of the extremely rare condition of physical evidence of sexual ambiguity, more recently defined as 'intersex,' the biological distinction between male and female cannot be argued. What it becomes, then, is a psychological distinction - a distortion of reality – identical to the cognitive disorder of anorexia. Anorexics look in the mirror and see obesity where a morbid emaciation actually exists. Similarly, a woman can *believe* that she is truly a man but that does not make it so. A man may sometimes *believe* that he is a woman, and at other times, a man, but his *true* nature cannot possibly be contorted as such. This functional denial of truth is not a projection of heroism or courage, as many will claim, but instead, a classic symptom of a mental disorder - a delusional psychosis. Altering biological facts to conform to feelings and emotions is not only contrary to science but also quite impossible. We have lost touch with our true identities as we fabricate and affirm artificial ones. Our culture has all but beatified Bruce Jenner, yet ridicules Rachel Dolezal, a young woman of full Caucasian ethnicity who nevertheless claims she is African-American. Why is it any less ridiculous for Mr. Jenner to claim that he is really a woman, than for Ms. Dolezal to claim she is really black? Maybe the extremes of hormone therapy and genital reconstruction surpass, in sheer boldness and insanity, a fake tan, cornrow braids, and a name change to Nkechi Amare Diallo, but the two instances are otherwise of an identical delirium. How can one re-create his or her 'authentic' being by self-evident prevarication or, worse yet, by self-manipulation and self-mutilation? Dismantling your true self is the antithesis of authenticity. Mimicking an alternative, fabricated self, by definition, is schizophrenic and should be treated as such with empathetic psychiatric therapy. Instead, many states have passed laws preventing psychiatrists from clinically attempting to reverse or correct this deviation from sound mental health, and the federal government has actually included sex-reassignment surgery as a covered Medicare procedure. It is only a matter of time before our enlightened culture criminalizes any attempt to ameliorate the perplexing conditions of homosexuality and transgenderism by a sympathetic and palliative return to nature and normalcy – not only psychologists as criminals, but priests and parents as well.

Patronization of unnatural longings for a false gender identity does both the individual and society great harm, but is especially a travesty when applied to children, often by their own parents, doctors and counselors. Warping young minds with the concepts of gender fluidity may be 'trendy,' but it is also insidiously deceitful.

Being naturally impressionable, as well as physically and emotionally immature, children who portray a tendency to gender confusion should never be encouraged to surrender to these oftentimes-fleeting episodes. Studies at Vanderbilt University have shown that children displaying transgender tendencies often lose those same feelings over time, prior to any medical or surgical treatment. Seventy to Eighty percent of the children by the study's end no longer experienced gender confusion (Wall Street Journal Commentary, June 12, 2014; Dr. Paul McHugh, former psychiatrist-in-chief, Johns Hopkins Hospital). Can you imagine the physical and emotional distress suffered by these children, as they would be subjected, unnecessarily, to hormone therapy and surgery? Instead of ameliorating their confusion, it is more likely that such appeasement will only exacerbate their mental torture and psychological damage, and, as such, is nothing short of child abuse. The apex of this abuse is found in the puberty blockers and cross-sex hormones that have numerous adverse side effects maliciously punctuated by irreversible sterilization in many cases. Psychologists who validate and promote this mental fiction in children are a traitor to their profession, and doctors who maim the natural sexuality of our youth are complicit in the pathology of their physical desecration. These are the true proponents of a barbaric and abusive 'conversion therapy.' Why is it now illegal to attempt to align a child's psychological perception of gender with reality, yet perfectly fine to mutilate sexual organs so as to appease a psychological illusion? Individuals experiencing gender dysphoria, especially children, are being psychologically and physically molested by the very people who claim to defend them.

Adults succumbing to the confusion of gender identity by resorting to sex-reassignment surgery fare no better. A January 2014 study performed by the Williams Institute at the American Foundation for Suicide Prevention has determined that over 40% of transgender individuals will attempt suicide at some point in their lives compared to less than five percent of the general population. Another study at the Karolinska Institute in Sweden showed an almost 2000% increase in suicide between reassigned men and women versus the non-transgender population, as well as a higher likelihood to seek psychiatric assistance (Plos One; February 22, 2011; Cecilia Dehejne, et.al.). Sex reassignment surgeries do little to lessen the psychological torment of the gender-challenged, and, in many cases, magnify their misery.

Homosexuality

While gender confusion on such a wide scale is a relatively new phenomenon, it has arisen out of, as well as spawned, numerous forms of gender deviance (i.e. lesbian, gay, bisexual, transgender, agender, amalgagender, bigender, demigender, gender fluid, asexual, pansexual, queer, gender-full, neutrois, questioning, androgynous, variant, masculine/feminine of center, nonconforming, nonbinary, gender apathetic, Two Spirit, unspecified, etc.) - an inane 'gender spectrum' driven by a society and media fixated on normalizing all things abnormal, even to the point of declaring such preternatural tendencies as 'blessings of liberty.' The 'umbrella' condition of homosexuality, however, has existed at some level since the beginning of mankind. While some cultures throughout history have shown toleration, or at least indifference, to homosexuality, only lately has homosexuality been afforded cultural esteem as a hallmark of social progress. Truly odd is the attempt to market this lifestyle as something decent, even honorable. Imagine a group of incestuous partners or serial adulterers organizing a massive parade to broadcast their 'pride.' Homosexuality and its by-products are certainly no cause for boastful celebration. It is one thing to continually falter in sin, feel remorse, and seek forgiveness. It is quite another to continually falter in sin and then attempt to extol its virtues. Equating homosexual love with the conjugal love of man and woman is nothing but an evisceration of the concept of human love and a blatant offense to natural laws as instituted by God.

There rages a great debate as to how sexual orientation should be utilized, if at all, in determining a person's moral character. No matter how the absolute value of sexual orientation is scored by society, however, the bottom line is that homosexual acts are a sin and an aberration of God's plan for human sexuality. The Bible is incontrovertibly clear on the subject. In the Old Testament book of Leviticus (18:22), there can be no confusion as to God's opinion: "Do not have sexual relations with a man as one does with a woman…it is an abomination." Many proponents of homosexuality, even religious believers, will invariably argue that the Old Testament's succinct objection to homosexuality is outdated. In addition, how could homosexuality be taken seriously as a sin when it was lumped in with other numerous (and ridiculous to modern sensibilities), codified proscriptions in Leviticus, such as eating seafood, wearing mixed linens, and having abnormally large limbs? If one is to follow that argument to its conclusion, however, then bestiality and incest should also be given a pass, as these two icons of depravity are parenthetical to the listing of homosexuality.

The New Testament, as well, in numerous passages, reemphasizes the indisputable stance of the early Church regarding homosexual behavior:

Romans 1:26-27:

[26] Because of this, God gave them over to shameful lusts. Even their women exchanged natural sexual relations for unnatural ones. [27] In the same way the men also abandoned natural relations with women and were inflamed with lust for one another. Men committed shameful acts with other men, and received in themselves the due penalty for their error.

1 Corinthians 6:9-10:

[9] Or do you not know that wrongdoers will not inherit the kingdom of God? Do not be deceived: Neither the sexually immoral nor idolaters nor adulterers nor men who have sex with men[10] nor thieves nor the greedy nor drunkards nor slanderers nor swindlers will inherit the kingdom of God.

1 Timothy 1:9-10:

[9] We also know that the law is made not for the righteous but for lawbreakers and rebels, the ungodly and sinful, the unholy and irreligious, for those who kill their fathers or mothers, for murderers, [10] for the sexually immoral, for those practicing homosexuality,

for slave traders and liars and perjurers—and for whatever else is contrary to the sound doctrine.

Despite a clear biblical consensus, however, the next argument posed by misinformed believers is found in the assertion that Jesus never mentions homosexuality (at least as recorded in the Bible). While true, it does nothing to prove that He condoned it. One cannot believe Jesus was providing affirmation for homosexuality simply by being silent on the subject. He was silent on many other aspects of human behavior that are, or have been, generally considered sinful as well. As such, it is unlikely that He automatically condoned those actions that He did not directly address. Maybe Jesus never uttered an opinion on homosexuality because it had been so clearly addressed in Scripture, and quite emphatically, at that. If He really intended to sanction homosexual acts, or at least not condemn them, one would believe that He, out of a need for clarity, would have made a distinct reprobation of the Old Testament/Hebrew laws regarding the same, much as He did to the 'eye for an eye' code of justice that He clearly denounced in Matthew's gospel.

In a desperate attempt to find an element, any element, of support for homosexuality in Jesus' words of the New Testament, some 'biblical scholars' reference Matthew 19:12: "For there are eunuchs who were born that way from their mother's womb; and there are eunuchs who were made eunuchs by men; and there are also eunuchs who made themselves eunuchs for the sake of the kingdom of heaven." The parsing of this verse from the overall context of Matthew 19 is itself evidence of a dishonest argument. This section of Matthew's gospel is speaking only of the permanence of marriage, and in no way is even a remote discussion on homosexuality. Furthermore, the term 'eunuch' refers to those who are in fact *incapable* of sexual activity (whether by birth defect, forced castration, or personal sacrifice), not those who are inclined to an unnatural sexual proclivity; in other words, a biological distinction, not one of sexual psychology. In effect, the discussion precludes *any* sexual activity, which would obviously necessitate a denial of homosexuality as well. Tangential arguments, contextual misrepresentations and weak translations aside, both Testaments of Sacred Scripture are inarguably of the same mind when it comes to homosexual behavior.

Homosexuality can be attributed to only three possible causes, none of which gives credence to its unworthy comparison to natural love. The first hypothesis is based on the supposition that certain people are 'born that way,' being predisposed to homosexual tendencies by way of a genetic difference…the 'gay' gene. These people would be destined, therefore, to a life of unavoidable and irreversible homosexual urges. The ensuing argument is that gays and lesbians are victims of their biological makeup, and thus possess no control over their sexual inclinations. In the first place, there is no evidence of any such gene ever being discovered by medical science, in spite of obfuscating attempts by some scientists and social activists to imply the opposite. Second, the entire hypothesis becomes a 'non sequitur,' cast as illogical by the phenomenon of identical twins (with identical genetic makeup). If one twin were homosexual, then it would stand to reason that the other would have to be as well, in every instance, because the supposed gay gene would be present in each. Obviously, this is not the case. Furthermore, if this hypothesis were true, it creates a frightening social precedent. Assume science can prove that certain people are genetically prone to drug abuse. Are these people then, as self-casualties of their genetics, entitled to (or, worse yet, encouraged to) continue drug use and abandon any attempt to overcome the problem, or to seek help, simply because they were 'born that way?' The drug abuser succumbs to a temptation that leaves him vulnerable to a gluttony that is physically unnatural and societally detrimental. He is reveling in the satisfaction of his own selfish desires. If the cause of homosexuality could actually be traced to a predestined, uncontrollable proclivity, then it should be treated as such – a disease. Just because one may have been born 'with an inclination' toward pride, lust, or greed, it does not at all follow that any of these propensities are acceptable, or, especially, worthy of celebration. Finally, this entire argument is a direct contradiction to the rationale behind the elevation and defense of the transgender lifestyle. While society must support the homosexual man (or woman) by never suggesting that he normalize his lifestyle *because* he was 'born that way,' at the same time, society is obligated to always encourage the transgender man or woman to change his or her original sexuality *in spite of* being 'born that way.' Such abstruse hypocrisy and naked intellect are emblematic of a society bereft of sound reason.

In recent years, there have come forth certain groups who have taken this hypothesis to a blasphemous extreme by boldly asserting that God has created them as homosexuals and, since God is all knowing, all-powerful and the essence of perfection, it is their destiny to live as such. In other words, homosexuality is God's will for them, their vocation of sorts, and it would be a travesty not to be faithful to their calling and fulfill this truth with which God Himself has blessed them. This convoluted reasoning is borne of a heretical confusion between God's omnipotent will and mankind's free will. How can one believe that God wishes any of us to fulfill our potential by means of an 'abomination?' We are all born with original sin and a lifelong inclination to a varied spectrum of evil. This is not of God's making; it is of our own. If the opposite were true, every weakness that we encounter within ourselves could be attributed to God's will and our concept of human evil would cease to exist…an argument conceived by the devil himself.

The second possible cause of homosexuality is argued on the nurture side of the 'nature vs nurture' debate. This view surmises that a person's environment or experience determines his or her sexuality. The suggestion is that, from the earliest days of infancy onward, a person's relationships with parents, family and friends, as well as his education, work, recreation and all measure of social interaction play a part in formulating sexual orientation. The unproven but realistic implication is that some 'abnormal' occurrence (or pattern) somehow affected the healthy sexual development of that person, whether poor role models, broken families, abuse of some sort, coercion, societal pressure, or any number of other possibilities. This social formula can be applied to many different types of human behavior. For example, a child who is reared in a stable home, and nurtured with love and guided with discipline, is more apt to become a good parent than one who is deprived of the same blessings. The deprived child, however, is not automatically barred from becoming a good parent, nor is he or she automatically exonerated for becoming a bad parent. Granted, it will be more difficult for the neglected child to attain well-rounded parenthood, but that child is not exempted from the task. Possibly, so it is with homosexual men and women who fall under this nurture diagnosis. People who are socially influenced to adopt a lifestyle of homosexuality, therefore, are not irreversibly or uncontrollably subjected to a permanence of homosexual activity.

The third and only other possible cause of human homosexuality lies in the conscious decision to engage in homosexual acts without any impetus from biological or social forces. While many believe this to be the most forthright evaluation of the topic, it is also the most easily addressed. Through free will, all sin, and therefore all evil, pain and suffering, is a derivative of the conscious decision. To knowingly partake of that which is contrary to nature, to God's miraculous blueprint of mankind's existence and to the succession of society, flagrantly ridicules the good and wholesome life, and is the touchstone for acts abhorrent to any moral culture.

A discussion of homosexuality from a strictly social viewpoint, outside the realm of spirituality and religious dogma, only results in further evidence of the damaging nature of homosexual acts. The factors that contribute to a healthy and productive society are each drained of their positive impact and self-actualizing powers which they naturally possess when they are overwhelmed by unnatural powers. Homosexuality as an unnatural, behavioral contortion is indisputable. The cornerstone of society is, and always has been, the family – the naturally functioning family whose members are each aware of their separate but equally critical roles to create, sustain, and enhance life, not only for the direct benefit of their own family unit, but just as crucially for the good of society as a whole. The recent and spiraling disintegration of the family is directly linked to a rampage of social toxins such as poverty, promiscuity, crime, violence, and a host of other maladies. Homosexuality, among other impurities, is magnifying this disintegration by its unabashed ridicule of, and contempt for, the very values that are essential to the natural family. Homosexual, and other 'alternative lifestyle' relationships, as they increase in number and acceptance, will unavoidably continue to sap society of its lifeblood.

Many in today's culture understand the injurious social implications of such lifestyles, not out of fear or loathing, but simply out of an intelligent understanding and a keen awareness of cultural anthropology. Short of that, common sense alone should suffice. Nevertheless, accusations of homophobia, hatred, judgment and discrimination are regularly directed at anyone who dares to disagree with such culturally damaging behavior. Judgment of actions is more than appropriate, and is even necessary, as we all have an inherent interest in the direction of our culture. Personal judgment should be none of our concern, as it is not in our purview to pass any verdict on the ultimate disposition of one's soul. We should neither disparage nor ridicule the person, nor discriminate in housing, employment or any other social structure outside of those that may condone the lifestyle or affirm acceptance. Compassion for the person, and an empathy for the disorienting tribulations they often experience, should be our only emotional response. Not to condemn certain actions, however, that are clearly anathema to natural law, scripturally described as sinful, and are, in our modern society, an overtly detrimental aspiration lacking any beneficent purpose, is an abdication of our responsibility for the right preservation of our culture.

As part of the social ramifications of homosexuality, one cannot ignore the many sexually transmitted diseases that are exacerbated by homosexual activity. According to the Centers for Disease Control, over 75% of many sexually transmitted diseases, including syphilis, gonorrhea, HPV, hepatitis-A, and chlamydia, are contracted and spread by sexually active gay men (CDC Fact Sheet: Reported STDs in the United States, 2016). Acquired Immune Deficiency Syndrome (AIDS) has for over 40 years crippled society by branding its mark of fear, pain and death on the collective psyche of humanity. Although virtually absent from current news, and despite new drugs that have slowed the disease appreciably, AIDS still leaves its scars worldwide. Its causes and epidemiology are still not fully understood, yet its modes of progression are rationally apparent. Evidence of bestiality being one of many causes of the onset of AIDS is realistic, yet merely anecdotal, as a possible determinant of transmission. In its early years, AIDS thrived at the hands of its most prolific agent, homosexual intercourse. Heterosexual promiscuity and drug use then joined homosexuality as chief transmitters of the disease. As such, the causes of AIDS are steeped in impurities and, as with all things immoral, innocent people are often affected. Newborn babies, marital partners, young children and hemophiliacs have all become victims of a preventable disease that, for the most part, is due to the actions of a people who have condoned unnatural sex, recklessly shunned the merits of self-control, and selfishly put other's health in jeopardy. As a society, we have done everything within our power to thwart AIDS and prevent its damage at the physical level, but we have done virtually nothing to attack its major cause – the embracing of immorality through defilement of the sexual act. As long as we ignore, or worse yet, condone and even encourage homosexuality as an acceptable and normal lifestyle, we will forever be haunted by the pathology of AIDS, the sexual revolution's most consequential contribution to society.

Gay Marriage

As the homosexual lobby at one time begged for mere acceptance, and now that it appears to have reached that goal across a wide range of society, one would think the din would have subsided somewhat. Shrill rhetoric remains, however, as the primary tool in *demanding* detractors to not only accept the homosexual lifestyle but also to qualify it with special legal protections under specific laws favoring sexual orientation, as well as a forced recasting of the entire institution of marriage. Just as the definition of truth is not malleable, neither is the inherent meaning of marriage.

Marriage, by definition, is an institution designed to be for one man and one woman. Objectively, that is all it can ever be. For millennia, marriage has been known as a religious sacrament, a legal contract, or a social compact, which acknowledges the binding of male and female only as the bulwark of the family, the most important component of any society. There are two fundamental elements of marriage that preclude any distinction other than male and female. Primarily, and most obvious, is the concept of complementarity - unique qualities between two entities that mutually fulfill what each lacks. Ironically juxtaposed to the otherwise hallowed concept of 'diversity,' this dichotomy is truly worthy of distinction. Physical, emotional and psychological differences between male and female unite perfectly to create a whole that is more potent, more complete, and more perfect than the sum of its parts. This is crucial to the sustenance of a wholesome and supernal relationship between two in marriage, and obviously cannot be present in any homosexual arrangement. Furthermore, this same complementarity provides the optimum conditions for the raising of children. Children require direction from both male and female idiomatic natures to develop their full potential – the loving affection, attention and discipline that masculine and feminine qualities provide in different, yet synergistic ways. The second essential element of marriage that can only be ethically fulfilled by one man and one woman is found in the sublime act of procreation. At its base or animal level, procreation ensures survival; at an elevated or human level, procreation extends the longevity of family and, therefore, society; at its apex or spiritual level, procreation allows us to participate in God's plan for humanity. Two men alone, or two women alone, cannot possibly fulfill the designs of any level.

The contemporary definition of marriage has been diluted to a level that looks at only one component of a very complex institution. Same-sex marriage advocates decry the attempt by society to regulate whom they 'love', as if marriage was solely about romance, compatibility and sexuality. This fragmented and wholly selfish definition of marriage portrays the woeful state of our culture's attitude toward the concept of children as an integral part of marriage - not all marriages, but a majority of them. When confronted with this observation, those same advocates will assert that, with questionable supporting evidence, the raising of children in a same-sex household is just as efficacious as it is in a traditional household. There are countless studies favorable to the concept of same-sex parenting, yet they are peer-reviewed with the "shackled caveats of small, non-representative samples", "conveniently available or selected groups of participants", or "severe, methodological limitations, including bias" (Emotional Problems Among Children with Same-sex Parents; D. Paul Sullins; British Journal of Education, Society and Behavioural Science: Jan 30, 2005). One of the most basic rigors of scientific research, random sampling, is completely ignored. Nonetheless, our culture insists that the 'science is settled,' in spite of the fact that none of these studies have been conducted using the scientific method. After weeding through the 'fake science', it becomes abundantly clear that the research was conducted with prejudicial inclinations and an obviously preordained outcome.

The singular topic regarding marriage and the welfare of children that opposing sides can agree on is the social upheaval caused by absentee fathers. President Barak Obama, himself a recent and politically expedient proponent of same-sex marriage, readily admits: "We know the statistics: that children who grow up without a father are five times more likely to live in poverty and commit crime, nine times more likely to drop out of school, and twenty times more likely to end up in prison. They are more likely to have behavioral problems or run away from home, or become teenage parents. And the foundations of our community are weaker because of it." If a father's presence is such an integral part of the physical, emotional, intellectual, and social development of a child, which our culture deems it most definitely is, then how can society, in the same breath, champion a two-mother household as a worthy alternative? Conversely, as the role of a mother is an absolute necessity for the optimal well-being of every child, how can society so adamantly hail the virtues of a two-father household? Again, the specifically unique attributes brought by male and female into the art of parenting are *both* essential to foster the integral formation of every child; a formation that is key to resolving a whole host of momentous social issues, not the least of which are poverty, violence and crime. As such, the state has a clear and compelling interest in defending and encouraging child-centric parenthood as it was meant to be – one mother and one father. Eschewing that responsibility, just so two gay partners may get a tax break, share assets, visit each other in the hospital, and inherit each other's wealth, is pathetically myopic and a dereliction of society's obligation to itself.

Modern society has attempted, not surprisingly, to falsely equate gay marriage with interracial marriage, where there is no reasonable corollary whatsoever. Comparing interracial marriage with same-sex marriage is a perfect illustration of the opacity of modern reasoning. The 1967 Supreme Court case of Loving v. Virginia brought an end to the anti-miscegenation laws that had been in existence since before the country's founding. The attempt to create a civil rights parallel between this case and same-sex marriage is a false-narrative effort that has recently been appropriated by gay marriage proponents. Citing judicial precedent among congruent cases is one thing; among disparate cases, it is nothing short of activism and obfuscation. Racial discrimination in marriage was correctly deemed unconstitutional because the definition of marriage has nothing to do with race. Homosexuality, however, is not the genetic equivalent of skin color.

In a religious context, and also without merit, some have pointed to two biblical passages in a feeble attempt to discredit the Bible (and all religion, for that matter) in its clear proclamation regarding sexuality in marriage. To that end, the passages are never reprinted in full and always taken out of context:

Deuteronomy 7:1-4: Driving Out the Nations
7 When the LORD your God brings you into the land you are entering to possess and drives out before you many nations—the Hittites, Girgashites, Amorites, Canaanites, Perizzites, Hivites and Jebusites, seven nations larger and stronger than you— 2 and when the LORD your God has delivered them over to you and you have defeated them, then you must destroy them totally. Make no treaty with them, and show them no mercy. 3 Do not intermarry with them. Do not give your daughters to their sons or take their daughters for your sons, 4 for they will turn your children away from following me to serve other gods, and the LORD's anger will burn against you and will quickly destroy you.

2 Corinthians 6:14-18: Warning Against Idolatry

[14] Do not be yoked together with unbelievers. For what do righteousness and wickedness have in common? Or what fellowship can light have with darkness? [15] What harmony is there between Christ and Belial? Or what does a believer have in common with an unbeliever? [16] What agreement is there between the temple of God and idols? For we are the temple of the living God. As God has said: "I will live with them and walk among them, and I will be their God, and they will be my people." [17] Therefore, "come out from them and be separate, says the Lord. Touch no unclean thing, and I will receive you.

The false claim that the Bible is condoning the discrimination of race in marriage and, therefore, possesses no authority to proclaim any opinion on same-sex marriage, is either woefully ignorant or an intentional fabrication. Even a cursory read of these two passages clearly portrays that the author is speaking about "believers vs non-believers" and the passages have absolutely nothing to do with race.

The next argument in favor of gay marriage is found under the now trite and predictable umbrella of 'equality', 'rights', and 'discrimination,' even going so far as to find a Constitutional entitlement to same-sex marriage. In its 2015 ruling (Obergefell v. Hodges), the Supreme Court not only found a non-existent right to gay marriage in the Constitution, but it also jettisoned our 'first' right of the free exercise of religion in order to do so. Justice Anthony Kennedy's majority opinion, prefaced with the following statement,

"The Constitution promises liberty to all within its reach, a liberty that includes certain specific rights that allow persons, within a lawful realm, to define and express their identity," is evidence enough of the opacity of activist judicial deviation. The ruling, which Justice Antonin Scalia scathingly referred to as the "mystical aphorisms of the fortune cookie," belies the dangers of judicial contortion to a "living" Constitution…*anything* can be declared 'constitutional' if one obfuscates with enough ideological prejudice. The Progressive pursuit of an ever-evolving Constitution, especially in regard to an attack on the vital institution of marriage, is tantamount to judicial tyranny, and merely a pretense to weaken the most momentous document of governance ever conceived.

The attempted link between fundamental rights and gay marriage is patently ridiculous. Marriage itself is not a right. Marriage is a responsibility, a privilege and a vocation. If everyone has a right to marry whomever they so desire, then how can we not allow a brother and sister to be married, or two brothers, or a parent and a grown child? Consanguineous relations are the next sexual taboo to fall, and the clamoring for marital rights will soon follow (New Jersey has already legalized incest between consenting adults). How can we now not prevent the marriage of one woman and two men, or three men and two women, or an entire community? Under the fallacious constitutional arguments now being made, how can we not acknowledge the right of multiple marriages? The once slippery slope is plunging into a vertical, breathless descent of dead weight as similar rights will now be claimed by pedophiles and all manner of sexual miscreants, for perversions have now been recast as protected 'orientations.'

Pedophilia is already being classified as an "ordinary" feeling and a "natural, unchangeable" sexual inclination of those who were "born that way," words reminiscent of the incremental social acceptance of homosexuality (TEDx Talk: *Why our perception of pedophilia has to change*; Mirjam Heine; July 1, 2018). The normalization of pedophilia is currently progressing in and around the fringes of the never-ending sexual revolution, patiently waiting for the opportune level of moral depravity to strike. The onslaught is imminent. The direct exploitation of innocent children has already commenced. A ten-year old boy in Brooklyn has been pimped out by his own parents for over two years. Appearing at a gay bar, the *3Dollar Bill,* in December, 2018, the abused boy performed in drag for adult males as they showered him with dollar bills. The rancid perversion is promoted by the main stream media as "inspirational" (Today Magazine; *Meet the 10-year-old 'drag kid' taking over social media with inspiring message*; June 18, 2018), "proud and fierce" (The Daily Beast; *RuPaul Loves 'Drag Kid' Desmond. You Will Too. Fiercely.*; February 7, 2018), and "fabulous" (Fatherly Newsletter; *Desmond Is Amazing and the Art of Raising a Child Drag Queen*; March 20, 2018). Not only are children being abused, their abusers are being celebrated. Harvey Milk, an admitted pederast (not to mention a statutory rapist), has been lionized by Progressives for decades. He is cast as a hero in film, honored by the US Post Office with a stamp in his likeness, recently had a Navy warship named after him, and most sadistically, finds his name on an elementary school in San Francisco.

Would it now surprise anyone to hear, in a few short years, of pedophile pride parades, inclusion, diversity, and exhortations for the civil rights to 'love whom we choose?' Or, a marketing strategy from NAMBLA (the North American Man-Boy Love Association) with catchy slogans such as"#SodomyIsSodomy," "Age is a Social Construct," "Born This Way," and "Imagine Being Discriminated against for Whom You Love"…they are simply waiting for the necessary level of moral depravity to strike. With the help of progressive politicians, degenerate Hollywood entertainers, a pliant media and corruptible psychiatrists, the normalcy of the sexual abuse of children is looming, as we are already being conditioned to accept the depiction of pedophiles as normal people who are simply misunderstood – as victims of discrimination and intolerance, and, of course, their genes. Fifty years ago, the idea of two men, or two women, on their wedding night was enough to nauseate the conscience of the most progressive among us. Now look where we are. The morally bankrupt will never be satisfied with the status quo…boundaries of degeneracy will constantly be pushed.

For thousands of years, marriage has been defined as being between one man and one woman. From a natural, social and legal perspective, that is quite an impressive precedent, yet it is now being blindly ignored, all for a sophomoric notion of fairness and an equivocation of justice. "The denial of the social and legal status of marriage to forms of cohabitation that are not and cannot be marital is not opposed to justice; on the contrary, justice requires it" (Pope Benedict XVI).

In a culture saturated with licentiousness and hedonism for more than three generations, it should come as no surprise that we have deviated from the healthy norm. The moral wrong has become the civil right. Insanity has taken the reins of our future. Reprobate minds attempting to refute the basic premises of biology, molding new rights from a cast of their own making, and embracing a stubborn and willful heresy of God's commands, each require a cultural hubris exceeding all powers of comprehension. If two women, or two men (or children, or animals, or any ad nauseam combination thereof), wish to live together as husband and wife and create their own personal compact, then that is their decision, yet it remains a union that is wholly sterile by nature. Such an arrangement can never be legally or socially coronated as a fundamental right. Deeming it a marriage is neither.

Contraception

"Let the little children come to me, and do not hinder them, for the kingdom of God belongs to such as these" (Mark 10:14). There is no greater earthly blessing than the gift of children, not only to parents but also to the whole of society. Through the eyes of a child, we can see the glory of heaven and the way by which we may attain it. Children are the channels through which we perceive the wonders of life. The joyful and willing reception of children, then, should be an automatic inclination for any society. Yet, for reasons that can only be found in the modern misinterpretation of "reproductive rights" and "sexual freedom", the exact opposite is often the case. This reasoning is unfounded, however, for, in the first place, we have no rights to reproduction. We are not the origin of life, and, thus, it is not ours to manipulate and control. Second, freedom shall never supersede life, as freedom requires life to have any meaning whatsoever. We have made an enemy of our own fertility, the very source of our existence and the most blessed gift of our humanity.

Contraception (etymologically "against the beginning," or "against thought") is viewed by many as one of the great marvels of medical science, and why? All we have accomplished is a way to prevent life – what a shameful editorial on modern medicine. Contraception willfully attempts to remove the Creator from the process of creation. Through the practice of contraception, we have entered into an area that is not of our domain. We are harvesting fruit from the tree of knowledge before it is even ripe. God is life; life comes only from God; therefore, life is God's domain, and His alone. Conception is God's initial manifestation of Himself to humanity. When we purposely prevent a life from coming into our world, we prevent God from coming into our world, and when we banish God, evil will gladly fill the void. By both logic and faith, then, it follows that denying conception is very much the same as denying God, and it is that denial that has become our culture's "original sin," the precursor of many of our society's afflictions.

The prophetic words of Pope Paul VI in his 1968 encyclical letter "Humanae Vitae" succinctly warn us of these intrinsic evils of artificial birth control and the cultural blight left by their virulent mutations. From the foretelling of an increase of "marital infidelity and a general lowering of moral standards," to "reducing women to a mere instrument for the satisfaction of {man's} desires," to the "danger of {forced contraception} by the hands of public authorities," all have come to pass as a result of widespread contraception.

Bishop Fulton Sheen, a Catholic priest and astute philosopher, analogizes further: *"The root principle of birth-control is unsound. It is a glorification of the means and a contempt of the end; it says that the pleasure, which is a means to the procreation of children, is good, but the children themselves are no good. In other words, to be logical, the philosophy of birth control would commit us to a world in which trees were always blooming but never giving fruit, a world full of signposts that were leading nowhere. In this cosmos every tree would be a barren fig tree and for that reason would have upon it the curse of God."* Honestly, one does not need to be a learned theologian to comprehend this causal connection. How can one even begin to compare the sometimes-harsh realities of being open to life with the desolate debilities to which contraception has led us? The growing prevalence of abortion, adultery, divorce, domestic violence, sexual abuse of all types, child abandonment, pornography, sexually transmitted diseases, and prostitution, not to mention government proscribed, forced sterilization and one-child policies, can all be traced back directly to the warped reasoning behind the accepted, and now sacrosanct, moral defect of contraception.

There are many voices throughout the entire cultural conversation, a strong majority to be sure, which glorify contraception as a pre-remedy for abortion. In other words, if we can prevent a life from forming now, we will not have to execute it later. How can one act that is contrary to life be considered a virtue simply because it precludes a subsequent act that is also contrary to life? Within the answer to this question lies our culture's unintelligible animosity toward the sanctity of life. This rationale is not at all a 'lesser of two evils' argument, as the result is essentially the same under either scenario – the wastage of implicit humanity, which is the original, albeit metaphysical, state of each and every person who has ever existed. No, this rationalization is more analogous to the precepts of selective eugenics, at least from the perspective of the progeny who were denied existence. For each of us fortunate enough to exist, our 'being' was made fertile by our parents in sacrificial submission to the will of an omnipotent God, not banished to a state of oblivion, and definitely not neutralized now to avoid termination later. A similarly relevant, yet more secular, argument can be made in the case of pornography. Contraception is to abortion as pornography is to sexual assault. Many will argue, with no evidence, that pornography actually reduces the occurrence of sexual assault when, in fact, pornography feeds the same mental inclinations that induce a predisposition to selfish, frenetic, and sometimes violent, sexual behavior. As with pornography and sexual abuse, contraception and abortion are borne of the same mind. The apple of Genesis is, in part, contraception, and the result of consuming it, abortion. Contraception is not at all the antidote for abortion, but rather the psychology of its cause.

Not only are there cultural ramifications attributable to contraception but there are also direct links to adverse effects on women's physical and mental health. A study demonstrating a link between contraceptive use and breast cancer was performed in 2014. An overall 50% increase in the risk of breast cancer, independent of family history, was found in women who had used oral contraceptives in the preceding year versus those who had not.

The higher the level of fabricated estrogen/progesterone in the contraceptives resulted in a proportionally higher risk of breast cancer (American Association for Cancer Research; *Recent Oral Contraceptive Use by Formulation and Breast Cancer Risk among Women 20 to 49 Years of Age;* May 21, 2014). Another recent study published in the journal *JAMA Psychiatry* has concluded that women who utilize hormonal birth control experienced a much higher rate of depression and were much more likely to seek psychiatric help than women who did not use birth control. For ten years, researchers in Denmark followed over one million women and determined that there exists a 23% increase in episodes of depression for women who use the 'pill' and other forms of hormone-altering birth control. Among teen girls, the increase was an astonishing 70% (Kaiser Health News; *Large Danish Study Links Contraceptive Use to Risk of Depression;* September 28, 2016). Counter studies friendly to the pharmaceutical industry have attempted to discredit any causative links between contraceptives and their hostile medical consequences, yet fall short of any evidence that can directly refute the positive correlation that exists. Various forms of birth control have been independently proven to increase the probability of a wide variety of adverse medical conditions, such as blood clots, Crohn's disease and ulcerative colitis, gall bladder disease, and the potentiality of breast and cervical cancer (National Cancer Institute: *Oral Contraceptives and Cancer Risk).*

Granted, many of the realities faced by married couples in today's society, from a strictly secular standpoint, lend an element of understanding to the use of contraceptives. There are certain times when having a child may impose severe hardships on the lives of a man and a woman, and even place what seems to be a severe strain on their marriage. Whether financial, medical, or emotional, these trials can become moments of truth for married couples who trust in God as the first member of their union. Whenever a child is conceived, it is by God's design. There is no earthly goal or worldly dilemma that is more important than the soul of that child. College educations, comfortable retirements, second homes, and time for oneself do not supersede the value of a soul. Likewise, there is no financial stress, fatigue, or pain of childbirth that will outlast the eternal bliss of that soul's salvation. Standards of living in this life are insignificant when compared with those of the next.

After the thorough examination of a rightly formed conscience, there may be times when avoiding pregnancy is necessary. God does not require an unlimited number of children to be our goal. He only requires that, in no way, will we exclude Him from the process. Natural family planning is the only form of birth control that neither alienates God nor precludes His omniscient wisdom in the creation of life, for two reasons. In the first place, natural family planning requires two elements that are absent in all other forms of birth control – acknowledgement and sacrifice. These two elements work hand in hand to generate a more divine vision of the miracle of conception, a vision that discovers conception as an event that we elevate to the pinnacle of human existence and not an event that we relegate to the depths of human control and prevention.

The acknowledgement of God's presence in the glory of conception is essential to cultivate a deeper understanding of life itself, beginning with the physical act which constitutes existence for each of us. The joys of sex are obvious, but hidden within this often times self-serving joy is the true meaning of a sexual relationship within marriage. When a husband and wife choose to refrain from intercourse after an honest and responsible evaluation of the possible effects of its outcome, they also acknowledge the fact that the act of sex was not created for the sole purpose of their own pleasure. They further recognize both the creative power of God in their union, as well as the potential life that may be laid to waste as a result of using unnatural forms of birth control. In other words, there should exist, above all else, a fundamental respect for both the Creator and the created, borne out of an awareness by every married couple of their subordinated role in the marital act. Natural family planning evokes this respect from both members of a marriage. This shared awareness of God's dominion over life, and of the spiritual rights of unborn souls, provides a primary link between husband and wife that will strengthen the vows of any marriage. Conversely, disavowing God's role and ignoring an unknown soul's potential will actually weaken the marital bond because God and human spirituality are the actual fibers of this bond. The theory comes full circle in stating that unnatural contraception, in its disrespect for God and human spirituality, is detrimental to any marriage and is a key component of the anemic state of the institution of marriage today.

Flowing from Divine acknowledgement is the second attribute of natural family planning – sacrifice. The moral art of sacrifice is a prerequisite of every marriage (especially those blessed with children), and, therefore, should be no stranger to the process that creates those children. While artificial birth control diminishes morality through selfishness, natural contraception enhances morality through sacrifice. If there are serious reasons why married partners should avoid the birth of a child, then those reasons should be given conviction, purpose and meaning through sacrifice. As with every other aspect of responsible living, certain pleasures must be foregone in order to achieve a necessary or desired end.

The power generated by this type of sacrifice, because it is incomprehensible to the modern mind, remains regrettably untapped. In the least, to deny oneself a fulfilled desire for the sake of another is obviously beneficial to both the individual and to society. To deny oneself a fulfilled desire in deference to God's will and the sanctity of life, however, is one of the noblest acts that humanity can perform. This is the legacy that natural family planning allows us to pass on from one God-fearing generation to the next. When we allow the author of life to write freely on the pages of our existence, the story unedited by our intrusive selfishness, and the ending made whole by our self-emptying trust in His will, it is then that we understand sacrifice not as a burden but as a liberating force.

The second reason why natural family planning is the only acceptable form of birth control is found in its name. Natural family planning is just that, natural. By following the natural rhythms and cycles of a woman's body, as ordained by God, we have been given the remarkably effective means of naturally spacing our children. There is no introduction of foreign agents that are hostile to the life creating process. Social acceptance of all types of unnatural contraceptives has anesthetized society's morals as they relate to the natural law. Artificial birth control is alien to both our human nature and our spiritual nature.

From a human, or earthly, perspective, it takes little philosophizing to realize how incontrovertibly unnatural birth control is. The main purpose of any life form is to propagate, to ensure itself a future. This is the natural law. To thwart this survival instinct through unnatural means is contrary to our own existence, our earthly reason for being. Natural family planning does not attempt to deny this instinct for it operates within the confines of nature and is unobtrusive to natural laws.

As they affect our spiritual nature, the ramifications of unnatural contraception are even more perverse. While our attempts to control the creation of life may blemish our collective human nature, their effects are merely temporal, as our human nature is finite. The scars on our spiritual nature, however, are much more than a temporary blemish. Every time we willfully and unnaturally prevent conception, we banish a soul for eternity. "Before I formed you in the womb, I knew you; before you were born, I set you apart" (Jeremiah 1:5). God has envisioned us, each before our conception into this world. To deny God's vision, His will for every one of us, born and unborn, is not simply an iniquitous error in judgment – it is a grave and blasphemous transgression against God. The introduction of birth control to our culture early in the 20th century was the damnable impetus that fatally severed this divinely inspired relationship between love and children, and in turn has led us down a path of familial dysfunction, a path forged by a defective understanding of life itself. The deliberate and unnatural prevention of pregnancy only serves to cheapen life, and as we devalue life, we need only travel a very short distance from prevention to termination.

Letter to an Unborn Child

From your moment of perception, aspire to master virtue, for it is through virtue that one distinguishes between good and evil, between what truly matters in life and what truly degrades it.

As you traverse each day, walk with patience, moderation and honesty, for your every step will tempt you with the tightness of their adversaries.

Be not afraid to cry in either happy times or sad, for tears both nourish goodness and cleanse the melancholy spirit.

Of all your mind's creations, prefer wisdom, as your every thought will father your every action and your every word.

Of all your actions, relish charity, for your every movement, however small it may seem, will in some way effect the condition of humanity.

Of all your words, crown prayer, as your every breath is but a gift and, thus, an extension of divinity.

Within the celebration of your finest accomplishments, allow thanksgiving to pass, for the smallest of your blessings is as a miracle to another.

Under the shroud of your worst failures, nurture forgiveness, as compassion for others' frailties is the forgiveness of your own.

Of your loftiest wishes, set none higher than salvation, upon yourself as well as your enemy, for from salvation is born perception.

Abortion

Countless human frailties have historically threatened the condition of mankind's existence in this world, whose future has been entrusted to our superior reason, foresight and intelligence. Many have been barbaric in their scope and outcome, destroying people or even nations of people for no other reason than the color of their skin, their politics, or their religious beliefs. Genocide of epic proportions has been committed by nation against nation, government against citizens, and neighbor against neighbor. All have been reflective of our evident fallen nature – reciprocal crimes of greed, power-lust, envy, and hatred – in essence, always the guilty against the guilty. There is not one, however, in its sheer scope and culpability, being perpetrated on the wholly innocent, that has been as intrinsically evil as the scourge of abortion.

America's darkest moment occurred in 1973 with the legal acceptance of the execution of unborn children, and since that time over 60 million innocent lives have been violently terminated…at the hands of their own mothers and fathers. The world was justifiably appalled as it learned about the 'killing fields' of the Khmer Rouge regime in Cambodia in the 1970's, when approximately two million citizens were brutally murdered, roughly equating to one-quarter of the Cambodian population. The world was likewise repulsed by the Nazi holocaust of the 1940's as millions of Jews and others suffered horrifying deaths; and sickened again a decade earlier by the estimated 50 million people who lost their lives in the Russian gulags. There have been numerous other examples of mass genocide throughout modern history, yet, tragically enough, their totals are dwarfed by the silent deaths of nearly 1.5 billion unborn babies worldwide since 1970. Their names are unknown and their faces unseen, as their lives were stolen before they drew their first breaths. How odd it is, when the worst of the world's killing fields is found in the mother's womb - once a blessed haven of protection and nourishment, now a venue of massacre, a funeral shroud, a torture chamber, a mass grave where more lives have been claimed than in all wars combined. The slaughter of the innocent is the most vulgar and reprehensible evil as it occurs in isolated violence and abuse. When it occurs widespread, however, promoted by governments and protected by courts, it is the devil incarnate. Abortion is, by far, the most contemptible human rights atrocity in the history of mankind.

Proponents of abortion advance spurious arguments from multiple angles in an attempt to defend the indefensible. Fathom the intellectual acrobatics needed to support a defense to the wanton destruction of life. From a 'God-fearing' perspective, those who claim to be spiritual, religious, or have a belief in any deity at all, and in the same breath defend the moral gangrene of abortion, are simply apostates of the most basic truths of creation. How could anyone believe that the Creator, the origin of life, would condone the destruction of that which He has created? In His own image? Even within a denial of God's existence, abortion is yet a foe of both rational thought and absolute moral conscience. The automatic rejection of abortion is not emblematic of a theocracy, but a civilized society. There remain, nonetheless, the obligatory invocations of civil rights, as well as numerous biological, ecological, legal, medical, ethical, and even philosophical rationales, all fabricated without recourse to logic, all enemies of the natural law found in each and every conscience, and all encapsulated in the 'culture of death' that plagues our society.

Civil Right

Advocates frame their defense of abortion as a civil right based on our culture's misconstrued concept of freedom and choice. In reality, the bedrock of abortion is neither freedom nor choice, but domination and duress. Even true freedom, the most noble of goals and the basis of all civil rights, must be valued from the proper perspective. Life precedes freedom. Harvesting some perceived notion of freedom at the mercy of life is an ignorant contradiction. Abortion and freedom naturally repel one another as abortion's version of freedom can only be achieved with the blood of the innocent. Excluding rape, 'freedom and choice' have already been granted to virtually all men and women who find themselves under the 'burden' of an unwanted pregnancy. The right of choice is granted at the moment when a man and a woman freely choose to have sexual relations. Many arguments in favor of abortion actually frame pregnancy as if it were some sort of arbitrary occurrence caused by random chance. On the contrary, every honest, thinking adult knows that pregnancy is the possible result of a personal decision. Once that decision is made, the choice has been declared and the right has been exhausted. In what kind of world, and under what strange definition of freedom, do the blameless pay for the acts of the guilty? The lives of the innocent have been consciously created by a choice, by an act of free will on the part of their parents. Abortion is the antithesis of freedom, and actually a form of slavery, as one individual voids the rights and controls the destiny of another by the threat of force. "How can the dream survive if we murder the children...every aborted baby is like a slave in the womb of his or her mother. The mother decides his or her fate." — Martin Luther King, Jr. Abortion is not a civil right but the ultimate act of selfishness and an immature evasion of personal responsibility – a crime of passion often for the sake of mere convenience or a sickening affirmation of promiscuity. Likewise, excuses due to age, perceived financial distress, and possible career impairment are not at all parallel to the personal responsibility pursuant to creating new life. Decisions of permanence cannot be held hostage by the tyranny of self-absorbed, temporary circumstances. From a cultural perspective, the absence of personal responsibility, coupled with the poison of self-absorption, is the birth of anarchy...and the birth of anarchy foreshadows the demise of all civil rights.

The concept of 'bodily autonomy' has recently been enshrined within our post-moral culture as an unassailable civil right. This newly discovered privilege has been used to excuse all manner of reprehensible, destructive behavior such as drug use, prostitution, pornography and, most recently, the 'right' to an abortion. The faux-libertarian argument is made that there can be no restraints on the individual (moral, legal or otherwise), as long as one's actions do not harm another. What constitutes harm? Does the abuse of drugs not harm parents, children, spouses, friends, and coworkers? Does it not exact a toll on society, either financially or culturally? Does not prostitution, or pornography, destroy relationships, marriages and families? And does not abortion terminate another's right to life, liberty and the pursuit of happiness? In fact, there is not one human action under the selfish ideology of 'bodily autonomy' that does not negatively affect another in some way. Where will the rights to our bodily autonomy end? Will parents no longer be obligated to provide for their children as that responsibility demands the use of our body? Will we no longer be required to work because our bodily autonomy is jeopardized? Will there be no constraints placed on our body at all, not even those willfully initiated by our own actions? As we continue to foolishly affirm the legitimacy of such 'rights,' even with their obvious hostility to reason, our culture is collapsing under the weight of a deep moral degeneracy…so deep that it will preclude even the right of existence to another human being.

Ecological

   Overpopulation has long been an excuse to further the abortion / contraception argument.   Whether decrying a lack of space or resources, the argument is moot. There are, undoubtedly, some areas of the world that are highly overpopulated, just as there are others that are sparsely populated. The globe as a whole, however, is more than capable of sustaining life at many multiples of our current population. Human ingenuity, the advancement of technology, ecological adaptations and perfected techniques of farming and harvesting, have all spurred to new heights, again and again, previous agricultural outputs thought to be at their peak. Supposed experts for years have posited the imminent crises of mass starvation and resource depletion, while offering abortion as a means of avoiding the pending calamities. From Thomas Malthus in late 18th century England who predicted the exhaustion of all food sources by 1980 (Essay: "Principle of Population", 1798), to 1968's "The Population Bomb" by Paul Ehrlich that foretold of mass human extinction by the end of the next decade, those with an evil hostility to the unborn have latched on to every "doomsday" scenario ever presented in order to advance the acceptance of abortion and contraception by means of fear-mongering.

The reality of the situation is quite the opposite of the scare tactics utilized by 'population experts.' From a space factor alone, there is enough land mass for every person on earth to have five acres each, including a half-acre of arable land (CIA: The World Factbook, Sept 30, 2013). Food and water scarcity is also a myth. There is presently enough food produced annually in the world to feed 10 billion people, nearly 1.5 times the amount needed to sustain the current population. The richest countries of the world waste more than 220 million tons of food annually, enough to feed the malnourished four times over (2012 Journal of Sustainable Agriculture). The world, likewise, has ample supplies of fresh water. Since 1900, the world's population has grown four-fold while extraction of usable fresh water has increased seven-fold (Peter H. Gleick; Water International, 2000). These facts do not minimize the plight of those suffering from real poverty, hunger and want that exist in the world. Nevertheless, these tragedies are not caused by overpopulation and are not global in scope. They are caused locally by environmental exploitation, failures of polity, greed, war and natural disasters. Overpopulation is a non-starter. Even if it were a real problem, the human condition begs that we utilize our God-given intellect and ingenuity to find an alternative solution and not simply resort to killing each other. Abortion could never be the solution to any problem, but especially not to a problem of fabricated existence.

Biological

Under the guise of a biological defense, those with a profane fidelity to abortion proffer a thoroughly unscientific and erroneous definition of life. According to them, an unborn child is not a child at all, not even a human being, but merely a glob of meaningless tissue, or 'uterine contents,' despite what common sense and medical facts prove to the contrary. The fertilized egg, or zygote, is a completely unique human being…not simply a cell or a part of the host, but a living being unto itself. Sick minds of the abortion culture, nonetheless, actually compare unborn children to 'parasites.' Upon fertilization, life exists. In the defense of life, there are many books and articles that outline the growth and development of the fetus, describing that within a few weeks the heart is beating, arms and legs move, and hands and toes have formed; and, within two months, the brain and nervous system, and the digestive, muscular and skeletal systems have all developed and are beginning to function. The advent of advanced ultrasound and enhanced sonograms has somewhat reduced the social acceptance of later-term abortions, as well as spurred legislation that outlaws abortion in most cases beyond the realization of viability. While these illustrations are useful in portraying a fetus as truly a baby in development, what about the first precious hours and days after conception? Just because we can see no major fetal changes taking place, and just because the fetus at this early stage really does not 'look' like a baby, does this make it at all more appropriate to discard it? By all scientific accounts, life begins at conception. A 2019 scientific study by Steven Jacobs highlights an international survey that found 96% of 5,577 biologists from across the religious and political spectrum believe that science itself has confirmed that life begins at conception (University of Chicago; *Balancing Abortion Rights and Fetal Rights: A Mixed Methods Mediation of the U.S. Abortion Debate*; Jacobs, Steven Andrew; June, 2019). Even without scientific testament, this fact is of a simple logic that cannot possibly confound even the feeblest of intellects. As the constraints of science are applied, this logic is only affirmed. Oddly enough, most of those who support abortion are typically of the same faction that has crowned science as our secular deity, yet in the case of abortion they refuse to pay homage to their god. In spite of the obvious contradictions, those blinded by ideology refuse to embrace this cogent and rational truth, even with scientific corroboration that compels acceptance.

Legal

Disoriented legal posturing has likewise been utilized to further the agenda of abortion. The declaration of abortion as a 'fundamental right,' arising out of the Roe v. Wade Supreme Court decision in 1973, was the result of a twisted redefinition of personal liberty; the crafting, out of whole cloth, of a new meaning for the word 'privacy;' and the maturation of the fabricated Progressive concept of 'substantive due process.'

Prior to the case reaching the Supreme Court, the lower federal district court in 1970 originated the odd coupling of privacy and abortion strictly on the merits of the ninth amendment to the Constitution, which declares, in its entirety: "The enumeration in the Constitution, of certain rights, shall not be construed to deny or disparage others retained by the people." The high court itself, in declaring a constitutional right to abortion, utilized yet another ambiguous amendment to codify its decision. The 'due process' clause of the fourteenth amendment to the Constitution states: "All persons born or naturalized in the United States, and subject to the jurisdiction thereof, are citizens of the United States and of the state wherein they reside. No state shall make or enforce any law which shall abridge the privileges or immunities of citizens of the United States; nor shall any state deprive any person of life, liberty, or property, without due process of law; nor deny to any person within its jurisdiction the equal protection of the laws." The imagination needed to find a right to abortion in those words is quite creative. In addition to being a judicial travesty, it is also a manipulation of the intellect. Supposedly brilliant minds arrogantly discarded the heretofore-unalienable right to life in favor of a vague and distorted understanding of privacy, the definition of which used to mean...well, the right to privacy, but now has become a sordid repository for all human actions which were once abhorrent but now socially acceptable. In perfect irony, neither referenced amendment even contains the word 'privacy.'

The principle of 'substantive due process' is a creative stratagem of those who have an affinity for judicial activism and Constitutional flexibility. Due process itself is a legitimate and necessary constitutional protection of individual liberty, a concept that dates back hundreds of years and finds its origin in the Magna Carta, the premier document of English Law from which the foundation for our own Constitution was laid. Primarily, the principle of due process prevents the government, outside of the law, from coercive actions against the individual. *Substantive* due process, however, is a legal artifice created in the 19th century that gives credence to the Progressive notion of a 'living and breathing' Constitution and a legislating judiciary. In other words, the concept relies heavily on subjectivity, implication and vagary, and specifies a desire to confound the Constitutional doctrine of 'separation of powers.' Supreme Court Justice Oliver Wendell Holmes, Jr. expounded on the dangers of substantive due process in a 1930 opinion: "{Regarding} the words *due process of law*…while it is too late to deny that they have been given a much more extended and artificial signification, still we ought to remember the great caution shown by the Constitution in limiting the power of the States, and should be slow to construe the clause in the Fourteenth Amendment as committing to the Court, with no guide but the Court's discretion, the validity of whatever laws the States may pass." The Supreme Court of 1973, in an application of the fourteenth amendment to its Constitutional meanderings regarding a fundamental right to abortion, took full advantage of both nebulous precepts hidden within 'substantive due process' - judicial creativity and a usurpation of Constitutional powers. Of the former, the word 'substantive' is a nebulous term meaning 'mostly' or 'considerable,' and, if granted enough imagination, it can, and will, ascertain anything that it is predisposed to discover, primarily under the auspices of a 'creative' judiciary. In its legal context, 'substantive' allows for personal opinion by idiomatic degree, and, even though used as a clarifying adjective to 'due process,' it actually creates a weakening of what was, on its own, a previously resolute concept. By the application of 'substantive due process' to the legality of abortion, we have been left with a finding based more on inventive sentiment and persuasion than established Constitutional principles. As that has occurred, more than sixty-million of 'we, the people' have been legally denied 'life, liberty, and the pursuit of happiness' by the tortured opinion of seven men.

Of the latter precept, the framers of the Constitution, wisely perceiving that too much power in the hands of a single branch of government would invite tyranny, delineated powers among the executive, legislative and judicial branches with intentional precision. The judicial branch of government, specifically the Supreme Court, has as its main power the interpretation of laws as they relate to the Constitution. The judiciary is expressly forbidden from making law (legislative) or enforcing law (executive). The Supreme Court retains jurisdiction over federal court and state court cases, but **only those involving issues of federal law**. Prior to the Roe v. Wade decision, states, through their legislatures, made their own laws regarding the legality of abortion. At the time, **there was no federal law directly related to the legitimacy of abortion.** The Supreme Court did not simply pass judgement on the constitutionality of each state's laws, but, in a blatant display of judicial activism, *created* a federal law deeming abortion a fundamental, Constitutional right, without the prerequisite federal legislation in place. Essentially, the Supreme Court was, and remains, in contempt of itself. Even if there had been existing federal legislation regarding abortion at the time of the Roe decision, the Supreme Court ruling was still unconstitutional. Amendment 10 of the Bill of Rights clearly states that any rights not specifically addressed in the Constitution, or enumerated by distinct wording to belong to the Federal government, are "reserved to the States themselves, or to the people." Unfortunately, these facts do not, in and of themselves, automatically deem the act of abortion to be illegal, but only confirm that the Roe decision itself was illegal, was made without standing, was utterly extra-constitutional, and that its proper adjudication must be returned to the States. Only then will the States be able to perform their incumbent, moral and Constitutional duty to abolish abortion outright.

Not only was the Roe decision unconstitutional, but also the Constitutional wording used to defend it actually defines its illegality. The legal basis for formulating a right to abort one's child was somehow coaxed out of a constitutional statement that actually *denies* government the power to "deprive any person of life." A subsequent argument then becomes, what is the legal, constitutional definition of a 'person?' In light of their conviction, as set forth in the Declaration, that "all men are created equal", the founding fathers make it quite clear that personhood is afforded to all as they are created. All men are not *born equal*, but *created* equal. "With consistency, beautiful, and undeviating, human life, from its commencement to its close, is protected by the common law" (James Wilson, signatory of the Declaration and Constitution, and an original justice of the Supreme Court). Furthermore, the apex of our list of 'unalienable rights' is the right to life of every such person. No addendum or footnote is referenced which makes any exception or accommodates any discussion or appeal. The word is unalienable and its intention is definitive and absolute. The loose weaving of arguments by abortion defenders regarding the definition of 'person' are tellingly of the exact same thread used by pro-slavery proponents as well as by the majority of justices in the Supreme Court's 'Dred Scott' decision - one of the earliest uses of 'substantive due process' - that a certain segment of humanity is of a sub-species not legally worthy of personhood.

Outside of a Constitutional definition, but still within the realm of the law, we have immaturely parsed the legal definition of 'person' within the vagaries of egocentric emotion. If a baby is wanted, it becomes a person the moment we learn of its existence. If a baby is unwanted, it is denied that status outright. If the murder of a pregnant woman constitutes two homicides, as it should be, and is, in many jurisdictions, then 'ipso facto,' the unborn child is legally a person. If the pregnant woman did not want the child, is that same child now no longer a person? If we can frivolously change legal definitions based solely on someone's feelings, then we have entered a very regressive era of sound legal understanding and practice. Just as obscure is the legal concept of 'viability.' A legal system that proclaims an unborn child is not a person at 140-days gestation, but magically claims that very child to be a person at midnight of the same evening, is law based more on some type of pagan sorcery than on ontological certitude.

The concept of 'implied consent' is utilized by our legal system under many different circumstances, and is fully applicable to the procreative act. Defined as "an assumption of permission to do, or to allow, something that is inferred from an individual's actions," the concept is widely applied to a host of other issues from commerce to illegal acts. Examples include:

- Drivers are assumed to consent to blood alcohol testing. The inference is that the driver understands that driving under the influence is illegal and that they may be subject to testing.
- Under canned spam laws, advertisers are permitted to send as much spam as they want to individuals who have opened only one of their emails, or requested any information from the sender, as it is assumed those actions affirm acceptance.
- Many government entities are employing the concept in regard to organ donations. The legal reasoning is that if a person does not explicitly document that they, upon death, expressly forbid the donation of their organs, then they have given 'implied consent' to the harvesting of those organs.

Although noticeably absent from arguments regarding abortion, the application is perfectly appropriate and legally sound. A man and a women, being undoubtedly aware that sexual intercourse will possibly result in pregnancy (even in spite of contraception), both provide implied consent to the potentiality of life and their consequential responsibilities, simply by having intercourse. This rationale also applies to the pro-abortion argument that, as the host body, the woman has the autonomous right to deny that use without question. Under 'implied consent,' the act of intercourse automatically precludes that right, and affirms her acceptance of the 'use of her womb.'

The stated attempt to 'keep abortion safe, accessible and legal' has become the anthem of abortion rights advocates. One stanza of that anthem is found in the notion that abortion has always occurred, and will continue to occur even if the practice is outlawed. While this notion is no doubt true, the apparent reasoning is mindless. Apply this same line of thinking to any social crime or cultural sin. Assault continues in spite of laws that make it a crime. Should we legalize it because we cannot prevent it? Do we deem it acceptable simply by virtue of its existence? If this were the case, the fundamental concept of a properly functioning society based on the 'rule of law' would become impotent.

Medical

There are also various medical justifications that are paradoxically positioned as amicable to the concept of legalized abortion. The fact that these forced justifications are a clear anomaly to the fundamentals of medical science, and to the profession of medicine itself, seems to be lost on our current culture. For over two millennia, the 'Hippocratic Oath' was declared before man and God (originally gods) by every medical doctor. As part of the oath, each aspiring medical professional would pledge to "not give a woman an abortive remedy." Over two thousand years ago, the practice of primitive medicine understood that abortion was not a medical treatment, and that pregnancy was not a disease. Today's 'advanced' practice of medicine somehow cannot comprehend those medical facts, and actually has the gall to defend the noxious prescription. "In purity and holiness I will guard my life and my art", and "first, do no harm" have somehow become elective promises that are malleable, and obviously no longer applicable to many professionals in the medical field.

Medical arguments have long been used as a tool to further the cultural acceptance of abortion. In the early battles between pro-abortion and pro-life, abortion was championed as a legal option for the noble protection of the life of the mother, or as a remedy against the possible results of rape or incest. While society would hope that the sacrificial element of motherhood would honor innocent life above the mother's own, or that the value of this same life would far surpass the horrors of man's violent crimes, it is nonetheless, at least, understandable that a woman might consider an abortion in these cases. In defense of all human life, however, we should never punish the guiltless for acts in which they have played no part. For all the attention this subject garners, the instances of rape, incest, and possible death of the mother via childbirth account for less than one percent of all pregnancies. Pro-abortion fanatics often cite defense of third-trimester abortions as potentially necessary to save the life of the mother. There is not one example in the annals of modern medicine, however, where abortion has been the only recourse to prevent a mother's death. Conversely, abortion is, in instances of high risk, late-term pregnancies, less safe than delivery (either vaginal or by caesarian section).

In an effort to maximize the social acceptance of abortion, proponents gradually amended their mere defense of the life of the mother and broadened abortion's horizons by compassionately crusading for the 'health' of the mother. By their definition, the health of the mother would include virtually any level of self-diagnosed physical, mental or emotional distress suffered by a woman as a direct, or even indirect, result of pregnancy. The potential of a woman's diminished 'quality of life,' the financial stress of raising a child, or the interruption of a career are now sufficient excuses that exonerate parents from the willful denial of their own child's life. 'Compassion' for the culpable at the expense of the innocent is now a Progressive virtue, handing down the dictatorial verdict that another's life is not worth living. In the wholly selfish and warped domain of abortion ideology, extinguishing life, and hope, is preferential to enduring even the *possibility* of poverty, sacrifice and hardship, if only to mollify the self-induced emotional or physical discomfort of puerile adults.

Medical apologetics are also used to promote abortion in the rare instances of possible birth defects - pleas that are always framed in compassionate terms as being in the best interest of the child. In the first place, under their own arguments, how can one share any concern, or hold any benevolence whatsoever, for an inconsequential mass of lifeless tissue? Hypocritical piety abounds. Many blind partisans of abortion will advocate for the humaneness of terminating an unhealthy fetus, which they claim has no humanity to begin with. This moral fraudulence is representative of a culture practiced in self-deception. Second, medical tests that supposedly diagnose fetal anomalies are far from foolproof and are actually highly suspect in many cases. False positives, low positive predictive values, grossly incorrect 'high risk' predictions, and human error itself are not infrequent. In the case of Down's syndrome, which is extremely high on the list of reasons for medical abortions, there is a 20% chance of an incorrect diagnosis, and a 5% rate of false positives, meaning that for every one-hundred Down's syndrome diagnoses, at least five are incorrect (Mayo Clinic – Tests and Procedures – Quad Test). Lord Shinkwin, a Tory peer from Britain who was born with a rare genetic brittle bone disease, warns us all of the growing horrors of the elective abortion of the disabled. He contends that 90% of British pregnancies diagnosed with Down's syndrome are terminated. "There's something deeply disturbing about non-disabled politicians spouting equality and then in the same breath defending a law which is being used as a license to kill for the crime of being disabled…I ask what message it sends if, after birth, I'm good enough for the House of Lords but, before birth, I'm only good enough for the incinerator…Too many in the medical establishment still view congenital disability as a tragedy to be eradicated through abortion…The institutional prejudice runs so deep that the whole system is in denial. What hope for worried parents or their disabled babies?...The irony is that this isn't really about abortion. Ultimately, it's about power, the power of non-disabled people to determine the fate of other – disabled – human beings, whether we should live or whether we should die. Prejudice must not prevail."

Unfortunately, there are instances where certain birth defects do result in pain, suffering, and shortened lives – all of them heart wrenching for the babies and their families alike. Such rare instances, however, are often perverted by those who would manipulate circumstances and exploit tragedy to further abortion ideology. When 'medical proof' becomes a mere possibility, and 'incontrovertible evidence' becomes arbitrary and subjective, abortion once again becomes nothing but a crime of passion. Although the presumptions may be ominous, terminating the lives of innocent babies to avoid potential negative health issues, or even to prevent a possible subsequent death at a later point, is illogical, and an act of despair based on fear of the implicit. An allegorical parallel finds a man and his young son on a frozen lake for an afternoon of ice fishing: *The young boy wanders off on his own and falls through a patch of thin ice. The father, upon realizing that his son is nowhere in sight, searches the lake for a sign of him. When he comes upon the broken ice, he sees his son floating just beneath the surface but with his hand still grasping the top of the ice. He stops to think for a moment. He realizes his son may have fallen in some time ago. If that were true, it is more than likely that his son is beyond saving, and, even if he were to rescue him, his son would surely lead a life of debilitating defect, much suffering, and possibly die anyway. With a clean conscience, he releases his son's grip on the ice, and then quietly walks away.* Other than time and familiarity, there is no difference.

Camouflaged excuses hide the real reasons behind why a significant subset of medical professionals has such an affinity for abortion. Yes, for some it is based on a misshapen ideology. For others, it is politically motivated. For most, however, it is simply a matter of self-enriching economics. The abortion industry is obscenely profitable. The approximately one billion-dollar a year industry pushes its wares on mostly frightened and vulnerable women, hesitates to offer adoption as a viable alternative, opposes parental consent laws, avoids full medical disclosure by not offering pregnant women the option of an ultrasound or a waiting period prior to an abortion, and even resists initiatives to ban late term abortions. Why? Abortion is, first and foremost, a business. The industry cloaks its true intentions behind the false perception of an altruistic defender of women's rights, and a champion of women's health. In actuality, the women, and the babies, are nothing but instruments in a quest for financial gain. One needs to look no further than the government's most favored abortion mill, Planned Parenthood. The organization insists that its existence is essential for comprehensive women's health, yet an overwhelming majority of its locations do not offer *any* prenatal care, and *none* of their centers offer mammograms. In a sadistic twist to an already demonic business plan, numerous top level Planned Parenthood officials have all but admitted that the organization has sold, and currently sells, fetal body parts. Ironically, notwithstanding its depravity and patent immorality, it is precisely the fact that a fetus' organs are so medically valuable that, in turn, so strikingly defines a fetus' humanity. Common decency, even if it is our last shred of it, demands a total repudiation of an evil so vile and disgusting. Yet, we as a culture are more interested in vilifying a baker who refuses to make a gay wedding cake than a government lauded, taxpayer funded institution, which callously massacres the unborn, discusses their leftover organs while enjoying a light lunch, and creates a revenue stream from their mutilated bodies.

Ironically, the abortion industry, the self-proclaimed philanthropic stalwart of women's health, often achieves its financial gain at the *expense* of women's health. If the industry is such a dedicated warrior for the well-being of women, then why does it oppose any and all regulation, licensure and inspection of abortion facilities? Inexplicably, regulations hoping to prevent the death of, or severe health risk to, women from abortion complications are now seen as an 'undue burden' on those very women. There are more regulations imposed on veterinary clinics, hair salons and public swimming pools than abortion clinics, and yet in spite of this lax oversight, more than 175 abortion clinics/providers have been cited by health officials and/or sued for the violation of health and safety standards since 2009 (National Review 5/5/2016: Denise Burke; "A Virginia Abortion Clinic's Misconduct is Part of National Scandal").

Furthermore, numerous medical and scientific studies have shown a direct correlation between breast cancer and abortion, as well as an elevated suicide rate for women who have had an abortion. Since 1957, there have been sixty-six separate medical studies that have sought to determine if there is a causality between abortion and breast cancer. Fifty-three of those studies (over 80%) showed a positive correlation, while twenty-five studies (over one-third) were statistically significant (Breast Cancer and Induced Abortion: A Comprehensive Review of Breast Development and Pathophysiology, the Epidemiologic Literature, and Proposal for Creation of Databanks to Elucidate All Breast Cancer Risk Factors; Angela E. Lanfranchi, M.D., FACS, and Patrick Fagan, Ph.D.: Spring 2014).

Studies in Finland, Australia, Denmark and the U.S. over the past quarter-century have compared the suicide rate between post-abortive and post-birth women. All studies showed an increased risk of suicide in the former group. The U.S. study, which examined the medical records of over 173,000 pregnant women in California, determined that women who had an abortion were more than 2.6 times likely to commit suicide than those who gave birth to their children (Southern Medical Journal: August, 2002). Moreover, concerning women's mental health in general, a 2011 study published in the British Journal of Psychiatry revealed that post-abortive women were 81% more likely to experience mental health problems compared to control groups, and were 55% were more likely to have negative psychological episodes compared to woman who endured an unplanned or unwanted pregnancy.

Abortion is alien to natural laws, hostile to the practice of medicine, and poisonous to women's health. Over one million U.S. abortions per year are classified as 'health care,' yet less than five percent are for legitimate reasons pursuant to the life of the mother, rape, and imminent fetal death. The remaining 95% have little to do with health care, medicine, or reproductive rights. Political pressure, entrenched moneyed interests, and warped moral psyches all drive the intentional deceit practiced by a pro-abortion culture that is no friend to women. The physical and psychological damage that has been imposed on tens of millions of women in this country alone constitutes the real war on women. Abortion is rarely medicine; it is "the ultimate exploitation of women" (Alice Paul, early 20th century feminist, suffragist, and women's rights advocate).

Ethical

Except in the rarest of cases, the term 'ethical abortion' is an oxymoron. For the overwhelming majority of abortions, secondary, even tertiary, rights of the mother supersede the primary 'right to life' of the child, a right that she herself, in conjunction with her mate, willfully initiated. If a person freely performs an act that catalyzes a responsibility to another, there can be nothing ethical in not fulfilling that responsibility, even if the exercise of that responsibility may end up causing harm, however perceived, to the first person. As an example, *a young man gets behind the wheel of his car after a night of heavy drinking. He unintentionally strikes a pedestrian, rendering the injured party unconscious. He has no insurance. He flees the scene, knowing that he will likely be held financially responsible for the injured party's medical bills, possibly for life.* As another example, *a scientist goes into the field of medical research simply because it is a lucrative career. He inadvertently develops a simple pill as a cure for a rare fatal disease. After his discovery, he comes to the realization that only one person in the entire world is afflicted by the disease. The expense of bringing the new drug to market will cost him far more than he might hope to realize in profits. He destroys all records pertaining to his discovery. After all, it was only one person – a person he had never even met.* There is no ethic in selfishness, nor in the denial of personal accountability. When a man and a woman engage in sexual intercourse and the woman becomes pregnant, even if unintentionally, both she and her partner are ethically responsible for the life that their decision has created.

Abortion moralists will argue that there is no ethical imperative, no 'moral consideration' warranted for the wellbeing of a fetus, an argument they base primarily on the concept of 'sentience.' Sentient, meaning 'aware, conscious, or cognizant,' is simply a borrowed, artificial construct chosen to give abortion a compelling illusion of ethical gravitas. As such, the rationale proceeds in claiming that fetuses in early development lack self-awareness and consciousness, and, thus, are not afforded the designation of human persons. They may be human beings, but are not considered human persons. Consequently, upon their disposal, for whatever reason, our consciences need not drown themselves in unnecessary scrupulosity. With further reflection, however, as many medical ethicists have expounded upon, one must agree that the sentient state is absent, as well, from those in a coma, those under anesthesia, even those asleep. The drug addict and alcoholic are often non-sentient, by their own volition, no less. Are these conditions, though temporary, indicative of non-personhood? Are we not obliged to morally consider the inherent rights of these human beings, as well? Of course we are. Surely, a fetus is likewise *temporarily* non-sentient until the development of the brain stem and nervous system. 'Temporary' is a relative, and mostly subjective term. The criteria, to make any rational sense and to accommodate the entire spectrum of sentience, cannot be parsed to include only 'imminent' sentience, or a 'return to' sentience, but, in its moral fullness, an ultimate 'capacity for' sentience. To counter that position, abortion apologists argue further that the fetus, since it has not yet achieved 'original' sentience, can be denied any moral consideration whatsoever. If this position is assumed ethically correct, then one needs to explain why these very same 'ethicists' typically defend legal action against anyone who may harm, or even simply handle, the eggs of bald eagles. Yes, bald eagles are on the endangered species list, and animal rights activists afford them the capacity for sentience, yet how can their undeveloped eggs demand the status of 'bald eagle' if they have not yet achieved 'original' sentience? This irrational hypocrisy confounds any explanation as to why these pharisees of ethical mores are unable to afford the same level of moral consideration to our children that they do to our national bird.

Abortion partisans have suggested that right-to-life defenders practice their own version of subjective ethics simply by not having an abortion themselves. "Don't like abortions?...Don't have one." What a weak and utterly senseless argument, akin to the brainless assertion that you can prove your ethical disagreement with child rape merely by not raping a child, or any number of other idiotic comparisons. Imagine stating your belief, "Don't like slavery?…don't own a slave." The ensuing social indignation and cultural scorn in response to that remark should easily demonstrate the parallel depravation with the ethicality of abortion.

Philosophical

Pro-abortion arguments made in response to pro-life philosophy are typically fraught with invalid generalizations. Ad hominem attacks and non sequitur arguments have always been the preferred methods of defense for a defenseless position. The mendacious claim that pro-life advocates are not pro-life at all but merely pro-birth in order to enslave women has become a rallying cry for pro-abortion sycophants. In their estimation, the pro-life position has no integrity unless the person who holds that position has personally adopted unwanted children or is willing to provide financial assistance to the mother of unwanted children. Not merely an illogical rationalization, this 'straw-man' argument also lacks moral equivalence and is a false dichotomy that casts the consequences of one person's decision as the responsibility of another, with the only purpose being to deflect fault and assuage guilt. Similarly, then, would one have the same mindless temerity to claim that a 'pro-euthanasia' position is automatically nullified if the persons holding that position are unwilling to provide for the deceased's wife, or adopt his children, or retain personal responsibility for their psychological well-being? Following this absurd philosophy, the appropriate argument would then ensue that they are not truly 'pro-death with dignity,' but simply pro-death. Likewise, in the case of illegal immigration, the aristocratic Progressives who do not open their own homes within their 'walled' communities to all immigrants are not pro-immigrant at all but simply pro-immigration in order to propagate cultural change. The duplicity is transparent. Pro-life advocates should, and many do, continue to assist women who are struggling with an unexpected pregnancy by way of crisis pregnancy centers, adoption agencies, and personal financial support. This assistance, however, is not at all a prerequisite to being afforded the right to passionately defend the lives of the unborn. Additionally, the argument that men should be barred from holding any opinion on abortion whatsoever because they are not the ones who have to endure pregnancy is akin to the sexist notion that women should have no opinion on financial matters if they do not work outside of the home.

In attempting to find an answer to the meaning of life, many of us have reached the conclusion that, prior to answering that question, we at first, somehow, have the primacy to terminate the life whose meaning we are trying to define. "Why are we here?" is a question that begs for a chance to find out. Abortion is of an anti-philosophy and irrational existentialism, reducing the value of human life to a subjective utility, much like a decision weighing the benefits of whether to rent or to buy a house, or the singular notion that having children merely adds to one's carbon footprint. The most ignorant mentality lies in the question "Why bring children into such a hostile and tragic world?" The answer is as obvious as the question is incomprehensible. Through our children, we are granted a vision of the entire continuum of existence. The lifeblood that courses through their veins is the blood of both our ancestors who have been and our descendants yet to be. As such, children are the embodiment of our memories and our hopes. They are a continual cleansing of humanity, an endless rebirth of our collective self, which washes from us the stains that soil the world. Children, unencumbered by worldly values and untainted by the sins of their parents, are the only earthly beings who retain the potential to save us from ourselves. Children, beyond the age of reason, have a keen awareness of all that is inherently good. By their mere presence, children reduce the hostility and tragedy that we have created. If we are to experience the glories of life, and love, through the eyes of a child, we must, in many ways, become more like them.

Instead of emulating them, we are eliminating them. We are killing a great percentage of the only human beings who can claim perfection.

Conclusion

Any culture that patronizes sexual expression while depreciating the value of life in the same breath is a culture with serious cognitive deficiencies. Our society promotes 'free' sex with as many partners as possible while casting pregnancy as a disease, a cancer that needs to be eradicated. We encourage women to fill their bodies with hormones and chemicals to prevent pregnancy, and, if that fails, to then brutally butcher their own child by burning them with more chemicals, or by piece-work dismemberment, or by suction so powerful that the body and its organs are ripped to shreds, or by inserting scissors into the back of the child's brain and severing the spinal cord. This is not some chamber of horrors fiction, but a reality that has occurred over 3,000 times per day in this country alone; and yet those labelled as anti-abortion are chastised about 'obsessions' regarding sexual morality and a preoccupation with 'pelvic issues,' maligned about waging some fictitious war on women, and branded as extremists for attempting to save innocent life. In some ways, we have progressed very little from the pagan brutality of cultures past. We may perform our inhumanity behind closed doors, under the guise of medicine, with sanitized instrument and sterile conscience, yet, still, the wretched act cannot withstand moral scrutiny. A virtuous culture would recoil in disgust upon learning that the dead bodies of discarded humanity are ground up and discharged into the sewer system or cast off like so much garbage in a landfill. On the contrary, the appalling ritual of human sacrifice, practiced by the savages of civilizations long ago, has found a welcoming home in our self-proscribed, Progressive culture. We are not simply derelict in our duty to defend those who are unable to defend themselves, but are also complicit in their slaughter. Their voices cry out for justice yet we remain reprobate in our silence and abdication. This picture, more than any other, depicts a very disturbing self-portrait of our aptitude for evil, which, without a reversal, is avowed to grow more loathsome and heinous over time.

What appears to be an almost 'religious' affinity for abortion, by an alarmingly significant percentage of the population, displays a troubling, maniacal pathology. At a vile and blasphemous 'spiritual blessing' in Columbus, Ohio, a morally deranged mother, who had just immolated her child on the altar of reproductive choice, recited a poem in song that her unborn child purportedly sang to her moments before its murder. The 'service' was sponsored by the *Religious Coalition for Reproductive Choice* and was promoted as a "progressive voices of faith" gathering to petition God's blessing on an abortion clinic. The 'spiritual' event, billed as *Holy Ground: Blessing the Sacred Space of Decision*, was officiated by "ministers celebrating conscience and moral decision making." The high priests of child sacrifice drew little moral outrage, however, as our culture now yawns as we inject sacrilege even unto religion.

Kristine Holmgren, an abortion advocate, blogger and self-described feminist 'theologian,' disgorged the following (as part of a treatise on Mother's Day, no less): "Let's protect our liberties, and reclaim safe, accessible abortion and contraception as our birthright." Whether intentional or not, the vile use of the word 'birthright' is either evidence of a contemptuous arrogance or a vacant intelligence.   As secularism is quickly becoming our national religion, abortion has become its most hallowed sacrament. Militant zealots with a macabre reverence for abortion can be found throughout our society but most worrisome is their presence in the highest levels of government, education and business.

When the Internal Revenue Service allows a tax deduction for an abortion but not for a stillborn baby…

When a student has to get her parents' permission to go on a field trip or to take an aspirin in school, but not to get an abortion…

When public schools implant IUD's in girls as young as 12, without their parent's knowledge or permission…

When pro-life speech is the equivalent of engaging in torture, as the United Nations has purported…

When a twisted concept of 'privacy' grants a license for any woman to dispose of her unborn child for any reason, yet, oddly enough, genuine privacy is no longer recognized in bathrooms and locker rooms throughout the nation…

When the scientific community approaches incontinence as 'life' is defined as a single cell that 'may have been' found on an alien planet, yet cannot reach the same consensus for in-utero persons…

Public opinion on abortion, the most momentous debate ever engaged in the history of mankind, has laid bare the lethargic conscience of our society. If a culture – vis-à-vis its judicial system, educational methodology, widespread philosophical sense of reason, even unto the realm of its spiritual conscience – is able to pass a death sentence on unwanted children, and to afflict a preponderance of its people with an infection that sanctions this extermination of the perfectly innocent, then evil will eventually consume it in whole. Once an uncivilized and regressive form of barbarism, abortion has been recast as a fundamental right, both morally laudable and socially inviolable. The annihilation of our future, one soul at a time, has been codified into law. If we honored each baby aborted since 1973 with a moment of silence, we would be mute for over 100 years. The moral pendulum will only reverse course at the instant of humanity's reawakening to logical truths – that life enkindles, while abortion extinguishes, the hope of infinite possibilities. Presently, chipping away at the legal periphery seems to be the only realistic course of action to minimize, as much as possible, this abscessed, cultural feculence. Even a possible overturning of Roe v Wade will not signify complete victory. A changing of hearts and minds must occur. This is how abortion will end in America. At some point in the future, just as the nation's moral faculties awakened regarding slavery, abortion will once again be perceived as abhorrent and unthinkable: abortion as a prevarication of justice, not a legal right to privacy; abortion as a societal dysfunction, not a cultural progression; abortion as a medical pandemic, not an ally of women's health; and abortion, not as a choice, but as a detestable act of human sacrifice. The battle of Armageddon is waged on such.

Euthanasia

Abortion is not alone in our society's preoccupation with death. A culture that has contempt for God will allow evil to manifest itself in countless ways, all contrary to the sanctity of life. Being the coward that he most certainly is, the devil will attack the weakest and most vulnerable, and with willing accomplices, attempt to exile the Author of life to a wasteland inhospitable to our conscience. 'From conception until natural death' is not only a spiritual tenet, but likewise a cultural conviction within which resides a resounding wisdom. The unborn and the aged are the parentheses of our existence. To cheapen their worth leaves us all exposed to the desolate and perilous depths of our obsession with human expiry.

As with abortion, in regard to the origin and ownership of life, euthanasia reflects the mindset of the godless. Initially modeled as a seemingly compassionate alternative to living out one's last days, months, or even years in constant pain and suffering, euthanasia is still, in its essence, suicide – the self-proscribed, premature ending of a life as ordained by God. The will of God is the clarion expression of mankind's existence, even in the fear, pain and despair that may accompany end of life trials. His omniscience is declared in each breath we take, in each beat of our heart, and in our very last thought. The time we seek to sever from the life He has given each of us may well be the very same time He will use to secure our salvation. Faith requires the humble acknowledgement that God alone knows the significance of each and every moment of our lives.

Even if - but also because - we recklessly remove God from the equation of life, euthanasia yet remains a parasitical enemy of cultural virtue and retains the potential for monumental abuse. As human beings become the sole arbiter of the intrinsic value of any given life (even one's own), mistakes, ulterior motives and malevolence will, by the simple nature of man, occupy the vacancy of God's expulsion. In fighting to retain Canada's ban on assisted suicide, Mark Penninga, director of ARPA Canada, encapsulates the risk most eloquently, by lamenting, "It will be logically impossible for Parliament or any legislature or court to enact safeguards that will be able to withstand future legal challenges. As we see in Belgium and the Netherlands, it is only a matter of time before these so-called safeguards are considered an unjust limitation on someone else's rights, even allowing children or those who are depressed to be killed at the hands of the state..." (*Canada Strikes Down Ban on Assisted Suicide, Says it Violates the Right to Life*; Steven Ertelt; LifeNews; 2/6/15). It appears that the once sacred 'right to life' enshrined in the common law of nearly every civilized society is shamefully being exploited as the legal basis for a 'progressive' right to death.

If one were to follow a timeline of the progression of euthanasia in modern history, one would see a distinct parallel to Mr. Penninga's concerns. Starting slowly in the mid-19th century and moving cautiously and quietly for the next 100 years, the groundwork was laid for a growing debate that began in earnest in the 1960's (oddly enough following a very similar timeline to that of abortion). Initially offered as a merciful and dignified procedure under the strictest guidelines and in the rarest of cases, euthanasia has gradually gained more and more proponents who have sought to broaden the reach of assisted suicide to include the mentally ill, the depressed, terminally ill children, the aged, and the disabled. The ultimate goal appears to be unfettered access to state-sanctioned suicide on demand, for any reason whatsoever. "In medicine we know that what is permissible becomes habitual, and what is habitual becomes standard care, and what is standard care becomes obligatory" (Dr. G. Kevin Donovan, professor of pediatrics and director of clinical bioethics at Georgetown University). There is no mercy, or dignity, in a society that portrays such a cavalier disrespect for the immense value of every single life, while aiding and abetting the despair of the most vulnerable.

Genetic Engineering

A more recent ethical challenge has emerged out of biological science's newfound understanding of the human genome, and our resulting ability to manipulate and control cellular activity at the very genesis of human life. Genetic engineering is a testament to the breadth of human ability, to the brilliance of our God-given intelligence, and to the virtually endless promise of science. The potential to reverse or prevent many debilitating diseases is nothing short of miraculous. The potential for perversion and ruin, however, is nothing short of cataclysmic. Before we engage in such monumental progress, therefore, humanity must be humbled by the prerequisite of our fundamental responsibilities.

The practice of genetic engineering in agriculture, medicine, and product development is exceptionally promising, although great caution should be observed regarding the potential toxic side effects and unintentional, long-term repercussions, which are not yet fully comprehended. The genetic engineering of human cells, however, should be constrained by the most stringent ethics and most restrictive prohibitions. Genome manipulation should never alter the original integrity of the human host, no matter the inflation of expected benefit. Embryonic stem cell research likewise should be wholly repudiated whenever the exploitation of a fertilized egg results in its destruction. There has never been an ethic that was born of evil.

We are assured that medical and bio-ethics will prevent the abuse of this extraordinary new technology. Yet, we are the same people that rationalize the killing of our own children, sabotage our own procreation, and invent the most effective ways of murdering our fellow man. Repeatedly, we have been proven unethical, and, are thus unwarranted by our own actions to possess this level of dominion.

Animal Worship

Animals have a unique and quantifiable value in and of themselves, but can never be elevated to the same significance and worth as human beings. The growing number of people proclaiming that their love for animals exceeds their love for their fellow man is a further illustration of the declining cultural mores of the modern world. Secular humanism, a philosophy of Progressivism, has elevated the worth of animals (and even plants) while at the same time devaluing the worth of humans. Hostility toward the tenets of the Judeo-Christian culture, as well as a progression of agnosticism and atheism, have levelled the value of all living things on the same plane. Secular precepts hold that humans are not made in the image and likeness of any god, and, therefore, our inherent value is no different from any other living thing. These new-age tenets are not only blasphemous, but are also borne of the same minds that perpetrated the mass genocide of communist regimes during the twentieth century. For millennia prior to that, our forbearers understood the infinite value of humanity, and wisely reasoned that animals have no moral nature, therefore no soul; no faculty of reason, therefore no virtue; and no inherent responsibilities, therefore no inherent rights. There is no doubt that animals provide many people with some level of comfort, companionship and pleasure in their lives. Animals have been placed under the dominion of mankind for these purposes and others (i.e. food, clothing, labor, etc.). As such, animals are a gift from God and their proper use is both a blessing to, and a responsibility of, mankind.

There are many debates about the institutionalized abuse of animals that occurs widespread in zoos, farms, pens and slaughterhouses worldwide. Living conditions for 'kept' animals should be adequate for the sake of their comfort and health, not due to any innate animal rights but due to incumbent human responsibility. Animals killed for the food that they provide for humanity should likewise never be tortured and their death should be painless. Any being that can feel pain should not be forced to endure it when it can be so easily avoided. Killing animals simply for the sake of killing them, with no regard for their provisional use, should be naturally repugnant.

Animal abuse, however, should not be replaced with animal worship. The blatant and wholesale devaluation of human life in our culture has been simultaneously, and ironically, accompanied by a heightened, pagan-like reverence for animals of all sorts. Many other cultures throughout history, in the throes of disintegration, have experienced a similar phenomenon. The personification of animals, once reserved for children's books and movies, has reached such iconoclastic levels that many favor bestowing some human rights on animals. Others place more value on the raising of pets than on the raising of children. The death of 'Cecil the Lion,' as violent and unnecessary as it was, sparked more public outrage than the concurrent beheadings of scores of people in the Middle East. "Wherever there is animal worship, there is human sacrifice" (G.K. Chesterton).

Gaian Idolatry

The mythologies of ancient Greece, Rome, and other cultures have recently been given new life in our retro-Progressive culture. For many, the earth has been re-deified as Gaia, the Greek goddess, as she seems to have been resurrected sometime in the 1960's. The earth as a single, self-regulating being, with its own 'organs' of oceans, soil, and atmosphere, has given rise to entirely new gaian-inspired versions of biology, organic chemistry, and evolution, all under the auspices of a "Gaian philosophy." Having been widely dismissed by the mainstream scientific community, Gaian hypotheses have been refashioned to align themselves with a more mainstream concept of religion.

Beginning in 1970, the world established the observance of Earth Day each year on April 22. The concepts of ecological responsibility, air and water pollutant reduction, and sustainable recycling, were, and continue to be, worthy goals - all positive changes needed in a world that often overlooks humanity's insistent obligation of stewardship. What began as a celebration of nature and the promotion of environmental acts of conservation, however, soon became a model of Progressive extremism. A new church had been created with the earth as the supreme deity, complete with its own holy day, saints, penitential rites, tithes, evangelization, excommunication, canon law, and even its own version of the Ten Commandments:

The Ten Commandments of Our Mother Earth:

*1. Thou shalt love and honor the Earth,
for it blesses thy life and governs thy survival.*

2. Thou shalt keep each day sacred to the Earth
and celebrate the turning of its seasons.

3. Thou shalt not hold thyself above other living
things
nor drive them to extinction.

4. Thou shalt give thanks for thy food
to the creatures and plants that nourish thee.

5. Thou shalt limit thy offspring
for multitudes of people are a burden unto the Earth.

6. Thou shalt not kill
nor waste Earth's riches upon weapons of war.

7. Thou shalt not pursue profit at the Earth's
expense,
but strive to restore its damaged majesty.

8. Thou shalt not hide from thyself or others
the consequences of thy actions upon the Earth.

9. Thou shalt not steal from future generations
by impoverishing or poisoning the Earth.

10. Thou shalt consume material goods in
moderation
so all may share Earth's bounty.

© 1990 Ernest Callenbach

The newly created church, the ultimate in reformation, was commissioned by the governments themselves, and centralized within the United Nations. The primary antagonists of this secular

faith are the three 'C's: Conservatism, Capitalism, and Christianity –
each portrayed as the devil himself.   Newly canonized saints
include the likes of Bill Nye, Dennis Hayes, Senators Gaylord
Nelson and, of course, Al Gore, who has made his fortune by
demanding that everyone else reduce their 'carbon footprint,' the
extreme of mortal sins. 'Confession' has been naturalized within
'land acknowledgements' and the admission of unearned privilege,
while penance has been meted out with carbon taxes, reparations
and redistribution. Tithing has never been an issue as the taxpayer
has 'donated' billions upon billions of dollars to the cause;
evangelization has been contracted out to the media; 'original sin' is
defined as being born a white male; and 'canon' law has been deftly
created in legislative chambers and executive offices worldwide.
Redemption, no longer compulsory (or even necessary) for the
individual soul, is now required on behalf of the deified earth itself,
which demands eternal repentance but never offers forgiveness.
Natural rights have been usurped by unlimited government
intervention. With zealous hypocrisy, this newfound church has
adopted patterns of sociopathic behavior that it falsely accuses
other churches of practicing - silencing critical voices, vehement
public chastisement, judgement and condemnation,
'excommunication' through the aegis of 'cancel culture,' and even
retrograde inquisitions of anyone who strays from the doctrine of the
new faith.

Population control appears to be at the crux of Gaian philosophy,
under the covert designs of the sexual revolution, toxic feminism
and climate change that have been raging now for nearly fifty years.
Beginning with the subversion of motherhood, child rearing and the

family, to the fabrication of illusory and fashionable rights to reproduction and bodily autonomy, 'progressing' to contraception and abortion, and now to the latter day concepts of widespread homosexuality, gender fluidity, and transgenderism, the world seems strategically hell bent on creating an antidote for fertility. As more and more people subscribe to this warped vision of sexuality, fertility rates will continue their decline, with the sinister intent of drastically reducing the worldwide population.

The Individual vs. the Collective

"All that is valuable in human society depends upon the opportunity for development accorded the individual"
Albert Einstein

"Liberty is not collective, it is personal. All liberty is individual liberty"
Calvin Coolidge

"Madness is the exception in individuals but the rule in groups"
Fredrich Nietzsche

Of Individuality and Conformity

One can grip his convictions with the authority of a vise
A fatal idealism exuding its own life's blood
Poisoning a passion for consummate truth
Leaving him to decay in a self-quixotic quagmire
While stifling potential for collective renaissance
And persuasion now mingles with futility

From what appear to be the innocuous skirmishes between good and evil, to the unfathomable societal demolition of cultural bedrock, all the way to the crucial battle in defense of life itself, the recent war on morality is relentlessly waged. Furthermore, no venue in between the extremes is immune, as the war has permeated all aspects of our culture. The enemy storms all positions, constantly probing the points at which our defenses are the most vulnerable and relentlessly seeking cultural discord and enmity, primarily by the immolation of the individual on the altar of the collective. While he no doubt will attack each individual separately, he finds it much more productive to attack the collective as a whole, and, as that battle has been won, turn the collective on the individual. Collectivism is simply totalitarianism in its infancy.

Cultural morality must start with the individual. A society is moral only insofar as it is comprised of individual morality. Human beings retain, *individually*, by God's endowment, an absolute standard of moral capacity. When we, as a culture, fight a war against morality, we fight a war against the individual and, thus, as the absolute standard falls, we ultimately vanquish ourselves. We are then left with an equivocal, secular morality by consensus, an artificial morality that changes on collective whim. This distinction leads one back to the elemental thesis of our country's founding – the supremacy of individual rights coupled with their incumbent responsibilities. Furthermore, this distinction defines again the cultural hazards of moral relativism, for without the individual exercise of a resolute morality, civilization invariably yields to an illiterate virtue. Finally, this distinction further epitomizes the clear differences between Conservatism and Progressivism. Conservatism is of the mindset that created the era of the individual: self-governance, self-reliance, and personal responsibility, all bound by the covenant of a consummate moral code. Progressive ideology, which now permeates our culture, is the 'anti-individual' reaction to Conservatism: social collectivism, 'it-takes-a-village' mentality, group identity, and a victimhood non-accountability, all held loosely by bland euphemisms and a vague, metamorphic code of 'good.' 'Be Nice' and 'We Care' are the new standard bearers of 'good,' and, being subjective and variable, become weak substitutes for the conviction of absolute morality. As the individual forsakes the fixed certainty of immutable virtue and conforms to the collective secularism of relative mores, 'good' often approaches a facsimile of evil, or at least facilitates a dissolution of once honored cultural customs and behaviors that have exhilarated American society from its very beginning.

Many of our current cultural battles, ideologically speaking, can be reduced to the common denominator of social hierarchy.

Whereas cultural Progressivism places the 'collective' (i.e. the federal government) at the pinnacle of every societal function, cultural Conservatism inverts the social pyramid in favor of the individual. Whether discussing education, health, law and order, charitable giving, rights, welfare, immigration, etc., the question becomes which hierarchy is more efficacious in structuring the most vigorous and effective cultural systems. Up until recent generations, there can be no doubt that American society championed a 'top-down' system with the individual at the apex. Ironically, it now appears that Conservatism has become counter-cultural while Progressivism demands a rigid conformity without question…a forced compliance that has deliberately rendered the individual as modernity's truly endangered minority. "The opposite of courage in our society is not cowardice, it is conformity" (the late existential psychologist, Rollo May).

Individual*ity* is not individual*ism*. Individualism is a cultural cancer that exposes itself as utter selfishness, especially when it is divorced from morality. Individualism, not as its name would imply, is actually a precursor of collectivism. As the vanity of individualism projects itself outward, it breeds a mindset of identity politics, 'tribal' affiliation, and rigid group association, leading to multiple subsets of warring collectivism. Individualism was reborn during the 1960's second wave of Progressivism and, having been allowed to fester for half a century, has recently come of age. The 'me' generation, with its egocentrism and instant gratification, its 'my truth' mantra, its contempt for civility, manners and self-control, and its offensive speech, crude dress and spoiled rants, is presiding over the quickening pace of a cultural unraveling, if not the slow crumbling of a civilization. As each individual succumbs to this contagious distemper, the collective, in turn, languishes in regression. True individuality, on the other hand, is not about self-centeredness but the quest to become the best person possible, not for the mere advantage of the individual, but for the wellness and edification of an ordered society. As each individual subscribes to this altruistic desire, the collective, in turn, flourishes in compounding degree. Individuality is, most importantly, the antidote to Progressive manipulation and the armor that shields our intellect from the cultural dementia that surrounds us.

Common sense alone, then, would dictate that the individual, of sound mind and visceral moral conviction, would undoubtedly comprehend more fully than any other being or institution what is most wholesome to him or her, not selfishly, but in order to play an integral part in an authentic commitment to society. From there, the cultural hierarchy would move slowly down to the family, the community, and then to local and state governments, and finally to an intentionally limited federal government (the Constitutional model). The Progressive vision looks for an all-powerful federal government that would have the ability to control virtually every aspect of society and rule by edict down through the state and local government, with the individual, incapable of self-governance, living in serfdom (the totalitarian model). Actions versus words, facts versus feelings, results versus intentions, and intellect versus emotions – in the trenches of the ideological battles being waged, one would think that the weapons used would determine the outcome. In today's multifarious and confused culture, however, such is not always the case.

The American Dream

Millions upon millions of people have flocked to the shores of the America over the past two centuries willing to invest their hard work, sacrifice, and faith in the Constitution for the return of a real liberty that only self-determination can promise. The American Dream, at its core, was never about wealth, success, and materialism, but about the individual longing to seek a self-ordained destiny. The potential for that very freedom is now nothing more than a mirage clouded by an overly intrusive government, forced equality, and the Progressive doctrine of 'fairness.' The quest for the American Dream has been replaced by the Progressive fairy tale of an 'American Utopia.' Simply put, life is not now, and never has been, fair. By the nature of our humanity, we can never be equal. "Human beings are born with different capacities, if they are free, they are not equal. And if they are equal, they are not free" (Aleksandr Solzhenitsyn). When we attempt to force a synthetic equality, now branded as 'equity,' we actually diminish diversity and exalt a sameness that leads to a bland complacence and superficiality. The egalitarian ethos of a post-modern, Progressive America has only served to make us all equally subordinate to our potential. The only worthwhile and productive equality is the equality of opportunity, the singular and most valuable entitlement any culture can offer to the individual. From there, we are all tasked with making the best of our positive traits, minimizing our negative tendencies, and pursuing, on our own, the self-defined path we desire to forge in life. In success and in failure, acknowledging the absolute value of each, we must live with the results of our efforts.

Utopian America fails to see the positive attributes of failure. As such, lessons are no longer learned and corrections are no longer made. We go so far as to quash aspirations in order to prevent the discomfort of not reaching them. The champions of everyday life are rarely sought or celebrated – we are only homogenized participants. Our "everyone's a winner" culture, ironically (and intentionally), leads to the logical conclusion that there can be no winners. There is no longer objective value in winning, as that may entail others' losing. What we do not realize is that failure has the capacity to be the great teacher - a master who, if given the chance, can often impart wisdom and understanding that success is unable to fathom. Failure and success are not adversaries, but consorts that work together to define character and purpose. Failure is only worthless when it is disowned, thus becoming dereliction. We have run from failure and toward dereliction, and the results are what one could expect, especially among the youth, that no matter the effort expended, we should all expect the same outcome.

For generations we have been a culture exceptional on nearly every level; now, we are mired in a suffocating and pathetic mediocrity. In spite of its relentless sermonizing about the evils of largely nonexistent discrimination practiced by others, the Progressive reimagining of American culture has itself, nonetheless, bent over backwards to discriminate against merit and hard work. The Dream has been abducted by a self-absorption so all-consuming that it has foregone a demand for ransom. Feelings and emotions trump rational thought and concrete action. Adversity is an injustice to be avoided at all costs. Proclaiming the truth is deemed hate speech that causes some to cower in 'safe zones' and stroke their fragile esteem. Immature egos with delicate sensibilities are in a constant state of offense – a cross, a flag, the simple hail of 'Merry Christmas.' Actions no longer have consequences and personal misfortunes are invariably someone else's fault. Behavior is an individual responsibility no more as we blame anyone or anything but ourselves for our failings - the insolvent blame the bank; the criminal blame their upbringing; the high school dropouts blame the rich; the addicts blame a disease; the obese blame the restaurant; the looters blame the shopkeeper; the pregnant blame the child.

The American Dream has thus been diluted by the tears of the coddled masses. Through years of legislative actions and forced cultural transformations, it has now been decreed that the path to the American Dream can only pass through the collective, through the government itself, yet this version of the dream is a radically different dream altogether. As we attempt to level the playing field by promoting descent to a base level of 'fairness,' instead of the ascension of each individual to his or her highest potential, the Dream can now only be found in the subconscious fantasy of sleep. Upon waking, it soon dissipates. Once grounded by the anchor of morality and, at the same time, held aloft by our quest for excellence, the Dream is now entombed in this crypt of our national emasculation. Once guided by the beacon of the Almighty, the Dream is now only a memory, a delusion, a figment of our cultural imagination. As we willfully ignore the anchor untethered and the beacon shrouded, we will remain awash in a sea of tepidity.

The Collective State

Decades of animosity toward the individual and a growing cultural obsession with 'group' identities has led us to various renditions of a collective state - the welfare state, the nanny state, the administrative state, etc. They are numerous, they are suffocating, and they are intentional – purposely created, methodically administered, and always expanding, as a means of overarching control by Progressive fanaticism. They are always for the collective 'good;' for our 'safety' and 'security,' for 'fairness' and 'equality.' From birth, we are programmed to believe that we do not possess the wherewithal to take care of ourselves adequately. Our formative years are overwhelmed by an education system that undermines individual growth and favors 'group think.' As we enter adulthood, we find our every activity must be sanctioned with a government-issued license or permit, all of which are drafted with intentional complication. Along the way, we are incentivized into abdicating our responsibilities, even our morality, to the state as it bludgeons our weakening independence with infantile warnings, encumbering restrictions and coercive regulations, all accepted with the servile obedience of beaten dogs. As personal responsibility decreases, rules and regulations increase accordingly. With tentacles firmly secured in nearly every facet of life, the state, in effect, soon becomes the parent, the teacher, the physician, the banker, and the church - the consummate lord of our culture.

Ultimately, the profits from the state's addiction to power and control measure in direct proportion to the cost of our addiction to dependence – a usury taken full advantage of, yet one whose mere existence we are unable to even suspect. After a time of forced, belittling agency, we soon expect to be told what to do, then desire to be told what to do, then cannot even function on our own. Our commonwealth is sacrificed as we lie complacently while the state changes our soiled diaper. Eventually, as was their intent all along, we do not even bat an eye when we discover that they have been reading our personal correspondence, thieving our property, and surveilling our every move. All is well, as long as we are receiving our welfare benefits, corporate subsidies, minimum wage and free college tuition. The devolution of our independence and the culmination of state control seems to be a blind 'quid pro quo,' with each party unconcerned about the damage inflicted on our culture, and the eclipse of our national character:

Quid:
…A large segment of the population, approaching a majority, is exempted from taxation…
…Over 70% of all federal expenditures go to 'dependence creating' programs…
…In 1965, only one-in-fifty people were on Medicaid; today, one in four…
…In 2014, Americans received more than two **T**rillion dollars in federal benefits…
…In 2006, nearly one **T**rillion tax dollars was spent on corporate subsidies…

Pro Quo:

…Many communities are using RFID tracking chips to monitor recycling habits…

…At some public schools, home lunches are inspected to ensure they meet USDA guidelines…

…In many U.S. states it is now illegal to collect rain that falls on to your own property…

…In some locales, it is illegal to host a home Bible Study without a use permit...

…Tens of thousands of CCTV cameras surveil the public movements of virtually every citizen…

Alexis de Tocqueville, in his acclaimed book, *Democracy in America* (1835; 1840), foresaw the extent to which we would fall if we were to trade our individuality and independence to the state in exchange for a perception of benefit and absolution for idled personal responsibility: *"the sovereign power extends its arms over the entire society; it covers the surface of society with a network of small, complicated, minute and uniform rules, which the most original minds and the most vigorous souls cannot break through … ; it does not break wills, but it softens them, bends them and directs them; it rarely forces action, but it constantly opposes your acting; it does not destroy, it prevents birth; it does not tyrannize, it hinders, it represses, it enervates, it extinguishes, it stupefies, and finally it reduces each nation to being nothing more than a flock of timid and industrious animals, of which the government is the shepherd."*

Yes, by its very nature, ***the sovereign power will extend its arms over the entire society.*** Those arms are neither supportive nor embracing, as they are so virtuously marketed to the masses, but instead are rigid arms of restraint against the individual in order to control him.

Education

The education of children is, by all accounts, one of the most vital functions performed by society, and, its results, one of the most accurate measurements of cultural achievement. Education is the primary means by which any culture thrives over time, protecting the store of ideas by which it was formed, and passing down the knowledge, values and convictions that safeguard preservation from one generation to the next. From preschool through graduate school, there is no doubt that America funnels an enormous amount of resources into this, the worthiest of goals. The value of the results, however, does not match the value of the investment. If success was measured by the amount of money spent, then our educational system should easily be the finest in the world. Conversely, we all too often churn out barely literate students whose minds are filled with many opinions and little factual knowledge, with many entitlements and little responsibility, and, most despairingly, with a contempt for morality and an aversion for the foundational principles of their own country and culture. There are numerous and obvious reasons why, yet we do little to make the necessary changes. Instead, we continue with the same 'progressive' policies that have now failed at least two generations of children.

Primarily, the federal government should never control education. In fact, by constitutional omission, it is directly prohibited. While the federal government currently funds roughly 10% of the nations' elementary and secondary education budget, it retains much more than 10% of the control. With feel good names like 'No Child Left Behind,' 'Race to the Top,' and now, 'Common Core,' the federal government is garnering more and more influence over the materials that make it into the classroom and how those materials are suffused into the minds of our children.   How do overpaid bureaucrats in Washington D.C., or even in the state capitals, for that matter, know what is best for communities across the United States, all with different needs and, therefore, different objectives? One size does not fit all. All decisions regarding education, including curriculums, standards and best practices, should be made locally where individuals and families can have the most impact on the quality of the education that their own children receive. The taxes that pay for education should likewise be collected and disbursed 100% locally to eliminate any outside interference. It makes sense that local control of education is most effective, and that the impediment of mammoth departmental bureaucracies only serves to limit both the autonomous effectiveness of the teachers and the quality of the tools used to teach.

The federal government has no qualms about holding students hostage by weaponizing the entire school system in order to force social change. "Education is a weapon whose effects depend on who holds it in his hands and at whom it is aimed" (Joseph Stalin). Withholding school funding (taxpayers' money) from any district that does not implement the cultural excrement that the Department of Education mandates is nothing short of extortion. Such is their genuine concern for the children. The leader of our country, who is expressly forbidden to mandate expenditures from the federal treasury, threatens to withhold monies earmarked for the education of our children because he finds it more important to allow young boys to use the girls' bathrooms and locker rooms. His disturbing ideology, not to mention his regnant ego, is breathtaking in its psychosis. Meanwhile, the results of government intervention in education continue to be wanting. For decades, test scores measuring the efficacy of public school education have declined in proportion to the implementation of each new rendition of federal education guidelines. The latest embarrassment comes as a direct result of 'Common Core,' the federal government's most recent failed attempt to reverse the plummeting quality of American education under the misnamed, and functionally inept, 'Every Student Succeeds Act' of 2015. College readiness in mathematics, as measured by the 'American College Testing' (ACT) standardized exams, has consistently fallen nationwide. In 2018, the percentage of ACT-tested high-school graduates who met the minimum benchmark for math proficiency fell to its lowest level in fourteen years. A mere 40% of 2018 graduates surpassed the *minimum* requirement for the mastery of basic math skills. Students' average scores on the ACT math test dropped to its lowest level in more than 20 years—down to 20.5 (on a scale of 1 to 36), continuing a slide from 21.1 in 2012 to 20.7 in 2017. (ACT: *The Condition of College and Career Readiness – 2018*).

Dr. Walter E. Williams, a Professor of Economics at George Mason University, and a prolific conservative writer, unapologetically characterizes the state of public education as a "tragedy,' especially for poor, inner city children: "Several years ago, Project Baltimore began an investigation of Baltimore's school system. What they found was an utter disgrace. In 19 of Baltimore's 39 high schools, out of 3,804 students, only 14 of them, or less than 1%, were proficient in math. In 13 of Baltimore's high schools, not a single student scored proficient in math. In five Baltimore City high schools, not a single student scored proficient in math or reading. Despite these academic deficiencies, about 70% of the students graduate and are conferred a high school diploma...The Detroit Public Schools Community District scored the lowest in the nation compared to 26 other urban districts for reading and mathematics at the fourth- and eighth-grade levels. A recent video captures some of this miseducation in Milwaukee high schools: In two city high schools, only one student tested proficient in math and none are proficient in English. Yet, the schools spent a full week learning about "systemic racism" and "Black Lives Matter activism." By the way, a Nov. 19, 2020, Milwaukee Journal Sentinel article asks: "How many Black teachers did you have? I've only had two." The article concludes, "For future Black students, that number needs to go up." New York City is one of many school systems in the United States set to roll out Black Lives Matter-themed lesson plans. According to the NYC Department of Education, teachers will delve into "systemic racism," police brutality and white privilege in their classrooms" (Dr. Walter E. Williams; *Black Education Tragedy is New;* Dec 2, 2020). High School diplomas have become useless, fraudulent documents, as they are rubber stamped every year by educators who have not fulfilled their obligation to teach, given to students who have neglected their responsibility to learn.

Teachers Unions

Another deep-rooted and intractable problem in the US education system is the teacher's union. As with any union, their primary goal is money and power. Unlike most labor unions, however, the teachers union does not exist for the benefit of its members. Neither does it exist for the benefit of students, though it makes sure to surreptitiously project the illusion of being a benefactor 'for the children.' No, the teachers union exists solely for the benefit of the teachers union, with the sinister underlying goal of Progressive hegemony. As such, positive advancement in the education of our children is of no concern to the teachers union, a fact which becomes obvious when the results of education policy are scrutinized.

The union's rejection of merit-pay and education reform, coupled with lifetime tenure and the inability to fire even the worst performing educators, has played a large part in the pathetic results of test scores for years. The National Assessment of Educational Progress (NAEP) test, which is generally regarded as the standard for assessing the quality of the US public education system, reported in 2015 that two out of every three American children are below grade-level proficiency in virtually every subject. For minority students the results were even more atrocious, as a mere 16% achieved grade-level knowledge (The Daily Signal, *The Answer to Failing Schools? Give Students 'Backpacks Full of Cash'*; Bill Walton, October 24, 2017). Out of the 34 developed nations ranked by the Organization for Economic Cooperation and Development, America's schools consistently rank in the bottom half in nearly all areas of testing. China ranks considerably higher in virtually every category and many second world countries have recently surpassed the US as well. The union's response: we simply need to invest more money in education. On the contrary, in a 2011 study compiled by USC Rossier, results show that the US consistently spent much more on per pupil education than any other country in the world, yet ranked 10th in math and 9th in science. Japan, on the other hand, invests less than half of the US amount per student and comes in at fourth in math and third in science. How could that be? The answer can be found in the priorities of spending. The return on investment in the US would most definitely improve if the funds were directed more heavily in favor of curriculum, supplies and technology, rather than on ancillary expenditures in sports, resort-grade school buildings, and in creating unneeded administrative positions, the number of which has exploded even as enrollment has dropped, with pretentious titles such as 'Manager of Innovative Partnerships,' 'Enterprise Infrastructure and Operations Team Leader,' and 'Supervisor of Accountability.' Worse yet is the squandering of funds for gender inclusivity training, district 'equity teams,' racial disciplinary guidance, 'designated pronouns' committees, 'bias response' teams, 'white privilege' seminars, and other asinine social engineering endeavors.

School Choice

Disdain for school vouchers offers another prime example of the federal government's, as well as the teacher's unions, ersatz concern for the well-being of students and their families. By denying parents the choice of which school to send their own children to, whether public or private, the government has sentenced some children (primarily poor, inner city, minority children) to grossly underperforming schools and, worse yet, unsafe school environments. Self-ascribed advocates of all things 'fair,' of 'choice' and 'opportunity', have turned a hypocritical blind eye toward a policy that actually espouses and promotes these goals. School vouchers are a prime example of the equal opportunity afforded by real 'social justice,' yet are reviled by the very same cultural warriors who otherwise clamor for equity.

Not only is school choice an obvious, common-sense educational policy in theory, it is also of proven benefit in practice. Throughout the country, private schools, parochial schools and charter schools have far surpassed public schools in educational quality. As one example, in 2004, Congress piloted the D.C Opportunity Scholarship Program (DCOSP) in Washington, D.C. For over fifteen years now, the program has been an unarguable success. By any measurement, the DCOSP's impact on the education of thousands of low-income District families has dramatically improved their children's' futures. From higher test scores and safer schools to drastic improvements in graduation rates, the voucher program is direct evidence of the clear benefits of alternatives to public education. The reluctance of public school officials to acknowledge the educational opportunities of privately administered schools, and their successes, is unfortunate, but quite telling. Politicizing the education of our children, at the expense of those children, is indicative of the lack of true concern for the efficacy of their education.

School Violence

Burgeoning school violence has become commonplace over the past two generations. From mass killings to countless incidents of isolated violence, children must now deal with drug-sniffing dogs, metal detectors, and police presence, all amidst constant fear for their safety. Years of not enforcing simple rules of conduct, not demanding respect for authority, with no expectations of even the basics of civility, has left the schoolroom languishing, and the process of learning, severely crippled. To make matters worse, recently mandated racial quotas for discipline, 'therapy' circles that replace definitive correction, and suspension and expulsion rates that result in negative reviews by the Department of Education, have all been harmful to the climate of learning, and the safety of students. In further tribute to diversity, a 2014 civil-rights guidance issued by the Departments of Justice and Education threatened public schools with potential penalties and loss of grant money if their disciplinary policies lead to disproportionately higher rates of discipline for students in one racial group, even if those policies were written without discriminatory intent. This perverted 'guidance,' which warps common sense and ignores reality, evidently theorizes that holding minority children to a different standard is in the best interest of promoting racial equality. When put into practice, however, it only trades a pretense of equality for a genuine menace to the well-being of all students, teachers and administrators. Progressivism has instituted 'zero tolerance' for relatively benign incidents such as wearing a pro-second amendment t-shirt or chewing a pop-tart into the shape of a weapon, yet the frequent occurrence of actual criminal activity, gang infiltration, drug use and oftentimes violent disrespect are no longer reported to police or even properly disciplined. The leftist desire to shut down the so-called 'school to prison' pipeline has only served to expose our children to a daily regimen of, at best, a disruptive and ineffective education, and, at worst, potential violence unheard of in generations past. An ultimate irony is found in the Progressive mindset that defends the 'right' of behavioral offenders to remain in school in spite of their disordered conduct. One may understandably wonder, then, what became of the rights of the well-behaved students, eager to learn and not held back by the "soft bigotry of low expectations" (President George W. Bush).

Sex Education

The exclusion of God and the exile of moral convention from the classroom have had the effects that one would expect: a deteriorating respect for authority, an increase in violence, and, most sadistically, an unhealthy obsession with all things sexual. When preschoolers are indoctrinated with the normalization of alternative sexual lifestyles, disordered family structures and gender fluidity, there is obvious sinister intent. When children as young as ten are instructed in the ways of masturbation, contraception, sodomy and abortion, there exists a manifest, inexplicable perversion. The sexualization of innocent children is now a core component of the public school curriculum. Primarily under the auspices of Planned Parenthood, the sexual revolution has found its way into the classroom and is corrupting young minds without apology, no longer even attempting to hide its incomprehensible diabolism, as we abandon our own children to lifetimes of sexual depravities, dysfunctional relationships, incurable diseases and spiritual torture. We forbid the teaching of religion to our children, yet we mandate the teaching of immorality. The logical deduction that there is an obvious connection between the forced absence of that which is good, and the ascension of that which is evil, is never made. Deranged reasoning is the serpent's apprentice. When God was expelled from the public schools over fifty years ago, we should have walked out the door with Him. Instead, we stood idly by as He was replaced with the devil himself.

The cost, financing and educational quality of post-secondary education has likewise become symptomatic of a culture that has lost touch with the proper ambition of education. Whether for-profit or not-for-profit, colleges and universities throughout the country have become mere tools of the Progressive trade. As evidenced by a preponderance of left-leaning professors and administrators, whose bias is not only rehearsed and apparent but also force-fed into impressionable minds, the typical college campus is no longer a forum for ideas, debate and learning, but a convention for cultural change. There are now more 'administrators' than professors at Yale University. To further the obvious insanity, at least at Yale, there are actually more 'administrators' than undergraduate students (The Federalist; *Yale Now Has More Administrators Than Undergrads Thanks To A Mammoth Bureaucracy*; Spencer Lindquist; November 11, 2021). An investigative report by *Econ Journal Watch* in 2017 has documented the extent to which Progressivism has infiltrated the college campus. In the fields most susceptible to the designs of Progressive hegemony, the ratios of Progressive to Conservative leaning faculty (under the auspices of Democrat vs Republican voter registrations) is astonishingly one-sided: Economics (5:1); Law (9:1); Psychology (17:1); Journalism (20:1); and History (34:1) (*Faculty Voter Registration in Economics, History, Journalism, Law, and Psychology*; Mitchell Langbert, Anthony J. Quain, and Daniel B. Klein). Many university Progressives are outwardly hostile to the diversity of independent thought, going so far as to deny free speech rights to all who disagree with their version of new age socialism. The withholding of 'tenure' from any professors who do not cow to Progressive dogma is indicative of overt ideological intimidation. Progressivism's main goal is not the education of the mind but the manipulation of the psyche. College students are not only paying an unwarranted amount of money for an inadequate education, but also for sinister indoctrination.

The toll that most students and their parents must pay for a college education has far surpassed, in many instances, the benefit of that education. The average cost of a four-year bachelor's degree at institutions of higher learning, including tuition, room and board, can now easily exceed $100,000. Highly skilled and well-paying professions now require master's degrees or even doctorates, which can add another hundred thousand dollars. Young graduates who have to take out loans for these astronomical sums begin their working careers at a huge financial disadvantage. Many are graduating with degrees that require decades, in some cases, to achieve financial equilibrium under a cost-benefit analysis. For these students, the new government loan-college degree-gainful employment paradigm has become, "the lending of money we don't have to kids who can't pay it back to train them for jobs that no longer exist" (Mike Rowe, *Dirty Jobs*). According to *studentaid.ed.gov,* outstanding college loan debt is approaching $1.5 Trillion. The amount in 'default' status or delinquency (90 days or more late) for those who have already graduated is approximately $165,000,000,000. Nearly one in four students are not current with their loan payments. This is a financial catastrophe, not just waiting to happen, but already here. The total debt service required to pay back these loans is affecting our culture, and the overall economy, in many negative ways. Graduates in their mid-to-late twenties are also of the age for marriage and children. Having and raising children becomes severely handicapped when young married couples are saddled with such an enormous amount of debt. In addition, significant earnings that would have been recycled into the economy, such as buying a home, a car, or investing in savings and retirement, are now being syphoned away from productive use and, for a decade or more, thrown down the bottomless pit of debt servitude. Studies have shown that those with a college degree do earn more over their lifetimes than those without a degree, but that once important distinction is not nearly as impactful as it used to be. In some cases, the converse may now be true, as a great many graduates with a less marketable education have had to settle for jobs that do not require any degrees, and yet the massive debt still follows them.

For years now, we have been led to believe that a college degree is a necessity for a successful future. College, however, is not for everyone. Automatically sending nearly every high school graduate to college is actually a detriment to those students who do not possess the tools to succeed, while also a detraction from the quality of education for those who do possess the ability. Additionally, even for those occupations that have historically required some type of degree, there are other, more effective and affordable ways to achieve the goal of a fulfilling career. For most professions, the benefits of furthering education can easily be eclipsed by on-the-job experience. 'Earning while learning' used to be the most efficient way of achieving competency in virtually all fields of employment. The very simple and effective archetype of apprentice-journeyman-master, which has existed for hundreds of years, can be applied to almost any vocation. The symbiosis between teaching and learning is perfectly fulfilled on an individual, organic basis, rather than our current, impersonal and cumbersome, 'assembly-line' educational philosophy.

Conclusion

     Why, then, have we moved away from an educational design that worked so well prior to the metastasizing of the Department of Education? Considering that socialist ideology has dominated the classroom for decades, it should come as no surprise to learn that the Progressive infiltration, at all levels of education, was by design. A politicized, socially engineered education system has been the primary objective of our public education system for over fifty years. The national cancers of 'identity' politics and multiculturalism were propagated in this conservatory of the newly chartered Progressive schoolhouse. The unity of national identity was, and remains, purposely sacrificed for the discord of group identity. Supplanting fluency in American History with African-American studies, Mexican-American studies, Women's studies, and Queer or Gender studies only reinforces these group divisions. Law schools throughout the country have sacrificed conventional precepts of law and order, some unknowingly, others purposely, with the Marxist application of 'critical race theory,' which suffuses racial leverage and identity politics into every facet of our culture. The devolution of our entire school system from a classical, liberal arts education to an activist-controlled experiment for cultural change is apparent. Facts have surrendered to 'experiences'. The mastery of language, literacy, and literature has been cast aside to make room for the study of Ebonics and 'Food Talks: The Language of food.' Exiling the likes of Shakespeare, Dickens and the Greek and Roman classics, in deference to the 'Twilight' series and Steven King, or, worse yet, in favor of state-sponsored pamphlets of propaganda regarding the Federal Reserve, climate change, and, ironically enough, the praises of central planning, amounts to nothing more than, at best, the dumbing down of education, and, at worst, ideological warfare - in either case, definitely not educational quality. The transformation of mathematics from a precise science to a more flexible and arbitrary discipline typifies the denial of absolutes. The immolation of philosophy and the abstract sciences, including a subversive animosity for reason and judgement, the targeted disappearance of a civics curriculum, derision for the study of etiquette and proper manners, the abandonment of the Trivium (grammar, logic, and rhetoric), and termination of the proper study of the Constitution, in order to accommodate courses on 'Zombies in Popular Media,' 'The Science of Harry Potter,' 'Lady Gaga and the Sociology of Fame,' and 'Fat Studies,' leaves no doubt as to the depths reached by a dysfunctional education system. Emphasizing the teaching of the five pillars of Islam while decrying the memorization of the Ten Commandments as a violation of the separation of Church and State is an obvious display of the marked activism of an agenda-driven education. Furthermore, the outright repression of free speech while championing diversity, and the inability to distinguish that hypocrisy, is evidence of a profound intellectual decay, a decay that is intentional and premeditated.

Agents for Progressive change actually desire the less educated masses, for they are that much easier to deceive, to 'mass form,' and then to recruit. "Let me control the textbooks and I will control the state"…"He alone, who owns the youth, gains the future." (Adolph Hitler). The control of education is one cultural battle that has been patiently fought, and now decisively won, by Progressives. For over fifty years, the intentional disregard for logic, the bastardization of critical thinking, the banning of value judgments, and the denigration of moral authority, in conjunction with the elevation of the 'social sciences,' personal entitlement, susceptibility to endless offense and 'triggering', participation trophies, and instant gratification, has molded the exact type of mindset that many Progressives desire, numbing the psyche and forming the character traits and psychological profiles that are the most easily manipulated. At every stage of education, they have monopolized control of young minds and intentionally sown discord between children and their parents. They revel in their victory, knowing that these are the delusions that will shape our culture for years to come. As testament to the damage wrought, over two-thirds of public school-educated millennials are unable to define communism and socialism, yet nearly half prefer either of those ideologies to capitalism (Victims of Communism Memorial Foundation: *Annual Report on US Attitudes toward Socialism,* Oct, 2017) . Less than a hundred years removed from the self-evident evil of Communism and its calculated murder of over 100 million people, and despite the countless manifestations of the innate failures of socialism throughout the world, American youth remain purposely uneducated in the flagrant deficiencies of collective philosophy…and those immune to the deception know exactly why.

Over the years, every aspect of our education system has become complex, obtrusive and counterproductive, and the poor results are patently obvious. We are no longer teaching our children *how* to think, but indoctrinating them in *what* to think. Political correctness has thoroughly saturated the learning environment, and weighed down the social compact of education with the ballast of artificial equality, tolerance for mediocrity, the flattery of grade inflation, feelings over facts, the diversity of truth, and hostility toward virtue. As such, there is no other reason to combat the tyrannical cultural control of education than in the honest realization that it has nothing to do with imparting knowledge and everything to do with marketing a secular agenda by manipulating the minds of young children…eerily reminiscent of despotic societies of the past. By simply concentrating more on the simple, tried and true basics of education than on impractical and expensive degree mills, forced cultural revolutions, redefining morality, and driving a Progressive agenda, society will be all the better for it, as we transform children into young adults who are morally grounded, individually confident, productively independent, and instilled with a lifelong passion for learning…the true purpose of education. The results achieved by the "little red schoolhouse" education of generations past, even in its plainness and simplicity, easily surpass those of our current, elaborate, and 'sophisticated' educational models.

Health

Modern medicine and societal health, from a cultural perspective, have experienced both monumental, extraordinary achievements as well as epic, and often avoidable, failures. On the one hand, scientific and technological advances have improved our ability to prevent and treat many diseases, increased our average lifespans, and improved end of life care. On the other hand, health care complexity and affordability, contamination of our food and water, centralized medicine, misleading marketing and conflicts of interest have all had a hand in the deterioration of our overall health and quality of life. A combination of individual irresponsibility, degraded social mores, government malfeasance and corporate greed, have, in many ways, offset the finest medical breakthroughs and advancements of recent generations, such as the virtual extirpation of many diseases, the advent of non-invasive surgeries and organ transplants, and our ability to fight complex infections that a few decades ago would kill indiscriminately.

Personal health is the quintessential illustration of how our culture has surrendered the individual to the devices of the collective. Health care should be rendered, as it once was, based on an obligation to the individual, not the aggregate. Health insurance, which has become the bane of affordable and functional health care, places the wellness of the individual at the mercy of the group. Responsibility for a healthy life, and the liability of ignoring that responsibility, should be singular in nature. Ultimately, there is nothing that affects each person's overall health more than individual lifestyle choices. From moderation in diet, exercise, and rest, to the bad habits of smoking, excessive intake of alcohol, fat, and sugar, and the abuse of drugs (legal or otherwise), the lifestyles of decades passed were typically characterized by a preponderance of good habits and a minimum of bad. We grew our own food (natural, nutritional and untainted); we were granted all of the exercise we needed in our daily tasks; we obeyed our natural rhythms of sleep. We lived simply…and we lived well. We now ingest massive amounts of contaminated food, chemically laden and genetically modified, all with the FDA stamp of approval. Most of us sit at a desk all day and on the couch all night. We are patronized by the likes of Dr. Phil and Dr. Oz, and fall prey to miracle drugs and claims of endless youth and beauty, all peddled by modern-day snake oil salesmen, or turn to the synthetic happiness promised by all sorts of pharmaceuticals and illicit drugs. We live a congested and complex life…and we live poorly. Our self-regulated immunity to a rotten lifestyle has faded, and our quality of life has diminished with it.

Our physical health, of course, is primarily a function of both what we consume, and our level of activity. There cannot be a more shameful sight, at least as it regards our collective health, than to visit your local grocery super-store and witness the majority of customers who are grossly overweight, many so obese that they cannot walk without the aid of the now ubiquitous scooter/wheelchair. Some people have limited culpability, as they regrettably may have no control over their condition. Too many, however, suffer from a combination of zero physical activity and the over-consumption of the wrong type of foods. We all have our weaknesses, and we may make, from time to time, unhealthy choices. However, there is something wholly unnatural in the fidelity to consistently bad decisions.

A national examination of conscience also needs to be performed in order to address what we are NOT consuming. Throughout our food chain, from our farms to our kitchen tables, nearly one-third of our food is wasted. The US government actually pays farmers not to grow certain foods; millions of pounds of fresh vegetables are bulldozed into landfills for no other reason than improper labelling and packaging; grocery stores and restaurants fill dumpsters with perfectly edible but "unattractive" food; households throw out, on average, over 1000 pounds of food annually. Totaling nearly 3 trillion pounds per year, the UN Food and Agriculture Organization estimates that this unprecedented waste of food worldwide could sustain three billion people. Again, government interference, corporate self-interest, and individual apathy have created a global squandering of criminal proportions.

Drug and Alcohol Abuse

Possibly the most severe cultural dysfunction related to our health is our entrenched addiction to alcohol and recreational drugs. There exists a widespread epidemic when a large segment of the adult population favors perceived, temporary euphoria over their health, livelihood and relationships. Temperance is again sacrificed on the altar of immorality. Our culture's susceptibility to addiction has become a public health crisis, rationalized with the consent of deceptive self-prescription. Drug and alcohol abuse are not diseases in the typical sense, neither physical nor mental. They may result in diseases, but they are not a malady in and of themselves. They have been cast as such, however, with claims that uncontrollable addictions are beyond the control of the afflicted, as if ingesting the agents occurred by chance or force. Self-abuse is an individual decision, and dealing with the resulting effects should be, primarily, an individual responsibility. Should it be a criminal matter for an adult to use recreational drugs? In a free society, the answer is no. However, the user has the responsibility of moderation and self-restraint, and, short of mastering that control, is fully responsible for the deleterious outcomes of abuse. In a culture where individual responsibility is honored and expected, there would be no welfare for the addicted and no unemployment dollars for the young man so stoned that he has no ambition. Safety nets for those unable to help themselves are one thing. Safety nets for those who willfully self-destruct is quite another. Sole reliance on the financial benefits of social programs likely increases the occurrence, and virulence, of these types of contagions, as the enabled individual is more likely to engage in destructive behavior knowing that he or she has limited risk and little responsibility for its outcome. A culture that champions sovereign expectations of each person is neither coldhearted nor unsympathetic. On the contrary, compelling individual accountability would reduce much of this behavior and save many from the ruinous outcomes of self-indulgent decisions. Our culture of drug-use would not exist in its current state if we, as a people, held personal decisions liable for personal consequences. Making excuses for injurious behavior, and deflecting fault from where it should be squarely levelled, has only served to usher in the drug pandemic that is presently ravaging many communities across our nation. In the first fifteen years of the new millennium, opioid-induced deaths have seen a nearly 500% increase, culminating in the death of over 30,000 people in 2015 alone (CDC Wonder Database). As a society, we wring our hands in frustration, not understanding how such an infirmity could take hold of so many people. Oblivious to the root cause, we seek pretenses to excuse the individual and exonerate the gross deterioration of our culture. Blaming the problem on the red herrings of economics, income disparity, government prohibition, or excessive drug marketing, is simply an immature denial of guilt. While all of these may have lent themselves to an intensifying drug dilemma, they are not the primary determinants of our self-ruin. Specifically, arguments regarding either the legalization or criminalization of drugs does not get to the crux of the matter. Alcohol has been legal since the end of Prohibition, yet continues to ruin an untold number of lives. It is not the substance that is our nemesis, but the lack of interior order. Pretending that the precipitous decline in individual morality, and the outright rejection of God in our society, are not at all responsible for our drug and alcohol-induced cultural degradation is incredulous, and has only made the problem much more intractable.

Health Insurance

While most of the health issues that we face are due to our own decisions, there are numerous and very potent external forces that are cast as health benefits, but are actually detrimental to good health. These forces are normally out of our control, or, at least, we allow them to be out of our control. Typically, such negative health factors are borne of the conceit of an over reaching government and the avarice of big business, which, when combined, produce a dangerously powerful mechanism that only serves to deliver a reduction in health care quality coupled with the distress of exorbitant cost. Under false pretenses and always packaged as being in the best interest of the people, or to save us from impending doom, the white knights arrive with the magic solutions to save us from ourselves, all the while consolidating their power and profit. Most of these solutions are formulated to relieve symptoms, not eradicate the infirmity. The result is that we no longer have a health care system, but a disease management system, primarily because money and power are not found in the cure, but in the endless treatment.

The concept of health insurance, which was originally hailed as the answer to the rising cost of medical care, has become the single most catastrophic element of a failed health system. To force a third party into the system was the death knell of the once simple, and very effective, doctor-patient relationship. Insurance companies know little about medicine and zero about the relationship between you and your doctor. They have become another layer of bureaucracy, another cost center added, and are making decisions that affect our very lives based on actuarial tables and probabilities. Did they at least achieve their original objective of making health care more efficient and affordable? On the contrary, they brought with them broker companies, carrier companies, administrator companies, trust companies, etc…all taking their piece of the health cost pie, and together are responsible for a massive increase in the annual rate of medical care price gouging. To wit, the US spends an average of nearly $13,000 per person annually on health care, compared to other countries' average outlay of $6,125. The difference of $6,875 more per person multiplied by over 330 million Americans results in excess spending of $2.25 trillion a year on health care…often with inferior results.

So what is the plan to fix this problem that has only exacerbated over time? Did we remove the third, fourth, fifth and sixth parties in hopes of cutting back the added costs and overhead, and to return to the natural alliance of doctor and patient? No, we added a seventh party…the federal government, the ultimate interloper, under the auspices of the 'Affordable Care Act,' with more promises of reducing costs and increasing quality of care, all while being able to keep our current doctors and health insurance policies if we so desired. We quickly found those promises to be nothing but expedient lies, as two years into the debacle scores of people have lost coverage, premiums and deductibles have increased (drastically, in some cases), and many find that they can neither keep their doctor nor their preferred insurance policy. A large percentage of those previously uninsured have gained coverage, and those with pre-existing conditions cannot be denied coverage. As such, some individuals have benefited, but at a severe financial cost to all others that is unsustainable. A lack of price transparency, the economic reality of mounting costs as a direct result of medical care subsidies, and the disregard of basic supply and demand fundamentals, have all been intentionally abused to maximize price-gouging profits, and simultaneously have touched off the financial implosion of medical care. As the downward spiral gains momentum, we find the government has secured more control, the insurance companies promised more revenue, and the people, overall, for whom the ACA was supposedly created, have been saddled with higher costs and fewer choices. By design? As the ACA website rollout was an utterly embarrassing disaster, wasting billions in taxpayer dollars, and as more and more federal insurance co-ops have failed (nearly 67%), wasting billions more and cancelling health coverage for 800,000 people (Centers for Medicaid and Medicare Services, 7/13/16), it appears that the Affordable Care Act was either the most poorly written and implemented law in our nation's history, or it was simply *intended* to be an epic failure in order to then foist the implementation of single-payer health insurance on a blind and compliant populace - a scheming government takeover of nearly 20% of our national economy and, even more importantly, the absolute control that comes with it. Deliberate complexity, self-destructing promises and designed unaffordability are corroboration of a failed government intrusion into health care, countering the Progressive premise that the ACA was created to be the savior of a collapsing medical system. Until we remove both government and insurance from our health matrix, and return the economics of health care to a "first-party" purchase and a patient-centered system buttressed by personal choice, cost-control incentives, legitimate competition and free market principles, instead of burdened by bureaucracy, regulation, cost-inflating subsidies and special interest favoritism, we will continue to be encumbered with a health system rife with abuse, waste, poor quality and overwhelming cost.

In order for a government run health 'collective' to function properly, dictatorial controls must be enacted…hence, the Affordable Care Act's nearly twelve million words spanning almost two thousand pages. Without a strangling grip on every minute particular, the law would be destined to inarguable failure. Stifling mandates were thus beset upon the industries of medicine, pharmacy, and insurance. The heavy burdens, however, did not encumber the targeted entities as they were promptly transferred to the shoulders of the individual. Health collectivists actually hold this government control of health care as evidence of cultural progression. Is this a sign of advancement, or a sign of despotism? The answer, as always, is found in the details. Buried in the bowels of the Affordable Care Act is a potential catastrophe to personal health and individual freedoms. The 'Independent Payment Advisory Board' (IPAB) was quietly commissioned by the ACA to control the inevitable explosion of Medicare spending. Although not yet enacted, the very fact that it was devised, and then affirmed by legislative action, should be frightening to any culture founded on personal liberty. The IPAB was designed as a board of fifteen *unelected* bureaucrats whose sole responsibility would be to manage senior health care by recommending the type and level of health procedures to be performed, and the regulation of their cost. Price fixing and monopolistic control of an entire industry is illegal, but evidently not when dictated by government fiat. Those who condemned such tyrannical controls, and extrapolated the inbred potential for 'death panels,' were silenced and branded conspiracy theorists. If unelected government officials are able to deny individuals and their doctors the right to determine what medicines and procedures are the most beneficial to their health needs, then conspiracy is no longer a theory but a fact, and the potency of death panels is not at all a misnomer. In spite of the undeniable deficiencies inherent to the Affordable Care Act, many Progressives continue a push for a 'medicare for all' health system that will only magnify the ACA's failures, ration care, and stifle medical innovation. Chief among these deficiencies is an inevitable apportionment of care. If every American citizen has access to 'free' medical care, the entire health care system will be instantly overwhelmed. When demand exceeds supply by such a wide margin, the only possible outcomes, pursuant to the basic premises of economic science, would invariably be a massive increase in costs (taxes), and/or the necessity of health care rationing.

Massive healthcare conglomerates have also added to the downfall of medical care. Again, the personal relationship between doctor and patient is critical. Over the past half-century, we have moved from a personal doctor, to a doctor's office, to insurance companies and third-party (even fourth-party) administrators, to bureaucratically burdensome and impersonally dictatorial health systems. Heavy layers of administration and oppressive government regulation have drastically driven up the cost and reduced the overall efficiency of healthcare delivery. Over a 40-year period, from 1970 through 2010, the number of doctors in the US increased by roughly 150%. The number of health administrators, however, increased by over 3200% (Bureau of Labor Statistics; NCHS; Himmelstein/Woolhandler). For every one doctor, we have added more than 20 administrators/bureaucrats whose only contribution to the medical services industry has been substantial delays and soaring cost increases of health care. According to a study published in *Health Affairs,* a health care policies journal, layer upon layer of administrative costs account for more than 25% of all medical related expenditures. One out of every four dollars spent has little to no positive impact on health care and, instead, only supports a gigantic health care bureaucracy.

The 'Medicalization' of America

Just as the insurance industry and the government have conspired to radically change the concept and practice of healthcare, so have pharmaceutical companies and the government. In cooperation with the Food and Drug Administration, big-pharma's mad scientists relentlessly pursue chemical answers to all of life's challenges. Some prescription drugs have played an important role in the control of diseases and the eradication of others. Many more, however, especially recently, are of marginal worth. These are the drugs endlessly advertised by pharmaceutical companies; drugs that only mask symptoms and do not really treat the disease, allowing us to continue the poor habits that caused the ailment in the first place. Have a problem…take a pill. No longer do we need to take responsibility or change behavior. These are also the drugs whose endless side effects are laughably often worse than the underlying condition; or the drugs that even contribute to the onset of other, completely unrelated diseases. Even with massive regulatory intervention, we now find ourselves susceptible to a seemingly infinite list of potentially unsafe 'magic potions,' all of which are lining the pockets of giant pharmaceutical companies, a cartel that has deluded our culture with biased research, demonstrably false claims in medical journals, and obvious financial conflicts of interest. Dr. Marcia Angell, a former editor-in-chief of the New England Journal of Medicine and currently of the Harvard Medical School, claims that sponsorship of most clinical research has been commandeered by the pharmaceutical industry itself. Dr. Richard Horton, the editor-in-chief of the British medical journal *Lancet,* declared, "…much of the scientific literature, perhaps half, may simply be untrue. Science has taken a turn toward darkness."

Pharmaceutical companies and their principals are major donors to political parties and individual politicians. In a mutually beneficial alliance with the government, these drug monoliths spend massive amounts lobbying the government for favorable treatment – and favorable treatment they get. Research and development regulations and medical patents have become conduits of obscene profits for pharmaceutical companies, often at the expense of the consumer. Government regulations have created a scenario in which it takes at least ten years to develop a new drug, according to the Pharmaceutical Manufacturers Association. During that period, it is illegal to market the drug. Therefore, the pharmaceutical industry makes the best use of that time by actually marketing the disease instead. The deception runs the entire gamut of the immoral spectrum, starting with, at least, an exaggerated portrayal of the prevalence or severity of the targeted condition, all the way up to, in some cases, the outright fabrication of new diseases. They actually create and market the disease while patiently waiting for government approval of the 'cure.' The pharmaceutical industry spends $19 on marketing a new drug for every $1 spent on research and development (British Medical Journal: *Analysis: Pharmaceutical research and development: what do we get for all that money?*; Donald Light and Joel Lexchin; May 18, 2012). To advance the fraud, pharmaceutical companies masterfully utilize their marketing pipeline - hospitals and doctors' offices across the country (some gullible and uninformed, some complicit through legalized bribery) - as their 'sales' team. Furthermore, the massive cost of bringing a new drug to market (indirectly mandated by the government's regulations) substantially represses any competition. Only the largest companies can absorb this cost and these companies are rewarded with the long-term monopoly of a government-stamped medical patent, which is different from other product patents that only protect narrowly defined innovations. The length of patent protections enforced by the government have become absurd. The Food and Drug Administration is prohibited by federal law from approving a comparative drug for seven to twelve years (potentially with many more years of extensions), even if a patent does not protect the originally approved drug. During the virtually endless timeframe of most medical patents, this scheme, implemented by Big Pharma and enforced by the government, also allows pharmaceutical companies to raise prices with impunity, as all competition has been driven from the market. In addition, frivolous patent claims prevent, or at least delay, the issuance of many generic drugs.

The history of the drug *deflazacort,* marketed and sold by Marathon Pharmaceuticals, is a perfect illustration of this pharma-government complicity. In an article for 'Mises Wire,' entitled *"Why some pharmaceuticals are so expensive"* (August 13, 2017), Gilbert

Berdine, an associate professor of medicine at Texas Tech University Health Sciences Center, pulls back the curtain on the sordid tryst between the Food and Drug Administration and the pharmaceutical industry. Developed in 1969 for the treatment of muscular dystrophy, *deflazacort* only recently received FDA approval. Ironically, but not surprisingly, the approval was issued the year after Marathon formed a political action committee. Variations of the drug have been used around the globe for decades, and, until recently, were allowed to be imported into the US at an average cost of $1,500 annually. Marathon, who did not play any part in the initial conception of *deflazacort,* won FDA-approval by simply performing additional analysis on old clinical trial data. Under the FDA's protection, Marathon is now selling the drug for $89,000 per year while the import of any one of three-hundred generic versions of the drug (with the exact same chemical composition) has been banned. This is not a case of legitimate patent protection, but a collusion of monopoly between Marathon and the FDA. At nearly 60 times the cost, this is clearly a case of government backed price gouging. With the conspiration of the FDA, Marathon now holds a monopolistic privilege on a drug that it did not even invent. Very few people are willing or able to pay such a prohibitive amount, even for a commodity of great benefit. Under free market competition, Marathon would likely not be able to sell even one dose. So, the heavy hand of government intervenes again. Public financing through the auspices of Medicare and Medicaid remove free market constraints and allow Marathon to continue taking advantage of exorbitant prices. Since the end-user is not paying for the medication, they have no concern for the price.

The user, in effect, has become each and every taxpayer, and, without concern for economy, the bloated and unsustainable government health insurance programs continue toward insolvency.

The entire system, purportedly put in place to benefit and safeguard the consumer, is nothing more than a sham, a protection racket. Pharmaceutical companies lobby the government aggressively and contribute heavily to politicians, while politicians write the laws that protect the pharmaceutical companies. Lawyers stand on the periphery, initially constructing and defending the patents, then suing for the inevitable side effects. This triumvirate of medicine becomes obscenely wealthy on the backs of the macerated individual, who finds himself at the mercy of the cabal, unable to afford even the most basic of needed drugs, and goaded into other pharmaceuticals of highly suspect utility. Medicines of true worth, divorced from the free market and controlled by a pharma-government pact, have now become a luxury.

Chronic Diseases

Yet another recent medical phenomenon has had a major impact on our personal well-being, and is creating severe physical, emotional and psychological distress. The growing prevalence of 'chronic' diseases has severely diminished both our quality of life and our life expectancy. We may be approaching the first time in modern history where the current generation will not outlive the previous. The occurrence of food allergies, digestive disorders, autism, ADHD, Alzheimer's disease, asthma, diabetes, and many other maladies, have recently exploded in numbers. A few have always existed but not at the near epidemic levels we are currently witnessing. Others seem to have appeared almost as if by spontaneous generation with no known pathological history. Some blame vaccines; others blame genetically modified foods or industrial chemicals, fluoridated water, environmental toxins, pesticides, or pharmaceuticals – there are any number of potential culprits, with almost all of them being of latter-day origin. Our society can trust none of the players in this dangerous game, as they all have hidden agendas and ulterior motives. Corporate mega-farms, food producers and agricultural conglomerates, the Food and Drug Administration, giant chemical companies and manufacturing concerns, the aforementioned pharmaceutical enterprises, the US Department of Agriculture – all enemies, then cohorts, depending on the mission of misinformation at hand. Quite possibly, all could be complicit. Countless studies are performed castigating one or the other, followed by a similar number of counter studies exonerating one or the other…an unholy and unspoken compact that portends collusion, or at least breeds intentional distraction, and results in more questions than answers, the only constant being the alarmingly waning health of the populace.

For decades, the federal government, again through the Food and Drug Administration, has been lecturing Americans on what foods to eat and what foods to avoid. In order to diminish the impact of ballooning rates of chronic heart disease, the government, beginning in 1977 and in cooperation with the expertise of medical science, targeted cholesterol as the ultimate villain of American diets, in spite of the fact that not one scientific study had been performed testing the validity of the premise. As we have been bombarded with scientific literature, food pyramids, Ad Council advertisements, and label warnings, 'bad' cholesterol became the scapegoat for multiple diseases, the poster-child for settled dietary and nutrition science, and the largest uncontrolled experiment in history. Not only was the remedy a failure to begin with, but it has now become worse than the disease itself. Inflammation in the artery walls, not cholesterol, is the primary culprit of the heart disease plague, as it is inflammation that allows the cholesterol to attach to the blood vessels in the first place. If there were no inflammation, the cholesterol would move through the arteries unimpeded. The focus then should have been on determining what caused the inflammation. Neither fat, nor eggs, nor red meat, nor dairy – generally none of the foods much maligned by the FDA – are at all responsible for the inflammation that has caused a meteoric rise in heart disease over the past half-century. On the contrary, excessive consumption of their mandated replacements is the actual culprit. When medical science insisted that we eradicate all saturated fat from our diets and instead consume foods high in polyunsaturated fat, such as soybean, corn and other vegetable oils, the processed food pandemic was upon us. Coupled with massive amounts of carbohydrates, sugars, and omega-6 preservatives, that which has been slowly killing us turns out to be exactly what the doctor ordered. Our digestive systems were not made for the constant and repetitive ingestion of these poisons, as they relentlessly damage the lining of our blood vessels, causing our bodies to naturally respond with inflammation and, in turn, allowing cholesterol to attach to the vessel lining and impede blood flow.

The results of this medical malpractice are found in the fact that nearly half of American adults suffer from obesity, the onset of diabetes, and/or heart disease, resulting in over 600,000 deaths annually (Centers for Disease Control and Prevention; *Heart Disease Facts*) - an avoidable tragedy whose scope, if not stemmed, will eventually rival the worst plagues of history. Yet, our politically correct society now promotes obesity as somehow virtuous.

Disorders, Syndromes and Addictions

Inchoate disorders, syndromes, and addictions have also become more commonplace - actually fashionable - so prevalent that it is almost as if they were infectious diseases. No longer do we have character flaws; no, we now have uncontrollable syndromes. No longer do we experience ordinary human experiences; no, we now have unmanageable disorders. We need not take personal responsibility for our thoughts or actions, as they are the direct result of inveterate addictions. The myriad 'conditions' have become so numerous that we are running out of alphabetic combinations to name them all…from Uncombable Hair Syndrome (UHS) all the way to Male Pattern Baldness (MPB). The *Diagnostic and Statistical Manual of Mental Disorders* lists over 365 different disorders with more being added every year, creating a disease-mongering culture in which every possible human condition, weakness, and fault has been 'medicalized.' Your children are not misbehaving…they have 'Oppositional Defiant Disorder' (ODD) or 'Disruptive Mood Dysregulation Disorder' (DMDD); you are not impulsive, overspending or living beyond your means…you have 'Compulsive Shoppers Syndrome' (CSS); you are not gluttonous…you have a 'Binge Eating Disorder' (BED); you are not forgetful and unorganized…you have a 'Minor Neurocognitive Disorder' (MND); your teenager is not lazy and selfish…he or she is suffering from 'Adolescent Benign Focal Crisis' (ABFC); you are not vulgar and have bad manners…you have an 'Anti-Social Mood Disorder' (ASMD); you don't abuse drugs…you have an 'Uncooperative Drug Addiction' (UDA). While a normal culture would find most of these 'crises' patently ridiculous, ours has been programmed to give credence to the conviction that we are a slave to our emotions, thoughts, limitations and defects. As such, we constantly seek excuses for our poor behavior and thus, never expend the effort to self-correct the anomalies…we just pop a pill and blame it on someone or something else.

Far from being humorous, our reaction to some recently diagnosed disorders have been both medically irresponsible and a cultural injustice. Attention Deficit Hyperactivity Disorder (ADHD) was 'discovered' some fifty years ago. Since then, on average, one out of every ten children (some as young as two years old) are prescribed amphetamines such as Adderall and Ritalin, all to control what was once considered, for the most part, normal childhood behavior. We have essentially classified childhood itself as a disease. Undoubtedly, there are some children who have a severe form of the condition and require some type of intervention, but the scope and severity of the response is reprehensible. Being naturally prone to a lack of focus, distraction, day dreaming, tantrums, impulsiveness, agitation, and other 'symptoms' of ADHD, all children display some, if not all, of these tendencies at some point in their young lives. With no inclination toward any attempt at pharmacological restraint by parents, teachers, and even doctors, the prescriptions are hastily written with no apparent concern for the potentially adverse effects. In a ten-year period near the end of the last century, there was a 2000% increase in ADHD prescriptions, with the use of psychotropic medication tripling in children aged two to four years old (Journal of the American Medical Association, *Trends in the Prescribing of Psychotropic Medications to Preschoolers,* Feb 23, 2000). More recently, in 2011 alone, nearly fifty million prescriptions were written to mask, not cure, the symptoms of ADHD (US Drug Enforcement Administration-Office of Diversion Control, *Special Report: ADD/ADHD Stimulants in NFLIS, 2007-2011,* November 2012).

The long-term use of these psychotropic drugs can cause unexpected negative outcomes and dangerous side effects. In the first place, the children exposed to these drugs are never given the chance to overcome the targeted behaviors in a more normal, and permanent, way. Instead, many will likely need to stay on the drugs indefinitely, and at gradually higher doses, in order to maintain the desired effects. In addition, because of ADHD medications' masking effects, there may be unknown underlying conditions that will never be diagnosed (therefore, never treated) and, in some cases, even aggravated. Second, amphetamines are addictive by their nature, potentially leading to other substance abuse, and they have inherent side effects such as sleep deprivation, hallucinations, and appetite suppression. Finally, and most troubling, as with all psychotropic drugs, there is the potential for suicidal thoughts and actions, not to mention the fact that nearly all mass murders in this country have been committed while under the influence of some sort of mind-altering drug.   Little emphasis is given to the much simpler, and safer, treatments of nutritional diets, proper sleep, exercise, practiced discipline, setting behavioral expectations and incremental / achievable goals, all of which have been shown to be effective in overcoming the often-temporary behaviors defined by ADHD. These, of course, take time, patience, and parental involvement – qualities that are sorely lacking in many households. It is much easier to force your children to ingest mind-mutating stimulants and achieve almost immediate relief than to give your children the time-consuming attention they need to properly address the perceived problem. Giving otherwise illegal and addictive drugs to our two-year old children who are in the prime of their physical and mental development is bizarre, and should be inconceivable. The extent of shortsightedness and the potential for great harm to children on such a wide scale, by their own parents and doctors nonetheless, is egregious neglect, bordering on abuse…yet another cultural example of 'suffer the children.'

Mental Health

Our understanding of the psychology of the mind has lagged many years behind our comprehension of the physiology of the body. In many ways, the science of psychology is still in its infancy. Where there is injury to the body, the treatments are relatively normalized, concrete and definitive. Where there is injury to the mind, however, the remedies are more subjective and less precise.

By the mind's very nature, there are only vague ways of measuring progress and quantifying recuperation. Diagnosing the causes of mental illness is substantially speculative, for, in most cases, there is no empirical manifestation of the pathology. The science points to possible connections with biological, chemical, neurological, and genetic determinants yet will likely never move beyond studied conjecture, as the mind's depth and breadth is impossible to fathom. The essence of the human mind is both miraculous and confounding. Human perceptions are the ultimate enigma, conceiving at once the majestic, the mundane, and the malevolent. Our minds have created both the *'Pieta'* and the electric chair; formed each the persona of Mother Theresa and Pol Pot; developed the cure for polio as well as the curse of biological warfare; and concurrently offered both homage to God and fealty to the devil. Our consciousness is simultaneously diabolical and sublime, chaos and symmetry, espousing profound wisdom in one thought and ignorant folly in the next – it is what makes us uniquely human.

For the mind to achieve and maintain healthy function, it needs, above all else, order…a confidence in the absolute, and the surety of practiced resolution. Our culture offers - no, it commands - the exact opposite. The internal strife created by endlessly challenging our organic mental processes with the extrinsic and synthetic notions compelled by our culture is a malignancy that reveals itself in many ways – depression, eating disorders, anxiety, bipolar disorders, and addictions. While disturbing and unfortunate, this inundation of psychological distress, apparent in the broad and amplifying regularity of mental disease throughout our culture, should not be surprising. The littering of our psyche with a constant torrent of disquieting contradictions, unnatural deficiencies, and disorienting fallacies, is one of the primary causes of inner turmoil and emotional incontinence, creating a disordered mind that has become hostile to sound thought. How?...By being separated from God, severed from communion with perpetual truths, and disengaged from authentic reason. Truth has become the enemy of Progressive hegemony, and is now cast off as mis-information, dis-information and mal-information, a mere conspiracy theory. Why?...Because a mentally disordered populace is more susceptible to domination.

There is widespread cultural evidence that our dissonant and encumbered consciences have been programmed to accept that which a healthy mind would otherwise never entertain. The post-modern contagion of individual psychoses has resulted in an all-encompassing mass delusion. How else do you explain the idiocy of men claiming to be women, and the teaching of transgenderism and 'age appropriate' pornography to children? Or the resurgent infatuation with communism? Or open borders as immigration policy? Or the half-century of lawful abortion? As mental disease is no longer the exception, but instead has become the norm, our culture has been consumed by an epidemic of psychological madness. The growing prevalence of mental illness in our society is not by chance, but by the result of an intentional 'rape of the mind' by the diabolical totalitarians among us, as described by the Dutch psychoanalyst, Joost Meerloo. The French scientist, Gustave Le Bon, further describes this premeditated brainwashing of society leading to consensual psychosis: "The masses have never thirsted after truth. They turn aside from evidence that is not to their taste, preferring to deify error, if error seduce them. Whoever can supply them with illusions is easily their master; whoever attempts to destroy their illusions is always their victim." A more appropriate epitaph could not be etched on our cultural tomb.

Suicide

The culmination of this relentless abrasion of the mind can ultimately lead to the scars of all-consuming despair. As those scars are torn open repeatedly, the mental torment becomes unbearable, thrusting some toward the ultimate disorder of suicide. In the past, suicide was usually a singular act of passion, approaching the involuntary, usually directed inward as a response to a devastating blow to the psyche, typically motivated by perceived intolerable shame, financial ruin, or a severe and unrecoverable deterioration of health. While our modern society still experiences these specific acts of interior anguish, it has also witnessed a distressing increase in a more generalized and conforming version of suicide, now alarmingly driven more by what appears to be almost custom or ritual than exigent circumstance.

In a fifteen year period from 1999 to 2014, according to the National Center for Health Statistics, overall suicide rates in the US rose by nearly 50%, with increases in almost every age group and demographic (except older Americans, aged 75 and older). Most alarmingly, the number of young girls who committed suicide tripled over the same timeframe. Experts cast blame on various causes, including the economy, income stagnation and disparity, and the proliferation of mental health issues, among many others. While these reasons most assuredly play a role in some instances, there appears to be a rationale more deeply rooted, a portent of the obvious peril of our neo-cultural consciousness. When we remove God from every aspect of our culture, we simultaneously remove the virtues that He embodies. The one constant in all instances of suicide is the total absence of hope – the full omission of God - complete and utter desperation. Counseling and medication, likely more widespread now than any other period in human history, are at times helpful but decidedly are not a panacea at all for the chasm carved out by hopelessness.

In spite of, or maybe because of, the proliferation of psychotropic drugs and the prominent use of psychiatric counseling, suicide appears to be transforming into a cultural propriety. The romanticizing of suicide, especially among the younger generation, has led to the unhealthy view of suicide as liberating and heroic. The instances of entertainers and musicians taking their own lives has become daily news, further fueling the suicide contagion, and leading the emotionally immature to emulation. To advance prevention, suicide needs to be called out for exactly what it is, and exactly what it is not. Suicide is an extreme act of selfishness, as suicide does not eliminate mental misery. The individual may relieve himself or herself of the burden, but that burden does not disappear…it is automatically transferred onto the shoulders and into the psyches of abandoned loved ones. Suicide is not honorable, brave, liberating or inspiring…it is evidence of a mind that has lost accord with its Creator, denied its natural inclination toward hope, and traded its loftiest aspirations for non-existence, for nothingness. No matter one's level of depression or intensity of mental tribulation, the love of one's family, friends, and especially of one's God, is paramount, always and forever, to any perception of hopelessness, however entrenched it may seem.

Conclusion

As a culture, the amount of resources we invest in addressing health-related issues is astounding. The *National Institute of Health* alone has an annual budget approaching six-billion dollars. The entire healthcare industry comprises about one-fifth of our nation's total GDP, or over 3.5 trillion dollars. Some of this massive expenditure has been wisely spent, combatting diseases and healing the infirm. A much larger amount, however, has been pitifully wasted, and is little more than sewage as a by-product of poor individual choices, mercenary commercialism, forced government imperium, and cultural illusions that are more detriment than benevolence to our individual health. We typically live longer, but do we live better? The only undeniable reality is that we are forever mortal. As the hardest rock will return to sand and the largest tree to loam, so too will the healthiest man eventually return to the ground from which he came. Some of us are given many years, some few, the reasons being found only in the providence of God. If we spend those years devoted solely to that mortality, we will be caught up in the cultural morass of health as an end, instead of a means to an end. If we spend those years cognizant of the vital importance of genuine health in body, mind, and spirit, and optimizing our health so that we may favor living well over living long, not as tribute to ourselves but as homage to our Creator, we will begin to live those years to the fullest.

Rights and Responsibilities

Without morality as a master, our collective rights become ubiquitous while our individual responsibilities cease to exist. America, in the past 50 years, has become an entitlement nation. 'Social justice,' which once sought equality of opportunity, now seeks equality of outcomes (i.e. '*equity*'). Equity is as far from equality as tyranny is from freedom. "Equality, rightly understood as our founding fathers understood it, leads to liberty and to the emancipation of creative differences; wrongly understood ['*equity*'], as it has been so tragically in our time, it leads first to conformity and then to despotism" (Barry Goldwater). Poor individual choices must be borne, and remedied, by the collective. As it is no longer our responsibility to provide for ourselves, we are now 'entitled' to food, housing, and employment. We have a 'right' to free education, free birth control, free phones, free utilities, and free medical care. The United Nations has gone so far as to proclaim internet access a basic human right. These are not rights at all, but, when controlled and parceled out by the government, are actually "dependency, the rations of slavery" (Alexis de Tocqueville, *Democracy in America).*

In 1944, President Franklin Roosevelt designed a second 'bill of rights,' an economic bill of rights, as the crescendo of his 'New Deal.' Each new right, deemed 'unalienable' by Progressive standards, was necessary, claimed Roosevelt, to create an "economic constitutional order," and "to assure equality in the pursuit of happiness." By all accounts, the following list was only the first of dozens, if not hundreds, of newly fabricated rights, as ensuing generations have added many additional rights in order to ensure everyone achieves the "goals of human happiness and well-being":

- The right to a useful and remunerative job in the industries or shops or farms or mines of the nation;
- The right to earn enough to provide adequate food and clothing and recreation;
- The right of every farmer to raise and sell his products at a return which will give him and his family a decent living;
- The right of every businessman, large and small, to trade in an atmosphere of freedom from unfair competition and domination by monopolies at home or abroad;
- The right of every family to a decent home;
- The right to adequate medical care and the opportunity to achieve and enjoy good health;
- The right to adequate protection from the economic fears of old age, sickness, accident, and unemployment;
- The right to a good education.

This is not a list of rights, but a list of demands. If we all have an unalienable right to recreation, then there can be no end to our claims. Our original, unalienable rights, as enumerated in the constitution, are intangible by their nature, transcending this mundanity of wants, desires or even needs. In addition, the vague wording of most of these new rights is hampered by relativity. What is fair, adequate, good, or decent to one, may not be to another. Furthermore, within this convoluted line of reasoning, the rights of one person can only be attained at the expense of another. In the most honest portrayal, once someone else is forced to pay for a 'right,' it is no longer a right at all, but a liability to the person receiving it. Every desire, every whim, every need are now rights. Liberty is no longer a freedom to yearn for a better self but a license to demand whatever we want. We have created the temporal and subjective while ignoring the genuine and unalienable.

Our culture's self-defined, Progressive version of rights contends that all medical care is an entitlement of the highest order, an unalienable right, and should be provided free of any cost to every individual. The obvious fact is that, in the first place, absolutely nothing is free – someone must bear the cost - either personally, through family, charity, taxation or some other form of wealth redistribution. Second, critical health care is already provided to anyone who needs it, without personal liability, subsidized through higher costs borne by those who are able to pay. On its face, however, the idea that no one should have to file bankruptcy because of a medical emergency, or have to choose between food and the preposterous cost of most medical care, or be denied healthcare outright due to an inability to pay, should be an automatic inclination for any civilized society and is absolutely morally laudable – but it definitely is not tantamount to an unalienable right. Why does the government need to be involved in any of this, especially with its history of ineffectiveness, waste and abuse? Does the government hold a monopoly on compassion? In generations past, family and charity were the answers to these unfortunate issues, and both fulfilled their purpose well. For more serious/costly health issues, mostly religious-based institutions, funded by individuals and charitable organizations alike, provided free medical care with excellent quality and true compassion. Government intervention is not the answer to every societal challenge. In many cases, it is the cause, or, at least, the exacerbation.

Transferring these social responsibilities to the government is not only problematic but also unconstitutional, and opens a 'Pandora's box' of unforeseen consequences – unforeseen by us, but fully comprehended and feared by our forefathers. The government actually desires the fabrication of new rights, molding and encouraging the people's inclination for entitlement, and then casts itself as the only benevolence that can appease them – all to subordinate the individual and pacify the masses while solidifying dominion over them. The government has no business mandating and managing health care, and, when it does, we end up with the categorical failures under the likes of the Affordable Care Act (ACA). If the government is able to declare health care a right, it can, and will, declare anything that is even remotely health related a right, as well. Should the government be able to mandate that businesses pay employees for sick time and family leave? Many people fall ill, or even perish, from a lack of utilities, food, and proper housing…those with a poor education have shorter life spans…many deaths are the result of inadequate smoke/carbon monoxide alarms…are these all now rights? The physical and mental well-being of all people can be negatively affected by a lack of leisure, recreation, and vacation…are these now rights? Proper exercise is essential to good health and a long life…are a gym membership and a personal trainer, then, unalienable rights? Studies have shown that more lives are saved by using snow tires than are lost by some diseases. Should we have a right to snow tires? Under our culture's all-encompassing catalog of privilege, with intentional provocation by government, many of these otherwise facetiously framed rights have already been declared. We do not possess a right to any of these unearned advantages. What we do possess is the right to pursue them, should we desire, without interference or coercion from the government. Furthermore, the government, through its nuanced cultural reformation, will not stop with the compilation of innumerable new rights…it will also impose smothering restrictions, taxes, and legislation that intentionally deny us other, essential rights and, in so doing, radically reduce our freedoms. Many people were forced under the ACA to purchase health insurance that they neither wanted nor needed. When the government has the ability to force citizens to buy a product or service in order to secure someone else's 'rights,' we find ourselves on the precipice of subjugation. Yet, we only look down and venerate the chains of our servitude and feel secure in our yoke of tyranny. If the government retains that type of power and can operate at that level of authoritarianism with impunity, it can demand or withhold, implement or dissolve, create or destroy anything it desires, including rights, and 'we, the people' will have no recourse for remedy – precisely what the founding fathers portended.

Notice, also, how today all rights must be 'equal.' While every person has certain unalienable rights (simply by virtue of our Creator's benevolence and by the mere nature of our humanity), not ALL rights are unalienable. One could call these secondary rights, 'constitutional,' or 'common,' and, out of that subset, not all of these common rights are for every person. One has unalienable rights to life, religion, speech, self-defense, etc.; one should have common rights to own property, to due process, etc. One cannot, however, as an example, claim the right to attend Harvard. Young girls cannot have the right to become boy scouts. A male attending college cannot have the right to join a sorority. A confused man, transgender or not, cannot have the right to use the women's bathroom. An illegal immigrant cannot have a right to the benefits of citizenship. Two men, or two women, cannot have the right to marry. These are not rights, and denying them is not a heinous act of bigotry, hatred, discrimination and oppression, but common sense distinctions based on obvious variabilities. As our understanding of rights has regressed to the maturity level of a toddler, we have primed an entire generation to subscribe to the idea that they need only desire something, and it automatically becomes a right. The 'millennial manifesto' can be paraphrased as, "I want this thing, I deserve this thing, I have a right to this thing, but I don't want to work for this thing, so either lower the standards required to obtain this thing, or better yet, someone else must give me this thing."

Another indication of a culture that has lost touch with a proper understanding of rights is found in subscribing to group privilege. Only the individual possesses rights. The endowment of rights by government decree specifically for defined groups is not only culturally damaging, but also unconstitutional. The 'protected class' argument is a nonstarter, as it is the essence of discrimination and the epilogue of a free society. If the basic liberties of some are protected while others are denied, and if the laws favor one at the expense of another, we quickly return to the rationales and practices of monarchies, oligarchies, and the slave state. Most worrisome, however, is its suspicious origin in a clenched-fist, 'power to the people', neo-Marxist ideology. Similar to the justifications for affirmative action and progressive taxation, the resurgent communist canard of class oppression can only be rectified by forcibly taking liberties / rights / opportunities / possessions from one group, those cast as 'privileged,' and transferring the same to another group, the 'oppressed.' Freedom of speech, association, self-defense, and, eventually, all unalienable rights, then, will no longer be unalienable. Instead, they become, at first, malleable, and then, political weapons. The protected class of today can easily become the oppressed class of tomorrow, with the government alone determining the parameters. Then, the very concepts of 'equality under the law' and 'due process,' the underpinnings of all civilized societies and their legal systems, are forsaken, and we take yet another step forward on the plank of tyranny.

We find ourselves not only authoring an endless fiction of newly chartered individual rights, as well as undermining liberty with discriminatory group rights, but also inventing a 'hierarchy of rights,' where the rights of the nouvelle-favored often supersede the rights of all others. Culturally popular movements and groups such as atheism, abortion proponents, as well as the transgender and affirmative action population, are the sole recipients of certain rights that are not based on constitutional inalienability, or natural disparity, but instead on real, yet ignored, racism, sexism, and irreligious favoritism. A man has the right to become a woman; a woman has the right to extinguish the life of her child; the minority has a right to a college education; the homosexual has the right to marry; the pornographer has the right to publish; and the satanist has the right to worship an anti-god. However, the military chaplain no longer has the right to preach Christian doctrine; the vendor no longer has the right to free association; the common person no longer has the right to privacy; and the public school student can no longer enjoy freedom of religion while on school grounds.

While a majority of Americans is clamoring for more and more rights, they are simultaneously loath to more and more responsibilities. This correlation makes sense in that if an always-increasing number of our wants and needs are to be provided by others, then we no longer have the personal responsibility to provide them for ourselves. Rights without responsibilities are as knowledge without education, ideas without thought, and harvest without planting. The well of rights, of freedom, is only replenished with the proper discharge of our obligations. Rights and responsibilities are inextricably linked, and their union, self-promoting. We can live at the expense of others for a time, but as we quench our insatiable thirst for privilege while neglecting commitment, we will soon return to a font dry and barren. As rights continue to increase, and responsibilities similarly decrease, the bridge of self-determination will no longer be able to span the cavernous breadth between the two.

Our once bold proclamation of individual self-reliance has become a whimpering, then cacophonous, whine, full of excuses for why it is someone else's social duty to take care of us. Our capacity for responsibility has become so feeble as to be a cultural embarrassment. When the high school dropout demands a 'living wage;' or, the promiscuous father of five children with five different women cowardly vacates his parental responsibilities to the state; or, the able-bodied food stamp recipient illegally sells his EBT benefits in order to purchase drugs or make the payment on his 60" flat screen, or spends welfare dollars at the strip club or on his sixth tattoo…what a pathetic testament to the character traits that have become all too prevalent among a significant percentage of our spoiled populace, especially our youth. Too few are willing to plod the proven, yet slow and tedious, advance of responsibility through education, experience and hard work, instead demanding the worthless 'rights' of immediate gratification that we, as a culture, have now spent decades fabricating and glorifying in spite of an obvious lack of successful consequence.

The dissociation of rights and responsibilities resides in every class of people, throughout every demographic. There are those prosperous who are not immune to their own litany of claims for myopic rights, and who are oftentimes averse to their own responsibilities. 'Affluenza,' or the 'right' to 'maintain the lifestyle that I've become accustomed to' is the liquor that intoxicates the minds of some who are wealthy, while excusing their socio-economic transgressions and evading the heightened expectations of their social responsibilities. Those who have been blessed with good fortune, successful business acumen, or inherited wealth, retain a parallel liability of personal charity and social philanthropy - not as a forced and sterile taxable event but as a singular, moral obligation.

Welfare and Work

Our obverse cultural views on both rights and responsibilities have left our concepts of welfare and work quite disoriented. Every society has certain members who, through no fault of their own, are genuinely unable to provide for themselves. We retain a social imperative to afford them whatever resources they need to lead purposeful and dignified lives. There are others in society who may fall on hard times and need assistance to overcome a job loss, health concerns, or even unfortunate financial decisions…it is incumbent upon us to offer material, yet temporary, assistance to extract them from their condition. As individuals, we have the responsibility to care for these people without prejudice or the pride of superiority. In the past, the family would assume this responsibility. Again, the Conservative view of social hierarchy prevailed, as the family would logically possess, at first, the most compassion, but also, the most effective means of caring for a member. If there was no family, then the charity would move down the hierarchy…always beginning locally, then, if necessary, ending with a federal 'safety net.' Unfortunately, the average family of today has renounced what used to be its widely perceived responsibilities, and instead has gladly ceded the weal of its own members over to the government.

Overall, the welfare system in America has taken on a life of its own by far exceeding the original intent of short-term, temporary assistance programs - TANF/AFDC, Medicaid, SSI, SSD, food stamps (SNAP), WIC, childcare assistance, cash aid, Section 8 housing, utility assistance, Bridge Cards, Head Start, Unemployment Insurance, ACA, SCHIP, Healthy Start, school breakfast, lunch and dinner programs, the Earned Income Credit…in total, 79 means tested programs (state and federal programs only…plus dozens more locally). Despite such a multitude of programs and the massive financial investment required to fund them, poverty yet remains pervasive. Even in times of healthy economic growth, with low unemployment rates and increasing wages, poverty still rages on. How could that be? Rather than wage inequality, economic immobility and lack of privilege being the causes of poverty, might they instead be the result of a persistence of poor individual choices and a culture of dependence that perpetuates the need for welfare? Entrenched dependence, especially across generations, is loath to be corrected, and when it is eventually perceived as entitlement, is practically impossible to reverse.

Poverty, in some ways, is becoming less and less a conditional problem and more and more a behavioral one. Many recipients of welfare are truly in need and have used the assistance to pull themselves out of unfortunate financial circumstances. Many more have abused the system to a degree where it is no longer a safety net, but a way of life. Culturally, in many instances, we are simply subsidizing bad decisions and enabling fraud. Rewarding irresponsibility is of no benefit for the habitually needy for, in most cases, this will perpetuate their condition. Affirming constant dependency ultimately steals both the dignity and the potential of the recipient and, when pervasive, severely debilitates the national character. When one out of every two citizens relies on the government for some sort of assistance, there is something inherently wrong with the entire system. When one out of every six people cannot even provide for their own basic necessities, there is an ingrained dysfunction. When over thirty million children receive free or reduced-price school lunches (on top of other food assistance), we are witnessing a cultural decay that exceeds mere economic frailty. Contrary to rational thought, Progressivism actually holds that the proliferation of welfare programs is a measure of their success, as opposed to being obvious evidence of their outright failure. Objections to time limits, work requirements, and mandatory drug testing epitomize welfare policies that only serve to commit the impoverished to a chronic debility. A healthy, productive, and truly compassionate society would structure welfare programs in order to maximize the number of people being freed from the hobbling effects of dependency. Instead, the cradle to grave welfare state has largely become a Progressive petri-dish for irresponsibility; Section 8 housing, a breeding ground for criminality; bridge cards, all too often, a bridge only to dependency; false unemployment claims, a proxy for work; and fraudulent disability benefits, a surrogate for self-sufficiency. "Welfare's purpose should be to eliminate, as far as possible, the need for its own existence." - Ronald Reagan

The 'safety net' has frayed beyond the stage of irreparable rupture. This is not strictly an anomaly of time or economic conditions, but instead a common generational mindset that has permeated our culture now for decades. Once entrenched in the system, there is little incentive, and even less desire, to get out. In many cases, it is easier to be 'professionally needy' than it is to put forth the required effort to support oneself. We are facilitating laziness and perpetuating failure on a grand scale, and, in so doing, are redirecting valid assistance away from those who truly need the support. This is not welfare…this is a cultural travesty, a caricature of compassion. The level of entitlement abuse has the potential to be extraordinary. An able-bodied adult can now, quite easily, by moving from one social program to another, avoid work indefinitely. When the entire system is wrought with fraud, it becomes the truly needy's worst enemy in the form of exhausted benefits and onerous application processes. Though accurate records are not kept, one can reasonably extrapolate that corruption is likely rampant based on the prevailing cultural mantra of 'I deserve…'; based on the countless reports of inefficiency found within the appalling track records of any massive program run by the government; and, finally, based on our culture's diminished concept of work, a character flaw prevalent in an entire generation of young people, young men especially. According to a study by the *National Bureau of Economic Research*, young men aged 21 to 30 years old worked 12 percent fewer hours in 2015 than they did in 2000. Even worse, around 15 percent of young men worked zero weeks in 2015, a rate nearly double that of 2000 (*Leisure Luxuries and the Labor Supply of Young Men*, NBER Working Paper No. 23552, June 2017). "The democracy will cease to exist when you take away from those who are willing to work and give to those who would not" (Thomas Jefferson).

“By the sweat of your brow will you eat your food until you return to the ground…” (Genesis 3:19). While some may view work as a curse related to the punishment of mankind by God after The Fall, it can likewise be perceived as a vehicle of atonement for that original sin. On an even higher level, as with so many other examples of God fashioning good from evil, our earthly toils have the capacity to evince the innate dignity of humankind. Work is rooted in very fertile ground. Our labors provide the necessities that are the reality of survival. Work allows us to be self-sustaining and prevents us from relying on the efforts of others while also cultivating the fruits of a productive society. Work is our vehicle to freedom. Work is also the mother of charity…not the forced charity by a proxy of wealth redistribution but the honest, personal charity freely offered to those truly in need. Work nourishes hope. Welfare, as a way of life, as an end unto itself, nourishes despair.

Charity

America has historically been a very generous nation. Personal charity, in addition to the work of legitimate philanthropic and religious organizations, has served to alleviate human suffering the world over. More recently, as we seem to be resigning our incumbent duties of charity to the government, or to the countless mock charities throughout our culture that are suspect in their true intentions, in many ways we are not practicing true charity at all, but a facsimile that is frequently ineffective, and in some cases, counterproductive. Our modernized concept of charity is often based more on feelings than results. Actual consequences do not really matter, as long as we 'care.' 'Feeling good' about 'doing good' is, in some instances, paramount to the objective outcomes of this narcissistic altruism. The self-promotion of being seen by others as charitable appears to be a driving force behind many of our cultural compassions.

The War on Poverty

The Progressive concept of charity has summarily been classified as the 'war on poverty,' which began in earnest during the 1960's implementation of President Johnson's Great Society experiment. By its intentions, it was praiseworthy. By its actual results, however, a complete and utter failure, and wholly inefficient. Since that time, our nation has invested nearly *25 TRILLION* dollars in combating poverty by enforced charity. We currently pour over one trillion dollars annually into all forms of 'charity' (i.e. welfare – excluding FICA) out of federal tax collections of $3.18 Trillion and an annual expense budget of $3.8 Trillion (whitehouse.gov, 2016). Total federal assistance, then, consumes over 30% of revenues collected and over one-fourth of our nation's total annual expenses.

If the results of this investment had significantly improved the rate of legitimate, actual poverty, then one could at least make the case that spending this incomprehensible amount may have been worthwhile. The historical facts, however, prove otherwise. Prior to the 'great society,' the poverty rate fluctuated between 10% and 15% of the population. In the fifty years since, it has never left that range. The results are nothing short of obscene…twenty-five Trillion dollars later, there has been no demonstrative improvement in our society's rate of destitution. Why? The reasons fall along three fronts. Primarily, the money spent has been far too heavily weighted in outright cash expenditures instead of being invested in job creation, training, and retention – the 'feed a man a fish vs teach a man to fish' parable is apt.

Second, the federal government's penchant for convolution often overlooks, sometimes purposefully, straightforward and organic solutions that would be much more efficient and effective in addressing any social problem that comes before them, essentially exacerbating the very issues they are attempting to solve. One might think that a mere modicum of common sense and a glimmer of wisdom should be able to lead the 'experts' to the obvious realization that the main driver of poverty is individual choices and behavior. Instead of the present gargantuan bureaucracy, the multiple and reiterative government programs, the many trillions of dollars of debt, and the abysmal results nonetheless, the simple chronological sequence of education, employment, marriage and children has been proven to be a highly effective means of avoiding poverty. Known as the 'Success Sequence,' as formulated by the Brookings Institute scholars, Ron Haskins and Isabel Sawhill, this practical design for the widespread flourishing of all individuals, and ensuing generations, has been universally known and accepted throughout history. An American Enterprise Institute study by researchers Brad Wilcox (Senior Fellow at the Institute for Family Studies) and Wendy Wang (Director of Research at the Institute for Family Studies and former Senior Researcher at the Pew Research Center) found that 97% of millennials that followed all four steps of the "Success Sequence" were in the middle income track (or higher) by age thirty. Conversely, "31 percent of millennial high school graduates (who didn't follow the work and marriage steps by their mid-20s) are in poverty during their prime adult years." Parents, teachers, social scientists, political activists, and all who seek to minimize the afflictions of poverty would be wise to promote this elemental formula that our ancestors knew, by mere cognitive reason, to be the precursor of economic success.

Third, the duplicities inherent in the Progressive model of 'fairness' are exactly what is driving our government-based concept of charity, evidenced by, not just the welfare state, but also the earned income credit, a living wage, guaranteed income, and other wealth redistribution schemes. In other words, the dreadful results of our 'great society' experiment are due in large part to, not a sincere desire to lift the poor out of poverty, but to the primary goal of forcing a level economic playing field. Thus, we have endless Progressive attempts to demonize the rich, castigate 'big' business, pontificate about the evils of free enterprise, and caricature the abuse of labor at the hands of capital. Charity has thus become yet another ideological weapon where our culture's social conscience and natural compassion is exploited to advance Progressive goals under the guise of humanitarianism. Even when faced with an undeniable truth that their policies are at best, inefficient, and at worst, counterproductive to economic commonwealth, they yet continue their Marxist lecture, pandering to the proletariat's sense of victimhood and envy. Their solution to every perceived problem invariably requires the transfer of wealth from one group to another, never the promotion of self-advancement through personal responsibility for one's economic condition.   "Do not expect to build up the weak by pulling down the strong" (Calvin Coolidge). The poor are not poor because the rich are rich. The poor are poor because we pay them to be poor. The real problem is that large-scale, government-run charity programs *never* work because, for the most part, the recipients do not realize lessons learned from the behaviors and circumstances that put them there in the first place.

A further dissemination of the results of our charitable war on poverty is even more telling. The historic rate of poverty over the past fifty years, as measured by the federal government, is roughly 12% of the population. Based on the current population of 320 million, the number of citizens in poverty would average a little over 38 million. The annual expenditure of $1 trillion correlates to an insane $26,000 per person, or over $60,000 per household, each and every year. The median annual household income in the US is only $55,000. We actually 'pay' the poor, on average, $5,000 more per year (with little corresponding production) than the average family earns by virtue of productive work. Considering human nature, why would anyone seek work when one can 'make' more money by not working? "I am for doing good to the poor, but…I think the best way of doing good to the poor, is not making them easy in poverty, but leading or driving them out of it. I observed…that the more public provisions were made for the poor, the less they provided for themselves, and of course became poorer. And, on the contrary, the less was done for them, the more they did for themselves, and became richer" (Benjamin Franklin).

The long arm of government rules and regulations, in many instances, diminish actual and effective works of charity by the individual. When a 90 year-old Florida pastor is charged under the criminal code for providing free meals to the hungry without the proper permits; or, when a compassionate young man is threatened with criminal charges for providing free haircuts for the homeless because he does not have a license; or, when the Little Sisters of the Poor, arguably the most charitable of all organizations, is forced by government mandate to offer free contraception in its health insurance policies or face massive fines and legal expenses…it becomes clear that bureaucracy and administrative overreach actually inhibit our natural propensity for charity. Possibly the most arcane example of cultural madness regarding our society's attempt to reduce poverty is found in the adoption and foster care system. The last hope of thousands of neglected children lies in the flourishing patronage of a sound and expansive adoption and foster care network. While feigning interest in child welfare and poverty reduction, however, numerous groups dishonor those very concepts, as their pursuit is sacrificed on the altar of Progressive extremism. The American Civil Liberties Union, among other leftist organizations, is successfully banning major charitable and religious-based social service programs from participating in adoption and foster parenting because those programs seek to place children exclusively in families with a mother and father. A significant number of child placements are facilitated by these faith based concerns. Denying thousands of children the opportunity to grow in a financially healthy, stable, and loving home is tantamount to child abandonment, if only to pay extreme homage to a diseased political correctness. Our culture's efforts to minimize poverty should not be thwarted by actively inhibiting the requisite conditions that have been shown to be successful; or by hampering individual altruism with an endless list of mostly unworthy and counter-productive regulations; or especially by resorting to an ideological betrayal of the obvious and fundamental elements forever inherent to any healthy culture. Charity then becomes a 'means,' not to an 'end' of reducing poverty, but instead activism to an end of advancing Progressive ideals.

Government has neither the right nor the mandate to force charity, or any transfer of property from one group to another.   The government does not even have the competency, based on the dismal results of our war on poverty. While charity is our personal obligation, it is not in the government's purview. "I cannot undertake to lay my finger on that article of the Constitution which granted a right to Congress of expending, on objects of benevolence, the money of their constituents…Charity is no part of the legislative duty of the government" (James Madison – "Father of the Constitution" and fourth U.S. President). Sharing the wealth of one's own volition is of great worth...being forced to share it creates a watered-down charity, a mirage of virtue that has done little to solve our social woes. Taking a more active, first-person role in highly localized forms of charity is proven much more effective than the impersonal and institutionalized charity enforced by the government. If everyone were more cognizant of, and reactive to, the sincere needs evident in their own families and immediate neighborhoods, much of our poverty and want would be eradicated. Instead, we gladly renounce our personal obligations and yield to a cosmopolitan, pseudo-philanthropy that has constrained, to a large extent, real individual altruism. The mindset of the Progressive-socialist that the government, not individuals, can best manage charity in all of its forms has led to this burgeoning 'welfare' state and the passivity of personal goodwill.

'Pathological Altruism'

Additionally, our culture does itself no favors by offering unqualified charity to the 'self-inflicted' disadvantaged of our society as we only aid and abet them in continuing their personal degradation. As a charitable culture, it would be far more honorable to foster a change in behavior and help pull a person out of their seemingly hopeless conditions than to fashion the tools that only serve to validate their poor behavior. In many instances, we are promoting the problem instead of correcting it. Barbara Oakley, a researcher and Professor of Engineering at Oakland University, has classified such unintended consequences as 'pathological altruism,' defining it as "altruism in which attempts to promote the welfare of others instead result in unanticipated harm." This case can be made with a parent who provides financial support for an adult child who has a history of drug abuse. The parent acts out of unconditional, yet misguided, love and genuine concern. The grown child uses the assistance to finance his continued drug addiction and eventually succumbs to an overdose. The outright refusal of government entities to administer any cultural charity on the condition of drug abstinence is an appropriate corollary that highlights these frequent, far from anecdotal, and counterproductive outcomes. One may wonder just how many people who have died of a drug overdose were concurrently patronized by federal charity. 'Tough love,' whether by a family or by the government, is often the most effective charity.

Organizational Charity

Even as direct charity has all but disappeared from the family dynamic, organizational charity has swelled. Many charitable groups, both locally and globally, are perfectly legitimate, and effectively offer relief to those who suffer. Prime examples include the Salvation Army, St. Jude Research, Samaritan's Purse, and the Make-A-Wish foundation. Many others are practiced in deception and are nothing if not a counterfeit to charity, forgeries that do little but abuse our penchant for compassion. There are countless fraudulent 'charities' that are unquestionably illegal. There are also many charitable organizations, however, which are completely legal, yet whose principals often make millions in compensation and whose administrative expenses are so high that only a modest fraction of the donations received actually finds the people in need. Many of these charities masquerade as legitimate, behind the façade of 'not for profit.' Just because an organization is set up as a non-profit entity does not automatically denote charitable authenticity. Goodwill Industries is a 501(c)(3) non-profit organization that many view as a charity. While Goodwill does provide job placement services for those facing employment challenges, its core business model to facilitate those services is selling donated items and paying minimum wages to most of its employees. The fact that it is non-profit does not prevent the CEO of Goodwill, Jim Gibbons, from receiving reported compensation of $725,000 annually (goodwill.org - 2011 IRS Form 990). Disguising a business in charitable camouflage, when its principal receives nearly fifty times the hourly wage as most of the employees it is purporting to help, reeks of insincerity and detracts from the good works espoused. In 2010, the director of the American Red Cross, Gail McGovern, was paid over one million dollars (redcross.org – 2010 IRS Form 990). While the Red Cross performs much needed services worldwide, the optics of a charity whose director receives roughly twenty-five times the median income of the average American worker lends itself to cynicism, and to a perception of simulated charity. It would take over 40,000 modest donations of $25 each just to cover her salary. Additionally, many veterans related 'charities' play on our emotions of national pride and patriotism. The Vietnam Veterans of America raises millions in donations, yet only 25% of those gifts are actually spent on the welfare of the veterans themselves (Charity Navigator).

As they relate to charity, the precepts of a Progressive socialism on an individual basis are worthy of acclaim and serve to elevate the dignity of every person. *Individually*, we are called to be 'our brother's keeper.' Socialism, as impersonal and forced polity, however, has been proven corrosive to cultural weal through ingrained, cradle-to-grave expectations via government-mandated altruism. As with all socialist endeavors, the endgame of government 'charity' is absolute control, even over the organic, person to person benevolence that has defined true charity for millennia. Socialism demands, via taxation, that you 'love your neighbor,' but only with the government's consent, and under the rigid dominance of its central planning.

Furthermore, socialism under the guise of commerce is, in many cases, nothing but a concealed sham of self-enrichment. By focusing on groups instead of individuals, the harmony of humanitarianism between the giver and the receiver is never realized, as both are unable to form the bonds of mutual concern and appreciation that are hallmarks of true charity. Every single nation in history that has governed on the tenets of this unadulterated socialism has eventually passed away by ceding individual sovereignty and strength to group languor and apathy. In the cases of socialist/communist dictatorships, the results were far worse. Legitimate philanthropy and individual benevolence, along with free market principals and a passion for personal accountability, have helped far more people than any government-proscribed socialistic policies cloaked as charity.

Of Sacrifice and Selfishness

The line of distinction will wildly meander
When drawn by opposing hand
Between the imperceptions of sacrifice
And the seductions of selfishness

Inverted images will rightly confirm
The current malady of moral dyslexia
To be wary of entrapment will not suffice
For rationalization spans temptation without border

Lifelong adversaries, so shall it permeate all that is man
Perception is found in the ever-conscious effort
Of living one's life with some other purpose
Than the muted myopia of 'me'

Sacrifice and Selfishness

Individual instances of charity are always conditioned on some level of sacrifice. A majority in the Progressive movement views Conservatism as unworkable, as, in their view, it promotes greed, precludes sacrifice and would eventually fall to the anarchy of selfishness. Within the confines of morality, however, they could not be more wrong. On the contrary, Conservatism is practiced in the art of sacrifice, not selfishness. Selfishness *is not found* in taking care of oneself, or one's family, as this crystalizes commitment and sacrificial contribution to society. Selfishness *is found* in one's expectations that someone else will take care of them. True Conservatism is not in need of the 'compassionate' caveat, for Conservatism is forged in beneficent import, in the sincere desire that each individual possesses the freedom and acquires the ability to succeed on his or her own merits and hard work…the 'pursuit of happiness.' Sacrifice is the fuel, and Conservatism is the engine that motivates true progress, for the individual at first, but in charitable turn, for the whole of our culture.

Throughout much of her history, America has clearly understood that cultural cohesion, unified purpose, and personalized concern are what propels individual sacrifice and frustrates our propensity for selfishness. The means that were most proficient, and most utilized in earlier years, were found in family, localized associations, civic and religious groups, and charitable organizations, all independent of political interference and the alienation of state paternalism. These groups thrived at the intersection of communal goodwill, civic responsibility, and moral felicity for the well-being of neighbor – the perfect balance of authentic altruism. When infiltrated by political concerns, and by ulterior motives inherent in government, the purpose, once substantive, nimble and pure, becomes artificial, cumbersome and uninspired. The results, previously driven by the zeal of individual engagement, are now thwarted by budgetary concerns, dictatorial regulation, and impersonal administration. Verifiably more efficient and productive, the once cherished convictions of individual charity, given potency through local orientation and community involvement, will someday return to America, as the bloated and largely ineffective decree of government dictated charity will eventually implode under its own weight.

Racism!?

The 1998 murder of James Byrd, a young black man dragged to his death at the hands of white supremacists, is a recent reminder that racism, in the actions of a few mentally deranged people, will never be fully extirpated from our society. The prevalence of unabashed racism throughout much of our cultural history has no doubt left a hideous scar on our nation's conscience, primarily by denying the intrinsic worth of each individual no matter his or her ethnic heritage. Treating an entire race of people as chattel, denying opportunities based on skin color or country of origin, and laws affirming credibility to the outright discrimination of minority ethnicities, have all contradicted our nation's founding creed that 'all men are created equal.' Blatant racism has been all but eradicated from our legal and economic systems, in spite of vacuous arguments to the contrary, yet there still exists a certain level of bigotry in the individual beliefs of some with hard hearts and weak intellects. This bigotry, however, does not explain our society's degenerative obsession with the continuing false narrative of a collective, institutionalized racism, as well as with an unceasing parade of concocted racial injustices.

Slavery

Racism in America is admittedly a by-product of the inhumane practice of slavery. In America, slavery obviously had a disproportionate effect on the black population, which, even after emancipation, suffered yet the lingering effects of psychological bondage for many years. In her defense, however, the founding of America was the impetus behind the most notable anti-slavery movement in history. "Slavery was not created on July 4, 1776. It was refuted on that date—the grand anti-slavery statement of a people, the first time in human history that a people decided to form a government on the basis of equality," (Lucas Morel, professor of politics at Washington and Lee University; "*Lincoln and the American Founding*"). Slavery was not unique at the time of our founding. What was unique was the constitutionalized notion that "all men are created equal"…an idea that made American ground fertile for the eventual abolition of slavery. The Founding Fathers' belief in a Federalist system of governance afforded the new United States of America the vehicle which mobilized the beginning of the end of slavery. Indeed, many northeastern States immediately banned the practice of slavery, and within the first five years after the turn of the 18th century, all had codified the abolition of slavery, either outright or through gradual emancipation. Furthermore, the expansion of America into the 'northwest territories' (present day Upper Midwest), and eventually into all future territories from which states would arise, was conditioned upon the demand that each new state would enjoin the practice of slavery in their respective state Constitutions. The fact that Article VI of the *Northwest Ordinance* of 1787 forbade the establishment of slavery is a clear repudiation of the 'systemic racism' argument used against the founding of America, as well as nullification of the entire premise of Critical Race Theory. Finally, America is the only country that has waged a civil war, with much sacrifice and bloodshed, to finally and fully eradicate the abhorrence of slavery.

Today, while all people of good will find the idea of any form of forced servitude abhorrent, many on the left exploit the history of slavery in this country to condemn, not just the American practice of slavery, but also the moral character of most of her founding fathers and, therefore, all aspects of her very essence. As such, they conveniently ignore or gloss over many material facts. Up until approximately 150 years ago, nearly every nation and culture throughout history engaged in some form of slavery regardless of race. Motivations for placing all blame for racial subjugation on white America alone can be reasonably questioned when predominantly black African slaveholders marketed the first half of the entire slave trade, many freed blacks in America owned slaves themselves, and thousands of Native American Indians were also slave owners. The Cherokee Constitution of 1839, in contrast with the U.S. Constitution, legalized slavery based on race. In his 2004 book entitled, *Christian Slaves, Muslim Masters: White Slavery in the Mediterranean, The Barbary Coast, and Italy, 1500-1800*, Ohio State University history professor Robert Davis estimates that more than three-million white Christian's were enslaved in Europe, North Africa and the Near East. The number of black slaves in British North America was estimated to be 750,000. Decades after America freed all black slaves, white slaves were still being bought and sold throughout the Ottoman Empire. These facts do not make any instance of enslavement acceptable, but it is quite disingenuous to portray white American transgression as singularly evil.

Two generations of white students In America have been indoctrinated to believe that it is their 'whiteness' that caused slavery, and that each and every white person, historically and presently, is directly responsible for the evils of black servitude. Adam Kotsko, a professor at Shimer College in Chicago, encapsulates this widely taught, irrational sentiment by proclaiming to his students, "Whether or not your individual ancestors owned slaves, you as a white person have benefitted from slavery and are complicit in it." Would Professor Kotsko levy this same judgement as well on the thousands of freed black men or American Indians who owned black slaves, or on the multitude of black African slave traders? Of course not, because it does not play into the Progressive script of 'whiteness' being the sole cause of black mistreatment.

Critical Race Theory

The concept of *Critical Theory* originated in the 1930's as a critique on societal structures that are deemed inherently oppressive. Significantly influenced by a commingling of radical Marxist ideology and Freudian pseudoscience, critical theory purports a desire to liberate all of humanity from the innumerable, and unconscious, forces that prevent people from reaching their full potential and, ultimately, true freedom. Critical Theory forcefully infuses the idea of a Marxist 'power struggle' deep into any institutions, norms and traditions (not surprisingly, mostly Conservative) that it may consider an adversary, exorcising all demons that have plagued America since her birth. Thus, Critical

Economic Theory, Critical Gender Theory, Critical Race Theory, Critical Education Theory, Critical History Theory, Critical Legal Theory…all principles, standards and values must be rejected and overthrown in order to reach Progressive nirvana. This social philosophy hibernated for decades in academia until it was adopted heavily by the second surge of the Progressive movement in the 1960's, and can no longer be ignored as a fringe ideology.

Critical Theory has more recently matured into the mainstream cultural force of identity politics. As such, Critical Theory's most abhorred antagonists are the unjust, hierarchical dynamics of a mostly white, rich, Christian patriarchy; dynamics which are further claimed to be embedded in many of the rights and original principles espoused from the moment of our founding. Therefore, property rights, free markets, freedom of religion and association, and even free speech, are no longer unalienable, but are instead inherently oppressive, and must be regulated, even repealed, if necessary, to liberate the masses. Under critical theory, all Progressive roads are now bridged: the eradication of private property; the death of free enterprise; the exile of God, the rejection of religion, and the denial of objective truth; identity politics and victimization; the perversion of human sexuality; and media manipulation. Thus, the rise of the collective. History has shown, however, repeatedly, that each of those roads leads to economic slavery; to the deceptive rationale for Communism; to the elevation of evil, the glorification of sin, and the deflection of personal responsibility; to pervasive tribal violence; to the collapse of marriage and family; and to propagandized, psychological conditioning. Thus, the fall of the individual. Intentionally, only one road remains: cultural upheaval, shared misery and the eventual transformation of America – an integrated campaign of demoralization.

Critical Theory has of late invested most of its ideological capital in matters of race, as racial divisions have long been the agency of choice to fabricate the cultural friction necessary to dismantle the social structures most obstructive to Progressive passions. Initially cast off as a circus sideshow, Critical Race Theory (CRT) has now been purposely spread to every corner of our social compact, primarily by indoctrination through government, academia, corporations, and the media. Propaganda and 'reeducation camps,' disguised as 'workforce training,' have leached out of the chronic sociopathy of higher education and propagated widespread to every level of government and virtually every major corporation, given cover by politicians and propelled by media. By dividing our country into subnational identity groups, all apparently subjugated by the invisible 'white privilege' that is claimed to have permeated every fiber of our culture, the ensuing intersectional, race-driven warfare lays the groundwork for an eventual overthrow of the current order…by any and all means necessary. Critical Race Theory is wholly counterproductive to the plight of racial minorities, as it casts racism as a fixed and permanent, 'institutionalized' phenomenon that cannot, by its very nature, be remedied. Providing immunity from personal accountability only serves to intentionally hobble the upward mobility of those exploited by Critical Race Theory's contrived thesis of immutable subjugation.

Masquerading as science, with a thick yet transparent layer of cosmetics to hide its Marxist blemish, Critical Theories are nothing if not the perennial and adolescent Progressive narratives of victimization and envy, the hackneyed and dangerous Communist canard of oppressor versus oppressed, and the convenient and premeditated excuses for the inherent failures throughout Progressive ideology - in education, law and order, immigration, marriage and family, economics, welfare, and health. They are all labelled as 'theories,' yet are hostile to the scientific method. Their antagonists are nonsensically claimed to be both 'systemic' and 'unseen' at the same time, though there is no-real world evidence of their existence, except for, per critical theorists, their convenient invisibility. They purport a desire to vanquish a mystical 'oppression,' yet only serve to encumber the freedom that only self-realization can foster. They defend segregation while feigning inclusion. Specifically, Critical Race Theory claims to defend society from discrimination, yet is definitively unconstitutional under both the Fourteenth Amendment to the Constitution and the Civil Rights Act of 1967 for the intentional *promotion of* discrimination, which, in a perfect example of 'doublespeak,' renders them antithetical to reason. Discussions regarding Critical Race Theory do not even deserve the 'in good faith' presumption of civil debate, as any contrary argument is automatically, and intentionally, subjected to "the devilishly clever word games of the race-obsessed for whom vagueness and ambiguity are both a shield and sword" (GianCarlo Canaparo; *Sloppy Thinking About Systemic Racism;* The Daily Signal; Aug 12, 2021).

The 1619 Project

A byproduct of critical race theory, and the latest weapon in the Progressive arsenal of cultural warfare, is a melodramatic reimagining of America's founding. *The 1619 Project,* begun in August of 2019, is a theatrical, revisionist polemic from the mind of Nikole Hannah-Jones, an editorial writer for the New York Times. A self-proclaimed work of scholarly history, the project is a multi-faceted attempt to pre-date the founding of America to the arrival of slaves on US shores in 1619, reducing the entire history of America to one overarching principle – systemic racism. While a more detailed history of the effects of slavery on our nation may be warranted, claiming that slavery and racism alone are the source and summit of America's story is not only counterfactual, but also evidence of Ms. Hannah-Jones' obvious designs to keep the pretense of systemic oppression alive at the expense of honesty and credibility. With the likes of Hannah-Jones spouting disinformation, American culture is not encumbered by systemic racism, but systemic ignorance.

After widespread criticism of the factual integrity of the work, within a year of its release, Ms. Hannah-Jones then claimed that it was no longer a work of history, but now a work of journalistic commentary. When she believes no one will fact check the veracity of her virtue signaling as she accepts the 2020 Pulitzer Prize, the project is an erudite, detailed scholarship fully worthy of the accolades she initially received. When the work is eventually scrutinized and found wanting of truth, the project is nothing more than an editorial or opinion piece. Actually, it is neither…it is simply source material for what is, by and large, factually ignorant propaganda. In spite of its clear lack of scholarly weight, the 1619 Project is nonetheless finding its way into curriculums throughout the country (to date, 3,500+ K-12 classrooms), and is especially widespread in the obvious Progressive pustules of the northeast and on the west coast. This was a primary focus from its inception, as the education piece of the project was launched simultaneously with the journalistic piece, and is further evidence of the perversion of our education system to provoke radicalism.

If even a minimal amount of objective research had been employed, available historical documents would have shown that the first 'slave ship' arriving in Jamestown did not carry slaves at all, but indentured servants, which later included both blacks and whites who were employed by other blacks and whites for a set period of time, and who afterwards became land owners themselves. The immorality of "chattel" slavery did not appear widespread until the late 17th / early 18th century, nearly 100 years later (*TIME Magazine;* "The First Africans in Virginia Landed in 1619. It Was a Turning Point for Slavery in American History—But Not the Beginning;" Olivia Waxman; August 20, 2019). An argument can be made (and now, of course, is conveniently ignored) that the 'father' of legal chattel slavery was actually a black man, Anthony Johnson, who was the first recorded "slave-owner" in the British colonies. Mr. Johnson sued for, and won in civil court, the perpetual ownership of another black man, John Casor. This precedent played no small part in the ensuing legalization of slavery throughout the southern colonies.

Phil Magness, a Senior Research Fellow at the American Institute for Economic Research and author of *The 1619 Project: A Critique,* highlights many other historical inaccuracies strewn throughout the 1619 agenda. From what appears to be intentional omission of well-known and easily sourced facts that do not corroborate the 1619 premise, to obvious misrepresentations and, in some cases, "clear, unambiguous error," the project is simply an attempt to rewrite American history. In the first place, the image of the "first slaves" arriving in Jamestown, Virginia is little more than emotional rhetoric, as slavery in America was historically expansive among the native population long before the arrival of English settlers. Second, the project intimates Colonial America as being aligned with slavery unanimously, with the British Empire cast as largely anti-slavery, which is illegitimate on both counts. Early legal documents authored by the Pilgrims of Plymouth colony specifically codified the illegality of slavery (*'man-stealing'*). When the first ship of African slaves reached the shores of Massachusetts in 1646, the Pilgrims actually arrested the slave traders, set the slaves free, and funded their return trip to their native country. There were numerous laws fought for and passed in each colony that either attempted to abolish slavery outright, or at least limit its progression. It was England, King George, his emissaries and appointed governors who vetoed all attempts by the colonies to extirpate slavery from the New World. Furthermore, the disingenuousness and irrationality of the claims that the American Revolution itself was fought in order to preserve slavery completely ignores the contrary fact that the Revolution itself singularly set the stage for the exact opposite. Additionally, in its desire to perpetuate the undercurrent of oppression essential to the façade of its Marxist, class struggle ideology, the 1619 Project intentionally omits the outsized efforts of many white Americans who were instrumental in the abolition of slavery.

According to Mr. Magness, the most egregious examples of inaccuracy in the 1619 Project are reflected in its ignorance of economics. Claims are made, without substantiation, that the slavery economy laid the foundation for the American system of free enterprise, implying that without slavery, there would be no America as the economic powerhouse of the world, and that all of the wealth America has generated over the centuries is directly linked to the efforts of slave labor. In the first place, the slavery economy of the south was primarily agricultural and wholly dominated by only two products: tobacco and cotton. While plantation owners became very wealthy, the south's economy as a whole was otherwise financially depressed, due mostly to the misallocation of resources and unseen opportunity costs of more efficient economic endeavors. Ms. Hannah-Jones' economic thesis lacks any credibility by completely ignoring all other economic activity in the nation, especially the industrialization and manufacturing largely prevalent in the north, which in sum far surpassed the economic output in the south.

The relentless cry that our Founding Fathers, the Constitution they wrote, and the birth of our country itself, were all illegitimate due to the practice of slavery, intentionally ignores the many efforts to rid America of its birth defect. Yes, most of the Founding Fathers were either slave owners or were sympathetic to the slave trade at some point in their lives, as were most of the world's peoples at the time. However, the 1619 Project's complete disregard and omission of the many penitential efforts to end the atrocity of slavery in our young nation is a testament to its scholarly and historical deceit. To wit, from the mind and heart of both Thomas Jefferson and Benjamin Franklin themselves:

"Commerce between master and slave is despotism. Nothing is more certainly written in the Book of Life than these people are to be free" (Thomas Jefferson).

From a persuasion that equal liberty was originally the Portion, It is still the Birthright of all men, & influenced by the strong ties of Humanity & the Principles of their Institution, your Memorialists conceive themselves bound to use all justifiable endeavours to loosen the bounds of Slavery and promote a general Enjoyment of the blessings of Freedom. Under these Impressions they earnestly entreat your serious attention to the Subject of Slavery, that you will be pleased to countenance the Restoration of liberty to those unhappy Men, who alone, in this land of Freedom, are degraded into perpetual Bondage, and who, amidst the general Joy of surrounding Freemen, are groaning in Servile Subjection, that you will devise means for removing this Inconsistency from the Character of the American People, that you will promote mercy and Justice towards this distressed Race, & that you will Step to the very verge of the Powers vested in you for discouraging every Species of Traffick in the Persons of our fellow men (Petition from the Pennsylvania Society for the Abolition of Slavery; Benjamin Franklin, President of the Society; Philadelphia, February 3, 1790).

With very little probative effort, it is clear that *The 1619 Project* is yet another ideological diatribe that was created solely to advance the designs of concocted racism in order to further division. By the spurious yet standard attacks of revisionist history, educational propaganda, and the condemnation of free enterprise, the project continues the same tired but relentless Progressive tirade against America, her past and her present, in order to facilitate the calculated disintegration of her future. "The left has warped, distorted, and defiled the American story with deceptions, falsehoods, and lies. This project rewrites American history to teach our children that we were founded on the principle of oppression, not freedom. Nothing could be further from the truth. America's founding set in motion the unstoppable chain of events that abolished slavery, secured civil rights, defeated communism and fascism, and built the most fair, equal, and prosperous nation in human history" (President Donald Trump).

Racism as Ideological Leverage

The Progressive movement, therefore, masterfully utilizes charges of racism as an ideo-political cudgel, with the treble purposes of silencing its adversaries, delegitimizing every aspect of American origin, and recruiting impassioned, if not obtuse, partisans. In the culture wars, cries of racism are never an isolated means to an end, but are often used in conjunction with other Progressive tools and ambitions, namely the sabotage of law and order, the undermining of our nation's founding, the scourging of police, defending and even promoting illegal immigration, and the overthrow of capitalism, among many others. As further evidence of 'politicized' racism, a discussion of 'reparations' periodically rises to the top of the national discussion (typically, every four years), and it is nothing if not a sales pitch, a marketing tool, to attract votes. What if reparations were enacted by government force? Who would pay the reparations and to whom would they be paid? Would descendants of black slave owners be on the paying end or the receiving end? Would descendants of Union soldiers who lost their lives in defense of freeing slaves be financially penalized? What amount would be deemed necessary to fully absolve America from its past sins? What recompense would prompt those who have never suffered slavery to forgive the rest of us for transgressions we have never committed? These questions are not meant to be answered because, if they were, there would no longer be a means to extract votes, and therefore, accrue power.

Culturally, 'racism' has become some sort of mystical invocation - our society's ultimate taboo - under which there is no longer a basis for rational thought or sound reasoning. Racism is nothing but theater, and is apparently everywhere: devil's food cake, gun ownership, breastfeeding, SpongeBob Square Pants, the nuclear family, limited government, equality under the law, manicured lawns, vascular disease, prostate cancer and diabetes, credit scores, Mount Rushmore, adopting black children, national borders, criminality, proper grammar, the Tea Party, the Coronavirus, even children's stories penned by Dr. Seuss. Under the current avalanche of 'critical race theory,' racism is often an incongruous entrapment. 'Gentrification,' or the movement of whites into predominantly minority neighborhoods, is considered racist, while 'white flight,' or the movement of whites out of predominantly minority neighborhoods, is likewise considered racist. Most paradoxically, a valid claim of not being racist is now proof of racism. The notions of a strident work ethic, attention to detail and punctuality have incomprehensibly fallen to claims of racism…the denial of virtue if only to rationalize its absence. Modern day examples of faux racism are an affront to so many who have experienced true, sometimes brutal, racism. Now, simply *claiming* racism, without even a pretension of honoring veracity, automatically nullifies any defense. We are told that some groups are inherently racist, always, while others are immune or, at least, fully pardoned. The monotonous claims of 'critical race theory' are nothing if not a counterfeit of empathy and/or the vapid bleating of a fatigued intellect.

Pointing fingers and yelling loudly, rabid race-baiting acolytes never dare introspect. Even cursory self-reflection would yield the palpable conclusion that the true racists in our midst are those casting aspersions the most vehemently. The new racism is an end unto itself, subordinating character and suppressing excellence. Dr. Martin Luther King's most famous quote, "I have a dream that my four little children will one day live in a nation where they will not be judged by the color of their skin but by the content of their character," has been inverted with disdain, and without apology. Evidenced by promoting public policies such as affirmative action, and by decrying other policies such as voter ID and school vouchers, self-obsessed racial guardians wallow in the deepest recesses of true racism. Demoralizing certain races by declaring them incapable of achieving educational and employment goals independently, dishonoring them for not possessing the aptitude to procure something as simple as a photo ID, and belittling their ability to choose the best schools for the education of their children, are all obvious examples of prejudicial disdain. Condescension, humiliation, and disparagement are the tools used by some to keep themselves in power, and to keep entire races in the bondage of dependency – now that is true racism. "The worst enemy that the Negro [has] is this white man that runs around here drooling at the mouth professing to love Negros and calling himself a liberal. It is following these white liberals that has perpetuated problems that Negros have. If the Negro wasn't taken, tricked or deceived by the white liberal, then Negros would get together and solve our own problems. I only cite these things to show you that in America, the history of the white liberal has been nothing but a series of trickery designed to make Negros think that the white liberal was going to solve our problems" (Malcolm X).

Racism and Law Enforcement

The most obvious examples of culturally extemporized racism exist in the realm of law enforcement, for a reason. Progressives use the fabrication of systemic racism, coupled with the narrative of widespread police brutality, for dual purposes. Not only does the perpetual charade of racism ensure the dependence of minorities, but also, by casting all police officers as a primary source of that racism, it will concurrently set the stage for the eventual dismantling of law enforcement as we know it, and the creation of a more 'progressive' system of law and order, which will, of course, be controlled by Progressives. As with every other aspect of Progressive ideology, law and order must finally succumb to chaos in order to be rebuilt, and conform to the revolution of nihilism.

'Systemic,' or 'institutionalized' racism is the newest Progressive talking point. If it is repeated loudly enough and for a long enough time, numbed and conditioned minds will believe. More dangerously, it is also the linchpin of the diabolical legal premise of 'thought' crimes. In our racially charged culture, any police encounters, any criticism, any negative interactions at all with people of color are now spontaneously branded as crimes of racism, even absent any concrete evidence to establish that fact. No one has proven, or even attempted to prove, that *any* negative police encounter with a black man is based on racial animus, yet every police officer's conduct, whether legal or illegal, is elevated to the 'thought crime' of racism without any such substantiation. When any and all white officers are automatically found guilty in the court of public opinion of racist thought crimes when interacting with criminals of color, without even a shred of corroborating proof, that, in and of itself, is the epitome of racism.

Racism, if it were a defendant, is no longer innocent until proven guilty, not even guilty until proven innocent, but, in many cases, guilty *in spite of* being proven innocent. When a police officer shot and killed a black man in Ferguson, Missouri after the young man, Michael Brown, attempted to do bodily harm to the officer, ignored numerous warnings, and had a history of violent behavior, the incident was not racism at all. Mr. Brown's DNA was found on the officer's gun. He was not killed because he was black, but because he was threatening a police officer with evident violence. The situation is obviously a tragedy, but it is solely the fault of the young black man. Those who shout 'racism!' the loudest appear to be the ones who rely on its continued propagation the most. Politicians and race-baiters inevitably attempt to instill a collective racist motive where none exists, simply for the self-serving reasons of personal and political gain, as well as to manipulate and control the thoughts and actions of an ignorant populace.

The Ferguson incident spawned numerous movements, which were all based on an obvious lie. The 'Hands Up, Don't Shoot' mantra was an outright fabrication, which was perpetuated by many groups, including members of Congress, even after it had been wholly refuted. Yet, the idiocy does not end there. Many people peddle lies such as these, and many more follow blindly. The entire Black Lives Matter movement was founded on this lie. Accordingly, Mr. Brown's stepfather, ex-con Louis Head, repeatedly called for the residents of Ferguson to "burn this bitch down." Mr. Brown's mother, Lesley McSpadden, investigated for her own personal version of assault and felony robbery charges, was actually invited to the Democratic National Convention (while police were explicitly excluded) and was applauded wildly…for what? For raising a son whose criminal actions led to his death, ruined the life of an innocent officer, caused the destruction of large sections of Ferguson, cost the taxpayers millions of dollars, and did untold damage to race relations in this country? This cultural madness is truly of an alternate reality. Truth is once more a casualty of a mentally defective culture, and the collateral damage of a politically correct society. The victim became the perpetrator, and the perpetrator became the victim. What is proven not racist is perpetuated as racist, while what truly is racist is claimed to be not. By extension, 'Black Lives Matter', in its proclamation, is a racist statement. Affirmative action, in its application, is institutional racism - nothing but an attempt to right the wrongs of public policy based on the color of one's skin by creating a new policy based on the color of one's skin. Why is it illegal to discriminate against someone because of their sexual orientation, yet it is not illegal to discriminate against another simply due to their race? Reverse discrimination does not negate racism, it perpetuates racism. The 'Black Caucus,' 'United Negro College Fund,' 'Black Entertainment Television,' etc. are all racist endeavors, by definition: the exclusion, and/or separation of, or the preferential treatment of, any group simply because of their race...divisiveness at all costs.

The case of Michael Brown was not an outlier. There are many other similar examples of perceived racial injustice that are not at all racist, but instead are allegorical to a black culture that has been in decline for decades. How can sane people actually believe that law enforcement is indiscriminately targeting innocent black citizens, widespread and without any justification, simply because of the color of their skin? If that can be proven true in any given case, then yes, the incident should be treated as racism, and obviously prosecuted as a crime. Excessive use of force / police brutality does occur, but in recorded cases, does not involve proven racist motives. In those cases, nonetheless, justice prevailed, as it should:

…Chicago Police Officer Jason Van Dyke shot and killed seventeen-year old Laquan McDonald as he was acting erratically and wielding a knife. It was determined through dash cam video that McDonald was shot in the back while walking away from police. Officer Van Dyke was charged with and convicted of second degree murder…

… Portsmouth, VA Police Officer Steven Rankin was convicted of voluntary manslaughter in the shooting death of eighteen-year old William Chapman, after Chapman refused to comply with Rankin's orders, resisted arrest, and aggressively charged at the officer…

…Texas Police Sergeant Jason Blackwelder was convicted of manslaughter after his weapon discharged during a fight with Russell Rios who was resisting arrest, fleeing from police, and assaulting an officer…

…Bay Area Rapid Transit Officer Johannes Mehserle was convicted of involuntary manslaughter for the accidental shooting death of Oscar Grant, after Grant struggled with police and resisted arrest…

In all of these instances, racism as a motive was never proven, or even claimed, except by Progressive instigators. Criminal wrongdoing on the part of the police was determined by examining the facts and responding with equity. The tendency of racial activists to project these rare and isolated incidents as the norm and to instill in all of them a racist motive is nothing but calculated deceit.

Could it be that a full majority of these tragic outcomes are driven by an individual's criminal behavior within a sub-culture that ignores, or in some cases condones and promotes, such behavior? That question remains not only unanswered by our culture, not even simply ignored…it dare not even be asked. Instead, we draw back the curtains on a childish melodrama with actors well versed in ignoring personal responsibility and deflecting fault. In this adaptation of reality, the performers slander the truth and perjure themselves willingly, their vignette being delivered with a routine of calculated and unceasing denial, even in the face of clear and contrary evidence. The theatrical fiction has played out repeatedly in the past few years – Michael Brown / Darren Wilson, Eric Garner / Daniel Pantaleo, Jonathan Ferrell / Randall Kerrick, Freddie Gray / Brian Rice et.al, and others. The media ideologically markets the production, as they seek out, and routinely embellish, evidence of an America, especially its police, as perpetually racist. Only those incidents that fit their predetermined narrative are pursued and anyone who refutes their biased prevarications is either willfully ignored or subject to character assassination. The timelines and details of the tightly composed script are predictably similar, and only serve to whip the audience into a frenzy. Immediately after the first act, 'eye witnesses' and acquaintances of the slain concoct blatant lies and fabricate details; friends and family describe the deceased's spotless character; the media portray the criminals as young and innocent with boyhood pictures and grossly mischaracterized biographies, always omitting previous criminal charges and arrests; black leaders condemn racist cops; the President sends emissaries to the funerals; the 'aggrieved' riot and loot; the actual evidence exonerates the police…more rioting and looting…and the play moves on to another town. The final act of the petulant histrionics is what truly renders the entire performance a tragedy. Shining a bright, condemning light on the rare, but actual, occurrences of racism in law enforcement is denied its transformative power when overshadowed by the endless cultural shocks of dramatized racism.

The Freddie Gray case is another prime example of these all too numerous myths of racism. Mr. Gray was a career drug criminal with eighteen arrests over eight years. In 2015, he was apprehended under suspicion of criminal activity, and during transport to the Baltimore jail, died in the rear of a police van. Six different police officers were involved in some way during the stop, arrest and transport. Before any facts became known, the black community, Black Lives Matter movement, the media, and race-baiting demagogues, immediately claimed racism and police brutality. The case was definitely racially motivated, but not in the sense portrayed by the media. The Baltimore DA, mayor, and civic leaders (all black), prior to the collection and dissemination of any evidence, purposely stoked the flames of racial animus. Their prejudicial and grossly unprofessional behavior was itself worthy of prosecution. The city's homicide rate skyrocketed over the following weeks and the ensuing riots and looting were the worst experienced by the city of Baltimore in decades. Months later, after evidence and testimony were presented, three out of the six officers were fully acquitted of each and every charge by the presiding judge (also black), which led to the dismissal of all remaining charges. Truth be damned, however, as Mr. Gray continues to be portrayed as a martyr, his family has been awarded millions for a wrongful death suit, the district attorney heralded as a warrior for racial justice, and an unwarranted and escalating hatred of police has resulted in the cold-blooded murder of numerous peace officers.

More recently, the death of George Floyd on a Minneapolis street in 2020 at the hands of Police Officer Derek Chauvin has garnered worldwide attention. Mr. Floyd was apprehended for allegedly passing a counterfeit twenty dollar bill in a convenience store. During the encounter, he became belligerent and persistently resisted arrest. Officer Chauvin subdued Mr. Floyd face down on the street while kneeling on his neck for approximately nine minutes, with Mr. Floyd's death occurring at some point during that time period. On their face, the actions of Officer Chauvin are, at a minimum, an apparent indifference to the dignity and wellbeing of Mr. Floyd, and are, at a maximum, possibly criminal in nature. We will not know where on that spectrum Officer Chauvin's guilt lies until all evidence has been presented.

The incident, while still under investigation, has nonetheless elevated the "guilty until proven innocent" mob mentality of our culture, especially in regard to any confrontation between black men and police, even prior to any evidence being collected. The guttural response was so swift that, for some, it almost appeared gleeful. Charges were filed immediately and upgraded to murder in the second degree within days, apparently to pacify the millions of people who immediately took to the streets, most of whom protested peacefully. They were not mollified, however, as months of rabid rioting, property destruction, arson, larceny, assault, and murder have become regular nightly occurrences.

In what can only be described as reckless endangerment, the Attorney General of Minnesota, Keith Ellison, withheld police body-cam footage for nearly three months; evidence that counters the current narrative, and, quite possibly, partially exonerates at least some of Officer Chauvin's actions; evidence that could have prevented, or significantly reduced, the violence, property damage, loss of life, and destruction of many inner cities. As factual evidence and full-context video footage trickles in, despite being downplayed or completely ignored, it appears, unsurprisingly, that a rush to judgement may have been premature. If most of the initial video evidence appeared to be rather damning for Officer Chauvin, the latest does the same for the case against him. In the finally released body-cam footage, throughout the time prior to Officer Chauvin placing his knee on Floyd's neck, Floyd is seen and heard continuously ignoring any and all commands. Floyd refuses to place his hands on the steering wheel of his vehicle, then does the same when ordered to place his hands on his head. After Mr. Floyd is forcefully removed from his vehicle, he then refuses to enter the police vehicle, claiming he is claustrophobic. Repeated attempts to get Mr. Floyd into the police car were not successful. At this point, Mr. Floyd begins what becomes a continuous chorus of "I can't breathe," and, "I'm choking," *before* ever being restrained by Officer Chauvin. Mr. Floyd then *asks* to be laid on the ground.

Perfectly legitimate questions arise and understandable conclusions are reached. Officer Chauvin's employment of a 'neck restraint,' while optically disturbing, was, nonetheless, standard jurisdictional procedure in 'use of force' instances. Furthermore, the reason George Floyd was restrained on the ground for such a long period of time was because, in addition to asking to be laid on the ground, he also refused to enter the police vehicle. Mr. Floyd's claims of being claustrophobic in the police car were completely disingenuous, as he did not appear to have any such condition while in his own vehicle (with the windows rolled up). The relentless complaints of choking and not being able to breathe prior to being restrained would understandably raise doubts as to those same claims after being restrained.

    Autopsy findings were contradictory, as they declared that the death of George Floyd was a homicide, but that he died of "cardiopulmonary arrest complicating law enforcement subdual, restraint and neck compression." The report also found that there was no traumatic asphyxiation, or any evidence of tracheal damage. Mr. Floyd also suffered from coronary disease, and toxicology reports found significant levels of methamphetamines and fentanyl. Minimal research shows that methamphetamines cause serious cardiovascular adverse events and fentanyl creates severe respiratory distress and hypoventilation. Abusing both drugs simultaneously magnifies the adverse effects of each, and those effects are further exacerbated in the presence of cardiovascular disease. How could Officer Chauvin have known about, much less be culpable for, Mr. Floyd's preexisting cardiovascular disease. How could he have known that Mr. Floyd was also under the influence of meth and opiates, obvious factors in "cardiopulmonary arrest," even if they were complicated by "law enforcement subdual, restraint and neck compression?'

An unbiased view of the facts should lead to a rational, mature discussion of why events unfolded as they did, and a logical discussion of all of the possible determinants of Mr. Floyd's death. Instead, potentially exculpatory evidence is ignored by the media and replaced with feigned outrage, petulant drama, and endless racist pandering, which is really a series of publicity stunts whose only purpose is to inflame the adolescent passions of 'useful idiot' puppets who do not even realize they are being used by Marxist insurrectionists. Hence, the well organized and perpetual rioting and destruction throughout the country.

Of course, Mr. Floyd did not deserve to die for passing a counterfeit bill. A valid claim can be made that, if not for Officer Chauvin's actions, Mr. Floyd would still be alive, but the facts do not lead to proof that Office Chauvin's 'murdered' Mr. Floyd. Righteous indignation is more than warranted, as there appeared to be a wanton disregard for Mr. Floyd's welfare, possibly rising to gross negligence, or even manslaughter. Furthermore, a valid claim can also be made that without Mr. Floyd's preexisting conditions, drug use, refusal to follow legitimate police orders, and resisting arrest, Mr. Floyd would also still be alive. If the prosecutor, Hennepin County Attorney Mike Freeman, who is already accused of prosecutorial misconduct and bias against the officers involved, had approached his responsibilities dispassionately, without placing politics over the pursuit of justice, and if the media had the decency and professionalism to report all of the facts and not to add accelerant to the inferno of racial enmity, then, possibly, the national discord and months of anarchy would have been largely avoided, and Officer Chauvin would be charged and likely convicted with crimes that were commensurate with his actions.

Officer Chauvin is relentlessly portrayed as a pariah, and Mr. Floyd, a paragon of virtue, a cultural icon, which is the standard narrative in all of these instances. Notice that the word 'allegedly' is an adverb that applies only to the criminal activity of the 'victim,' but never to the actions of police. Additionally, Floyd's easily sourced, long list of criminal behavior, including theft, numerous drug charges, and aggravated robbery with a deadly weapon, does not preclude cultural canonization by the mass media. So, we paint murals of Mr. Floyd and build memorials in his honor, all in a warped adaptation of hero worship. As our society tears down statues of truly great men, even saints, we are now replacing them with statues of the ignoble, even criminals, all for a prevarication of social justice. We erect monuments for George Floyd, a drug addled, violent lawbreaker, at the same moment we destroy monuments for George Washington.

Ultimately, in our politically and racially charged culture, Officer Chauvin will be hard pressed to receive a fair trial. In spite of numerous extenuating circumstances, any one of which would provide sufficient grounds for reasonable doubt to anyone with a modicum of objectivity, our recently adopted 'mob rule' legal system has all but assured a guilty verdict. For nearly a full year, the jury pool has been influenced by nightly riots, arson, and deadly chaos, perpetrated by those who now define justice. Society has been warned that anything short of conviction on all counts will only intensify the violence and destruction. Furthermore, the flames of animus consuming the heretofore honored concept of 'innocent until proven guilty' have been theatrically fanned by a complicit media, progressive race charlatans, and even the most prominent of political leaders, among them the President of the United States. If the potential jury is not fully sequestered throughout the entire trial, and their identities not adequately protected, then their safety is in jeopardy, and a verdict without prejudice is virtually impossible.

As if further proof was needed to unmask the pretense of a correlation between police brutality and racism, a chronicle eerily similar to that of George Floyd occurred in 2016. Tony Timpa, a white, 32 year-old resident of Dallas, Texas was subdued by police in much the same manner as George Floyd. Mr. Timpa died after being bound and lying prone on the ground for nearly twenty minutes. An autopsy ruled that Timpa's cause of death was also a homicide, and that he "died from sudden cardiac arrest due to the toxic effects of cocaine and the stress associated with physical restraint." The three officers involved in the incident were indicted by a grand jury in 2017 on charges of misdemeanor deadly conduct. Prosecutors dropped the charges, claiming that the officers did not act recklessly. There was no 24/7 national media coverage, no shrines erected, no endless protests, no riots, no 'say his name' tweets, and no politicians condemning law enforcement. The only material difference between the case of Tony Timpa and the case of George Floyd was found in their respective levels of skin pigmentation, and the manner in which their stories could be exploited.

Cases such as George Floyd, Freddie Gray, and Michael Brown, and there are many more, have made the difficult and dangerous job of policing all the more perilous. The police are actually being instructed, albeit by implication, to ignore sound aspects of their training. Within objective controls and the strict constraints of probable cause, the skills of behavioral modeling, quantifiable patterns, threat perception and situational analysis all play a constructive and proper role in effective law enforcement. To disregard these natural, cognitive capacities in deference to some fictitious claim of racism is counterproductive and dangerous to both the police and the citizens they are charged with protecting. Ignoring current behavioral patterns because of past racial injustice, whether real or perceived, is dangerous naiveté. Does the blame for data-driven, proactive policing lie with law enforcement, or with the actions of a significant portion of a racial demographic that affirms a profile by consistent and widespread behavior? Criminal stereotypes are not the direct result of bigotry and racism, but of a specific group's frequent transgressions under distinct circumstances, and the pursuant and legitimate assessment of threat. Men commit the majority of violent crimes in our country. Is it sexist for police to perceive a higher level of threat from men than from women, and to act accordingly? Absolutely not…it is simply common sense.

A two-decade long overall reduction in violent crime in America can be directly attributed to these policing techniques that are now being so thoroughly vilified. Data-driven law enforcement has quantifiably reduced the occurrence of all forms of crime nationwide, but especially in the inner-city areas. Detailed crime data analysis and preemptive policing are responsible for double-digit decreases in criminal activity in cities and communities, large and small. Under these policing guidelines, crime prevention became the focus, not simply crime response. The results rejuvenated neighborhoods, provided safer streets, and created more productive economies (not to mention saving thousands of lives) - all cultural benefits derived from policies and practices now defined as racism. Since being implemented in the early 1990's, proactive policing is directly responsible for a nationwide reduction in crime of approximately 40 percent. In New York City, proactive policing over a two-decade period was responsible for an 82% decrease in the murder rate, from a high of 2,200 murders per year to less than 400 per year (The New York Times; *To See Its Value, See How Crime Rose Elsewhere*; Heather McDonald; July 22, 2013). In her book, *The War on Cops,* Ms. McDonald does not shy away from the facts even as she is stigmatized with the usual spike of racism. Her research as a member of the Manhattan Institute is summarized in a Prager University presentation, *Are the Police Racist* (August 22, 2016), as she defends law enforcement actions as evidentiary, not prejudicial:

"Does the truth matter? Not to groups like Black Lives Matter. That's tragic for many reasons, not the least of which is that black lives are being lost as a result. When it comes to the subject of American police, blacks, and the deadly use of force, here is what we know: A recent "deadly force" study by Washington State University researcher Lois James found that police officers were less likely to shoot unarmed black suspects than unarmed white or Hispanic ones in simulated threat scenarios. Harvard economics professor Roland Fryer analyzed more than 1,000 officer-involved

shootings across the country. He concluded that there is zero evidence of racial bias in police shootings. In Houston, he found that blacks were 24 percent less likely than whites to be shot by officers even though the suspects were armed or violent.

Does the truth matter? An analysis of the Washington Post's Police Shooting Database and of Federal Crime Statistics reveals that fully 12 percent of all whites and Hispanics who die of homicide are killed by cops. By contrast, only four percent of black homicide victims are killed by cops. But isn't it a sign of bias that blacks make up 26 percent of police-shooting victims, but only 13 percent of the national population? It is not, and common sense suggests why. Police shootings occur more frequently where officers confront armed or violently resisting suspects. Those suspects are disproportionately black...In New York City, blacks commit over three-quarters of all shootings, though they are only 23 percent of the city's population. Whites, by contrast, commit under two percent of all shootings in the city, though they are 34 percent of the population. New York's crime disparities are repeated in virtually every racially diverse city in America. The real problem facing inner-city black communities today is not the police but criminals. In 2014, over 6,000 blacks were murdered, more than all white and Hispanic homicide victims combined. Who is killing them? Not the police, and not white civilians, but other blacks…If the police ended all use of lethal force tomorrow, it would have a negligible impact on the black death-by-homicide rate. In Chicago, through just the first six-and-a-half months of 2016, over 2,300 people were shot. That's a shooting an hour during some weekends. The vast majority of the victims were black. During this same period, the Chicago police shot

12 people, all armed and dangerous. That's one half of one percent of all shootings.

Does the truth matter? If it does, here's a truth worth pondering: There is no government agency more dedicated to the proposition that black lives matter than the police. The proactive policing revolution that began in the mid-1990s has dramatically brought down the inner-city murder rate and saved tens of thousands of black lives. Unfortunately, that crime decline is now in jeopardy. As I write in my book, The War on Cops, police officers are backing off of proactive policing in black neighborhoods thanks to the false narrative that police officers are infected with homicidal bias. As a result, violent crime is going up. In cities with large black populations, homicides in 2015 rose anywhere from 54 percent in Washington DC to 90 percent in Cleveland. Overall, in the nation's 56 largest cities, homicides in 2015 rose 17 percent, a nearly unprecedented one-year spike.   Many law-abiding residents of high-crime areas beg the police to maintain order — precisely the type of policing that the ACLU, progressive politicians, and the Obama Justice Department denounce as racist. This is tragic because when the police refrain from proactive policing, black lives are lost. Lost because of a myth. The best research and data reach this conclusion: there is no evidence that police are killing blacks just because they are black. You now have the truth. Does it matter?"

This is not a discussion of immature racial stereotypes or offensive characterizations but statistically proven facts in an arena of life and death issues that have split-second consequences. The statistics are sobering and depressing, yet cannot be ignored if progress is to be made. Obviously, most blacks are not criminals, yet they do commit, based on quantifiable proof, a significantly higher ratio of violent crimes. When over 50% of a society's murders are attributable to a group (black males) which comprises only 6% of the population (FBI-Murders/Census Bureau-Population; 2013), there is legitimate cause for chastisement and scrutiny of the individuals in question. The numbers are even more telling when mathematically reduced to a 'per capita' statistic. If the populations of both black and white people were equal, and using the factual 2013 percentages of criminality, the rate of murder by black citizens would be nearly 600% higher than that of white citizens. Facts are not oppressive bigotry. Facts, however, can be shameful, and that shame, if neither deflected nor disowned, has the potential to be the stimulus for positive change.

The data regarding police killings tell a similar story. From 2009-2012, 448 black men were killed by the police in this country. During that same three-year period, nearly 18,000 black men were murdered by other black men (Dr. Richard R. Johnson; FBI Supplementary Homicide Reports; 2012). Where is the real outrage? While the flames of racism are theatrically fanned whenever a black person is killed by a white assailant or police officer, there is complete silence on the overwhelming majority of black lives lost at the hands of other blacks, as these lives do not support the narrative of a racist white America bent on oppressing all blacks. The intentional obfuscation prevails at all levels of society, but especially through the manipulative arm of politics, for obvious reasons. Representative Beta O'Rourke, D-Texas and currently aspiring for the Presidency, provokes these racial tensions by claiming, "black men, unarmed, black teenagers, unarmed, and black children, unarmed, are being killed at a frightening level right now, including by members of law enforcement without accountability and without justice" (*NowThis*, Aug. 21, 2018). This statement is a perfect example of a *faulty generalization* – a logically fallacious argument defended only by a staggering exaggeration whose sole intent is to inflame uninformed passions. Black men *are* dying at a frightening level, but primarily at their own hands or due to their own actions. A far more accurate assessment would be, "black men, mostly armed, mostly criminal, and mostly violent, are being killed at a frightening level right now, due primarily to their poor decisions, disrespect for authority, and criminal activity."

In actuality, contrary to the Black Lives Matter narrative, the police have much more to fear from black males than black males have to fear from the police. In 2016, the police fatally shot 233 black people, the vast majority armed and dangerous. Of those fatal shootings, only 16 black male victims of police shootings were categorized as 'unarmed.' The majority of that small classification was due to assaults against officers and violent resistance to arrest (The Washington Post: *Academic Research on Police Shootings and Race;* July 19, 2016). In contrast, police officers were 18.5 times more likely to be killed by a black male than an unarmed black male was to be killed by a police officer. Black males have made up 42 percent of all cop-killers over the last decade, though they are only 6 percent of the population (National Review: *CNN Fans More Hatred of Cops, in Touting Flawed Study;* December 21, 2016). 'Black Lives Matter', the race-baiting politicians and the mainstream media will never even whisper these statistics. To them, the only lives that matter are the black ones killed by whites, especially by white police officers. Whenever one of these tragedies occurs, there is an immediate and incessant media onslaught. Conversely, when a white person is killed by the police there is very little, if any, reporting, whatsoever. One could make a safe assumption that the majority of Americans believe there are no, or very few, whites who are killed by the police. On the contrary, the number of whites killed by the police are nearly two times that of blacks (CDC Fatal Injury Report Database; 2012), and there is rarely an outcry of police brutality in any of these instances.

There is truth in the claim that black deaths at the hands of police occur at a higher *rate* than other races (based on population). There are rational reasons for this fact. In a 2009 study involving the 75 largest counties in America, black males constituted 62 percent of all robbery defendants, 57 percent of all murder defendants, 45 percent of all assault defendants - but only 7 percent of the population in those counties (FBI – Uniform Crime_Reports; 2009). Again, this is clearly a cultural issue, not a racial one. The disproportionate crime rate by blacks is, of course, not due to their being black, but due to the decades-long disintegration of black culture. Many will blame the statistics on poverty, yet what is the primary origin of their poverty? Again, it is found in the decay of the black family and in the misguided efforts of failed government policy. Our society has a responsibility to acknowledge this glaringly obvious correlation and, at the same time, has the right to hold individuals accountable – not because of their race but because of their behavior. We also have the responsibility to continue, against all odds, to do what we are able to stem this tragedy. The first step in that long walk is, as always, found in proclaiming the truth, and the first obvious truth should be easily comprehended – that this cultural tumult would not even exist if the instigators would simply desist from illegal activity and obey police commands. This reality is so transparently self-evident, yet is never uttered for fear of further racist claims. Truth is neither racially slanderous nor ethnically derogatory. When objective reality is repeatedly confirmed, it is not one's prejudice that is apparent, but, instead, one's innate capacity for human reason. Unfortunately, the cost to those who speak the truth – truth that would improve, and likely save, lives if acknowledged and acted upon – is public deprecation and claims of racism, and by whom? By those who seek to further the Progressive falsehood of a culture saturated with racism, and the activist agitators who blindly follow them. Obviously, society should always hold the police accountable when there are clear and proven cases of racism and unwarranted use of force. Likewise, creating local oversight boards and reconciliation processes, along with policing transparency, a return to more community-oriented policing, body cameras and officers properly trained in de-escalation tactics, are all necessary to bridge the divide between the police and black communities. What is also required, however, is an acknowledgement by those same black communities that it is not systemic racism, nor lingering vestiges of slavery, nor the police, nor poverty, nor denied privilege, nor fabricated scenarios and statistics, but their own cultural/familial breakdown that is the primary cause of criminality, high incarceration rates, and adversarial confrontations with police. Decades or more ago, the former could have been rightly blamed for the suppression of the black population, but to claim the same for recent generations is to fabricate testament and disrespect sincerity.

Racism as Contagion

The epidemic of insistent racism has become so embedded in every facet of our culture that there appears to be no respite. If repeated loudly and persistently enough, the weak anecdotes eventually become truth, or at least are proffered as such. The fiction is embellished with incessancy until it becomes accepted, thus avoiding the scrutiny of absolute fact. Once reaching critical mass, then and only then can it be parlayed into the ultimate goal of systemic change. Calculated racism has infected virtually every social perspective, realized by the politicization of everything from education to health, from economics to religion, from rights to responsibilities, from the media to the boardroom, and even unto entertainment and recreation.

The recent and accelerating fad of professional sports figures kneeling or sitting during the National Anthem is an indication of this faux-racism being promoted by our own culture through the aegis of the media, education system, and our government. Colin Kaepernick, the previously employed quarterback of the National Football League's San Francisco 49ers, patented this disrespect and the lemmings have followed in droves. Nearly every sports program across the nation was initially shamed into participation, then, as it become rabidly popular, tried to outdo each other in order to display their 'wokeness' bona fides. The virtue signaling participants are supposedly protesting the 'racism and oppression' perpetrated on people of color who are stopped, detained, arrested, and/or killed by the police. The entire performance is a charade, akin to a group of employees claiming that they are all being targeted and oppressed because some of the poorest performing among them are being fired. One may also find it odd that Mr. Kaepernick, while wearing socks that depict the police as pigs, has an outspoken affinity for the Castro regime of Communist Cuba. The protestors claim that their right to free speech, in a venue of their choosing, is not being recognized. Disrespecting the anthem that heralds the very protection of that right is intellectually suspect, as the act of practicing that right nullifies the claim. The NFL itself, bowing in cowardice to the politically correct, will not allow any public indication of partiality to law enforcement, yet has defended the players' rights to protest injustices that have little basis in fact. Those who disagree with this blatant and public disparagement of our nation are labeled 'divisive,' when it is obvious that true division is being incited by the infantile meanderings of privileged, self-promoting athletes – the 'institutionally oppressed' who make many millions of dollars playing a game – with active persuasion from their masters of progressive anarchy.

'Systemic Racism'

Racial divisions and inequalities definitely exist in our country but they are not drawn by the heavy hand of entrenched oppression.

While there are still instances of individual racism in our culture, there is, however, *no* current proof of *institutional racism* in this country. On the contrary, modern America is the least oppressive nation in the history of nations. Racism has become an industry, and if not enough can be found, it is then fabricated in order to advertise its virtual perpetration. Although ignored or suppressed, fake instances of racism are orchestrated regularly, on college campuses (see Albion College), in the workplace (see Bubba Wallace), in the media (see Jussie Smollett), but primarily in the impressionable minds of a brainwashed culture. "The demand for racism exceeds the supply…to put it differently, there's an enormous desire to find racism, and there's not enough racism to be found" (Dinesh D'Souza).

If anything, we are awash in *institutional racial favoritism,* as evidenced by Equal Employment Opportunity quotas, Affirmative Action education policies, Minority Disadvantaged Business classifications, and Housing and Urban Development Affirmative Marketing programs. The expanding partiality of race-tested programs for many decades now has not translated into widespread benefit, but has served to sustain the false notion that certain races, by their very nature, continually need the patriarchy of government to assure, not just their pursuit of happiness, but their realization of it as well. Likewise, any accountability for personal decisions, and the positive results that those sound choices would provide, is betrayed when eclipsed by never-ending victimization. As is the same for any race, the poor judgments of dropping out of school, having children without the benefit of marriage, and the substitution of work with the near occasion of crime, are a more significant determinant of opportunity and success than any rationalized effects of racism.

The latest and most asinine narrative of systemic discrimination is found in many local and state government's declarations of racism as a national health crisis, primarily due to a lack of access to wholesome foods, or 'food deserts.' In essence, these declarations imply, with no supporting evidence, that society (read "white privilege") is responsible for the relatively poor health of people of color. Even the Centers for Disease Control makes the same specious arguments. There is currently zero substantiation of the so-called cause and effect relationship between racism and health, not even anecdotal evidence…just racially charged claims of 'discrimination.' Intentionally omitting other determinants from the discussion is indicative of ulterior motives. Yes, by many different measures, minorities in general do typically suffer more from poor health when compared to the population as a whole, yet the obvious cause is not racism, nor even poverty, but lifestyle choices. Those who persist in the exaltation of ubiquitous racism conveniently ignore other, far more causative factors, primarily individual behaviors and personal decisions, such as consistently defective diets with an inordinate intake of salts, sugars and fats, which eventually lead to hypertension, diabetes, and a myriad of other diseases. This behavior and its results affect all people, regardless of ethnicity, or socio-economic status, and has nothing to do with racism. There is truth in the fact that minority neighborhoods do not commonly have the same access to wholesome foods as other areas may, yet this is not due to some deep, hidden racism but more to principals of simple economics. Why are there fewer grocery stores in low income neighborhoods that offer healthy food options, and, if they do exist, why are they rarely successful? Because there is not enough demand. The attempt to create a direct link from poor eating habits and substandard health to racism is ludicrous. White supremacists are not behind the scenes preventing fresh food markets from locating to minority neighborhoods, or running them out of those neighborhoods with the intent of destroying the health of their residents, or forcing residents to eat three squares a day at the nearest fast food establishment. No, it is self-evident that the residents themselves, simply by their lack of patronage, do not perceive the value of these marketplaces, and therefore *freely choose* what food they wish to consume, and are solely responsible for the health outcomes of those decisions.

White Privilege

The same society that refused to address the root cause of this cultural devolvement now peddles racial privilege as the scapegoat. The concept of a socio-economic advantage, now racially charged as 'white privilege,' is due neither to one's whiteness nor to one's unearned social appropriation. It is largely a racially blind construct, and finds its value, not in birthright or in the hue of one's skin, but in the heritage of consistent and inter-generational decisions based on sound judgement, self-sacrifice and personal responsibility. This 'privilege,' this "invisible package of unearned assets" (Peggy McIntosh, Wellesley College Senior Researcher; *Unpacking the invisible knapsack*) that racial agitators claim the white population alone possesses, is an 'academic concept' unable to be comprehended because of our society's perception of race. In other words, the privilege cannot be seen, and is outside of the realm of perceived reality. What *is* perfectly visible and easily perceived, however, is completely ignored. By creating and supporting the narratives that marriage is unnecessary, that the black father is dispensable, and that every obstacle is insurmountable because of a relentless white racism, our culture has demolished the futures of black children for generations to come. More than fifty years of misguided and damaging Progressive policies have demeaned an entire race of people by convincing them that, collectively, they bear no responsibility for the woeful state of their own culture; that rioting, violence and looting is an acceptable alternative to respect for authority; and that victimization is paramount to accountability. When they are, in effect, told that they are unable to master self-reliance; that they do not possess the competency to succeed in college admissions and job placement on their own merits and hard work; that the government offers the only means to resolve their afflictions which were primarily created by that same government in the first place; that it is always the lack of privilege, and never the widespread dysfunction of the black family that is to blame for chronic poverty, crime and dependency – these are merely placations that frustrate a solution to the problem and, in turn, fertilize its perpetuation. Fear of a racist branding has only served to intimidate the very prerequisites necessary for remedy.

Conclusion

Senator Patrick Moynihan, in his treatise on the plight of black society in 1965, titled *"The Negro Family: The Case for National Action"*, presciently warned the entire country of the looming disaster facing the black population due to the disintegration of the black family. He, of course, was ridiculed and branded a racist. At the time, the out of wedlock birth rate among blacks was at 23%...it is now at a staggering 72%. The ramifications of this growing statistic have rained down nothing but misery on a significant portion of the black community – poverty, school dropouts, unemployment, incarceration, gang activity, drug use, and often, deadly violence. Moynihan, who was truly concerned about the welfare of the black population, was muted, while the voices of racial opportunists such as Al Sharpton and Jesse Jackson rose to the top of the national discussion - and the predicament of the black family has only worsened.

A more shameful depletion of cultural capital would be hard to find. The squandering of potential in the lives of so many is a travesty to our entire society. To look into the eyes of so many of the young and innocent, and foresee the idle hopelessness that will consume far too many of them, evokes a deep and depressing lamentation for the future of a large segment of our culture. An outright rejection of the individual's responsibility for self-realization, evidenced by entrapment in hardened generational pretexts of deflective culpability, and cemented by the patronization of government condescension, does not bode well for the near-term resurgence of the black culture. Despite the stark and discouraging odds, the many who are yet able to liberate themselves from cultural exploitation, and retain inner conviction of their true worth and full potential, are genuine profiles in heroism, and remain a testament to the memories, sacrifices and hopes of great Americans such as Frederick Douglass, Booker T. Washington, Harriet Tubman, Dr. Martin Luther King, Jr., Sojourner Truth, as well as countless others, a majority in anonymity and obscurity, who have risen from the ashes of historical subjugation and the chains of contemporary victimization.

Empathy is due to these individuals, and there are many, who are viewed through these prisms yet whose behavior is outside of their scope. These cold truths and sterile statistics must understandably add to the despair of witnessing a large segment of their culture willfully cannibalizing itself, all with the complicit prejudice of those who claim to be their saviors. These individuals, however, have no legitimate cause to castigate others whose rational deduction has naturally led to candid views of those obviously responsible but never held to account. Instead, any reprobation should be levelled squarely at the malefactors whose behavior has tarnished the reputation of the collective to begin with. The overall character of any group is largely determined by the behavior of a significant faction of its members. Making excuses for the poor behavior of individuals within that collective, or passing off any censure as mere racism, does them, their race, and society as a whole, no favors.

Immigration

Immigration has played, over the years, a significant role in the formation of our culture. We have yet to reach the era of nation-state extinction, but the relatively new normality of globalized travel and trade has nonetheless changed the dynamics of immigration. In the multi-cultural milieu of modern day societies, immigration takes on a new meaning with its own positive and negative ramifications. Every nation-state has the right, and the responsibility, to control, monitor and enforce immigration policies that are in the best interest of the state's cultural, political and economic identity. Furthermore, national cohesion must be at the center of all immigration law. If not, the attributes that define sovereignty are evanesced to a level of insignificance, and deep cultural disparities will eventually dissolve the bonds of core convictions that unify a nation. Throughout American history, immigration has been instrumental in the writing of our unique and embracive story - many different chapters that have all added significant worth to the totality of our culture. Over the past fifty or so years, however, immigration, both legal and illegal, has been deliberately utilized as an instrument for cultural transformation, power-lust, and the dilution of America's founding philosophies. The Progressive movement exploits all factors of immigration in a comprehensive attempt to realize these ends. The movement refashions the proper discernment of immigrant motivation, discounts the priorities of assimilation, defends an array of policies that advance an unrestricted flow of legal immigration, and essentially ignores immigration law in the irrational patronage of illegal aliens.

Motivation

Prior to roughly two generations ago, the full majority of immigrants arriving in America were motivated by purpose, drive, and a passion for America. Legal immigration, when controlled and conditioned, has historically augmented both cultural and economic weal. In 1790, James Madison perfectly summarized the cultural purpose and beneficial scope of national immigration. "It is no doubt very desirable that we hold out as many inducements as possible for the worthy part of mankind to come and settle amongst us, and throw their fortunes into a common lot with ours…not merely to swell the catalogue of people…(but) to increase the wealth and strength of the community." Madison's definition of "wealth and strength" is neither mercenary nor might, but a wealth of character and a strength of fidelity. They may have been 'tired, poor, and huddled masses,' but they came with enterprise, resolve, and initiative…and respect. In other words, the full blessings of immigration are not intended solely for the immigrant, but first must enrich the cultural constitution. Yes, immigration must be beneficial to foreigners, but only insofar as they, at first, possess the 'worthy part,' a love of America and the proper motivation to contribute to the enhancement of the national interest and to embrace the cultural identity. To accept all comers without condition is diametric to that intent. For over fifty years, our immigration policies have been a traitor to Madison's defined potential for an expanded, yet consolidated culture. The motivation of more recent arrivals appears to be driven, for many, by the generous benefits that can be won by citizenship rather than by the opportunities offered by, and the responsibilities required by, the once tolled 'American Dream.' Even as resident citizens, many immigrants find our flag and our culture to be so terribly offensive…yet, they expect and devour the benefits derived from that flag and culture. Some continue to proudly wave the flag of another country but have no intent, or desire, to return to that country. On a large scale, we are not inviting those with a deep and abiding affection of American ideals, but instead we are welcoming many of the idle, the apathetic, those who would exploit the benefits of citizenship, and, worst of all, those that desire to radically transform American culture. As of late, immigration policy, and, to a greater degree, actively condoning illegal immigration, seems to be directed more toward the benefit of the latter than the former. These traits not only suppress the national character but also intensify a drought of patriotism, and compound many of our economic woes, chiefly wealth inequality and immobility.

Assimilation

While the concept of assimilation should never attempt to erase the identity, customs or heritage of any group of immigrants, not requiring a certain level of cultural conformity is detrimental to national unity. Citizenship confers many rights upon immigrants, and it should likewise levy expectations that they adopt the language, cultural mores and traditions that have made this nation the type of country they chose to immigrate to in the first place. We are no longer as 'Americans' first when we value diversity over a more homogeneous sense of nationalism. We then become 'hyphenated'-Americans, with the honor and acclaim of our national identity taking a subordinate position. The more than anecdotal decrease in patriotism over the last half-century is indicative of this odd love affair with distinction. The willful decoupling of immigration and assimilation at the hands of Progressive ideology is a conscious effort to diminish national pride, promote apathy, and sever the cultural bonds meant to unite. Additionally, as they resurrect the toxic philosophy of the 'Communist Manifesto,' many Progressives strategically position class above nation in order to advance cultural turmoil, all while seeking to consolidate power through a permanent flow of immigrant voters. The Left's obsession with unfettered immigration, without the prerequisites of proper motivation and assimilation, is not at all rooted in compassion, but in a slow yet deliberate coup of America...our culture, our constitution, and our once honored core values.

Diversity Visas

Up until the mid-to-late 20th century, immigrant-citizens not only took an oath to defend and abide by the constitutional trust that unites us all, but also were expected to adapt to, and invest in, the cultural congruity of America. This assimilative priority is apparently no longer the case. Actually, based on government policies, business practices, and our society's infatuation with 'diversity,' the exact opposite appears to be true. The government itself, through its laws, regulations and administrative policies, has for decades been emphasizing our differences that divide instead of our ties that bind. Primarily immigration policy, but also school registrations, health questionnaires, job applications (EEOC) and census reports, all stress our contrasts, and reflect governmental intentions that appear to be going out of their way to make our categorized differences apparent and permanent. To illustrate the idiocy of such government policies, one need look no further than the aptly named 'Diversity Visa Lottery,' where the primary qualification for permanent legal residence in the US is based solely on diversity…not on individual motivation, not on the condition of assimilation, but simple diversity, for diversity's sake. This inexplicable appetite for diversity has proved nauseating, especially as it relates to the immigration of radical elements, as we welcome the likes of Sayfullo Saipov, a 2010 winner of the diversity lottery, who murdered eight innocent people in New York City in 2017 by mowing them down with a rented truck. Since 9/11, there have been over 100 Islamist plots targeting the American homeland. Nearly 90% of those plots were 'homegrown,' or carried out by immigrant radicals living in America (David Inserra, Heritage Foundation; *Attempted New York Bombing Calls for Renewed Vigilance Against Homegrown Terrorism;* Dec. 13, 2017). This should not be alarming when one realizes that our own government no longer demands, nor even expects, the proper assimilation of immigrants.

Birthright Citizenship

Continuing the concerted effort to promote a weakening of cultural bonds, the next tool in the diversity toolbox is found in the manipulated designs of birthright citizenship. For years, Progressives have indoctrinated the populace into believing that by simply being born on US soil (*jus soli*), one should automatically secure US citizenship. While they so desire this to be the case, they know full well that it is not. Nevertheless, as Progressives are wont to do, they will parse Constitutional words in context, and fabricate meanings out of context, in order to further whatever agenda they wish to force upon the rest of us, in this case the automatic citizenship of nearly half a million children annually born to the 'undocumented,' and the billions of dollars in federal benefits afforded to them, and indirectly, to their illegal immigrant parents. Proponents of unbounded immigration twist the meaning of the 14th Amendment to the Constitution to advance these calculated schemes. The passage in question is found in Section 1, which states: "*All persons born or naturalized in the United States, and subject to the jurisdiction thereof, are citizens of the United States and of the State wherein they reside.*" Now, to most citizens educated in the US public school system, this statement does indeed seem to affirm that mere birth within the US does define citizenship. However, the conveniently overlooked phrase, "*subject to the jurisdiction thereof,*" renders that argument moot. Illegal aliens, and by extension, their children, are not subject to the jurisdiction of the US and its laws, primarily by the self-evident fact that they have blatantly defied 'the jurisdiction of the United States' by entering the country illegally, not to mention by the second fact that they still owe allegiance to another country. If a proper reading, in full context, of the amendment does not settle the specious claims of the open border crowd, then simple common sense alone should. If 'jus soli' was a full determinant of citizenship, then the offspring born on US soil of any enemy combatant would also be a citizen of the US, automatically. Nonetheless, birthright citizenship is alive and well, and every year creates hundreds of thousands of 'anchor babies' which, in many cases, are nothing but their parents' pawns in gaming the generous benefits offered by the United States, in lieu of following proper and legal immigration avenues. Meanwhile, America's own citizens are strapped with trillions of dollars in debt. Birthright citizenship has spawned whole cottage industries of 'birth tourism' within the US, primarily in California. Newsweek magazine reported on a federal raid of twenty 'maternity hotels' in Los Angeles, Orange County, and San Bernardino County, where Chinese nationals paid up to $80,000 in order to give birth to their children in the US. Estimates are that 40,000 children are born annually to illegal aliens on a US travel visa (Newsweek; *Feds Raid 'Maternity Hotels'*; Melina Delkic; Jan 10, 2018). The acceptance and pursuit of these immigration policies was never intended to stop with the anecdotal birth of children to illegal immigrants, but further to act as yet another magnet to bring an untold number of foreigners through the borders of the United States.

Chain Migration

To overwhelm the immigration system and more aggressively affect cultural change, Progressives will not settle for simply promoting individual cases of 'compassionate' immigration policy, but will further attempt to multiply those effects by offering a welcome mat to entire extended families. Known as '*chain migration,*' the practice actually markets itself to immigrant's family members whom otherwise would most likely have no standing for legal immigration to the US. Judicial Watch, 'a conservative, non-partisan educational foundation promoting transparency, accountability, and integrity in government,' has detailed a 2018 report issued jointly by the Department of Homeland Security and the Department of Justice which, in today's dungeon of political correctness, would otherwise have never seen the light of day (Executive Order 13780: *Protecting the Nation From Foreign Terrorist Entry Into the United States;* Initial Section 11 Report; Jan., 2018). The report details that there have been 549 criminals convicted (not merely charged) of terrorism in American federal courts since 2001. Nearly 75% of those criminals were born outside the United States, and a significant number of those were afforded entry by virtue of chain migration. Judicial Watch writes: "*Among them is Mufid Elfgeeh, a national of Yemen who benefitted from chain migration in 1997 and was sentenced to more than 22 years in prison for attempting to recruit fighters for ISIS. Sudanese Mahmoud Amin Mohamed Elhassan came to the U.S. in 2012 as a relative of a lawful permanent resident and eventually pleaded guilty to attempting to provide material support to ISIS. Pakistani Uzair Paracha was admitted to the U.S. in 1980 as a family member of a lawful permanent resident and in 2006 was sentenced to more than three decades in prison for providing material support to Al Qaeda. Khaleel Ahmed, a national of India, was admitted to the United States in 1998 as a family member of a naturalized United States citizen. Ahmed eventually became an American citizen and in 2010 was sentenced to more than eight years in prison for conspiring to provide material support to terrorists*" (Judicial Watch; *3 Out of 4 Convicted Terrorists Came to U.S., Legally Via Current Immigration System*; January 17, 2018). These facts "reflect the challenges faced by the United States and demonstrate the necessity to remain vigilant and proactive in our counterterrorism posture," as well as, no doubt, "vigilant and proactive" in our immigration posture.

Deferred Action for Childhood Arrivals (DACA)

In June of 2012, then President Barack Obama unilaterally created new immigration law via an executive order, which shielded children of illegal immigrants (aka 'Dreamers') from facing deportation. Notwithstanding its patent unconstitutionality and a bold denunciation of the 'separation of powers,' the new edict, innocently named the 'Deferred Action for Childhood Arrivals' (DACA), is nothing but another in a long line of 'amnesty' programs whose sole purpose is to absolve current immigrant lawbreakers, and open the doors wide to future immigrant lawbreakers, all the while wholly discounting and demeaning the efforts and sacrifices of those who seek to immigrate to the US legally. Instead of punishing insurgency and rewarding compliance, the exact opposite holds true.

Crafted effectively with a heavy reliance on feelings and emotions, DACA has depicted 'Dreamers' as nothing but hard working, enterprising children, fully assimilated into American culture, who seek only to contribute to the betterment of their adopted society. President Obama, claiming the program would afford limited amnesty only to the children of illegal immigrants, promised a thorough vetting of each and every applicant, made assurances that only those with at least a high school degree would be accepted, and that no applicant could pose a threat to national security or public safety. His promises were, unsurprisingly, never kept. First, the 'children' in question (often referred to by Obama as 'infants'), by the program's definition, were as old as thirty, with an average age of twenty-six. Second, as is obvious, when the children were given amnesty, then, by extension, so was each and every relative residing in the country illegally, evidenced by the government's feigned concern of never "tearing family's apart," and the 'backdoor' promotion of 'chain migration'. Third, as stated in an article by Hans von Spakovsky, a Senior Legal Fellow at the Heritage Foundation, President Obama's assurances all but vanished once the 'administrative' legislation was implemented. (*DACA Is Not What the Democrats Say It Is. Here Are the Facts;* December 4, 2017):

…Obama's guaranteed 'prescreening' promise to ensure that applicants have no criminal record was shown to be a tactical lie, as only a few randomly selected Dreamers were actually vetted, and within five years of the program's implementation, the Department of Homeland Security had terminated the eligibility of well over 2,000 beneficiaries "due to criminal conviction, (and/or) gang affiliation."

…The requirement of obtaining a high school education also appears to have been waived, as "only 49% of DACA beneficiaries have (completed) a high school education…despite the fact that a majority of them are adults." Furthermore, even though a mandated high school diploma would imply fluency of the English language, the Center for Immigration Studies has estimated that "perhaps 24% of the DACA-eligible population fall into the functionally illiterate category and another 46% have only a basic English ability."

In regards to the pledge of preventing any criminal elements from taking advantage of DACA amnesty, the results seem to contradict the intention. A 2019 report by the USCIS has compiled cold, hard facts refuting Obama's promise: *"Newly released data shows that over 10 percent of Deferred Action for Childhood Arrivals recipients boasted arrest records for crimes ranging from hit and runs to vandalism, burglary, assault and possession of child pornography, among many others, when they were approved for residency…and of that 10 percent, a whopping 31 percent had been arrested multiple times. Published Saturday by U.S. Citizenship and Immigration Services, the data shows that of the 765,166 illegal aliens who were granted a detention waiver as per former President Barack Hussein Obama's DACA program, and 79,398 were granted the waiver despite having an arrest record. Of those roughly 80,000 DACA recipients, only 12,968 (or 16 percent) had been arrested in the past over immigration violations. The rest of the arrests pertained to the following other matters:*

Traffic violations: 25,305

Theft, larceny: 7,926

Drug-related: 6,892

DUI: 4,210

Battery: 3,421

Assault: 3,308

Obstruction, fabrication, false claim: 3,053

Disorderly conduct: 2,223

Contempt, bench warrant, bail: 2,112

Liquor-related (excl. DUI): 2,094

Vandalism: 1,956

Failure to appear: 1,816

Burglary, breaking and entering: 1,471

Trespass, unlawful entry, etc.: 1,410

Offenses against family and children: 1,360

Resisting/interfering/evading police: 1,278

Weapon-related: 974

Fraud, money-laundering, corruption: 869

Undefined threats, attempted crime/conspiracy: 810 581

Forgery, counterfeiting: 712

Undefined juvenile offense: 631

Stolen property: 616

Undefined ordinance: 596

Hit and Run: 587

Probation/parole violation, remanded: 445

Other illegal sex-related acts: 428

Robbery: 269

Fail to comply/obey: 267

Sexual abuse, statutory rape: 259

Contributing to the delinquency of a minor: 243

Harassment, restraining order violation: 243

Indecent exposure, lewd/lascivious acts: 227

Reckless conduct/endangerment: 188

Kidnapping, trafficking, false imprisonment: 173

Embezzlement: 154

Loitering, vagrant: 143

Riot, unlawful assembly: 73

Motor vehicle theft: 71

Accessory, accomplice, hindering: 66

Rape: 62

Organized criminal activity: 45

Curfew violation: 43

Gambling: 33

Cruelty to animals: 31

Arson: 24

Murder: 15

Street gang: 15

Smuggling: 13

Bribery, influence public servant: 10

Manslaughter, negligent/reckless homicide: 5

Of those approved DACA recipients with arrest records, a whopping 15,903 (20 percent) went on to commit additional crimes that resulted in them being arrested again" (BPR Business and Politics; *Nearly 80,000 DACA recipients have arrest records, U.S. Citizenship and Immigration report finds*; Vivek Saxena; November 17, 2019).

While these are a listing of dry facts, there are personal stories behind each one. This is not simply a tally of 80,000 crimes, but the completely preventable suffering of 80,000 victims, if not for the 'compassion' of Obama's DACA mandate. One such victim was Xinran Ji, a USC engineering student from Inner Mongolia. In 2014, teenage 'dreamers' Jonathan Del Carmen, Alberto Ochoa, Andrew Garcia, and Alejandra Guerrero viciously murdered Ji, without cause or care, by bashing in his head with a baseball bat and a wrench (ABC7 Eyewitness News; *USC Student Death: Four Suspects Charged with Capital Murder*; July 29, 2014). Evidently, only some 'dreams' are worthy of protection.

As a by-product of these many failed government programs, specifically the diversity lottery, birthright citizenship, anchor babies and maternity tourism, chain-migration, DACA, but also many others, our immigration policies appear to intentionally omit any real desire for cultural harmony, and, incomprehensibly reflect a dereliction of duty to safeguard the welfare of the American people. Betraying our once de-facto motto of '*E Pluribus Unum,*' or 'out of many, one,' the government's forced separation of citizens into hardened group distinctions, all meant to further our confounding passion for diversity, has not only weakened the national cohesion and the sense of kindred community, but has also left Americans exposed to the murderous enterprise of those who have only nefarious intent. The charade is not by chance…it is the intentional Progressive, vis a vis Marxist, strategy of creating an oppressor vs oppressed dynamic; of overwhelming the entire system to change the political demographics of the nation; of forcing social chaos and anarchy; and, ultimately, of ushering in the fairytale, Progressive 'utopia.' Additionally, and ironically, these policies have only served to perpetuate xenophobic divides.

Illegal Immigration

There is a frighteningly large contingency of citizens within our own country who, in addition to favoring mostly counterproductive legal immigration policies, are also essentially advocating for unlawful immigration. According to figures from *US Customs and Border Protection (2006-2017)*, an average of approximately 700,000 immigrants attempting to enter the country illegally are apprehended every year. The number of migrants who enter our nation undetected is, of course, unknown. Considering our mostly barrier free borders, however, and the fact that there are an estimated twelve million illegal immigrants residing within our country, the annual inflow of illegal aliens can be extrapolated as significant. Once within our borders, there are many who actually defend the right of illegal aliens to remain without penalty. Furthermore, these same people espouse a blanket amnesty that would bestow citizenship upon illegal aliens without preconditions - yet another in a repetitive 'one-time amnesty' - with the obvious implication being that they actually desire an endless influx of illegal immigrants. A cultural betrayal, this is precisely the intentions of the Progressive left who desire, or, at least, turn a blind eye toward, the rampant and chaotic illegal immigration of the past few decades. Porous borders. sanctuary cities, the justification of employment-document fraud and identity theft, and the covert desire to allow illegal immigrant voting (the State of California has actually passed laws that not only allow, but actively pursue, the ability of illegal immigrants to vote in local and state elections), each alone present more than enough evidence of a Progressive disdain for national sovereignty.

The very existence of a nation is predicated on borders. Much more than an organized etching of national boundaries, a nation's borders frame the history, character and values of its citizens and require, subsequently, a foreign, and domestic, respect for the same. Such respect has been replaced by an obvious disgust for the nation-state in general and a barely hidden contempt for America's preeminence in world history, thus driving the Progressive desire for unfettered illegal immigration. The entire charade is guilefully presented as compassionate concern for the plight of the immigrant. While this is no doubt a legitimate altruism held by some, the intent of these blatantly un-American policies for others is not forged by any real charity for the welfare of immigrants but by an overt hatred of America and a Marxist attempt to weaken the bonds of American nationalism, all as potential for the fulfillment of 'one world' passions. For the majority, however, the driving force behind both unqualified legal immigration and uncontrolled illegal immigration is power, and in order to attain and sustain that power, there are those willing to 'divide and conquer' to the detriment of a nation. Remembering that divisiveness is the primary Progressive tool used to facilitate their quest for power, proponents will always position one class against another simply to amass power by pandering to as many groups as possible in order to achieve an overall majority. In the case of illegal immigration, they will even go so far as to favor the welfare of illegal immigrants over American citizens. When presented with overwhelming evidence of the damage caused to America by illegal immigration, Progressivism simply rationalizes its treacherous, calcified ideology and resorts to a denial of what its own senses know to be true. The false compassion for the welfare of illegal immigrants is patently obvious, as Progressives largely ignore the skyrocketing rate of human trafficking. As such, they are nothing if not complicit in perpetuating this *new slavery*, which is an affront to the human dignity of those for whom they feign such deep concern.

While it is flagrantly prejudicial to broad stroke all illegal immigrants as drug runners and gang members, the criminal element of the approximately twelve million illegal immigrants in the U.S. is not insignificant, and cannot be ignored. While most illegal immigrants do not commit crimes once residing in the US, one cannot overlook the fact that every single adult illegal immigrant is a criminal nonetheless based solely on their unlawful entry into the country. Beyond that fact, there is also overwhelming evidence that illegal immigrants are demonstratively more apt to engage in criminal activity than the population as a whole. A thirty-three year study in the State of Arizona has shown a material discrepancy in the rate of criminality by illegal aliens when compared to legal residents *(Undocumented Immigrants, U.S. Citizens, and Convicted Criminals in Arizona: Illegal Aliens, DACA-Age Youth More than Twice as Likely to Be Convicted Criminals; Craig Bannister, January 31, 2018)*. The results of the study "provide a uniquely accurate picture of illegal immigrant crime because it relies on comprehensive state records of every prisoner incarcerated over a 33-year period, delineated by citizenship status…and, unlike other studies, these data do not rely on self-reporting of criminal backgrounds." The study concludes that Arizona's illegal immigrants are "at least 142% more likely to be convicted of crime than other Arizonans; 165% more likely to be convicted of murder; and 189.6% more likely to be convicted of manslaughter…undocumented immigrants are also much more likely to commit sexual offenses against minors, assault, DUI, and armed robbery…45.4% more likely than other criminals to have been gang members, and 133% more likely to receive sentencing enhancements for being classified as dangerous." Furthermore, "if undocumented immigrants committed crime nationally as they do in Arizona, the study finds that, in 2016 alone, they would have been responsible for over 1,000 more murders, 5,200 more rapes, 8,900 more robberies, 25,300 more aggravated assaults, and 26,900 more burglaries than legal US citizens. Those eligible for Deferred Action for Childhood Arrivals (DACA) make up a four times higher percent of the prison population than their share of the overall state population…while illegal immigrants from 15 to 35 years of age make up a little over two percent of the Arizona population, they make up almost 8% of the prison population." There are, of course, other studies that uphold the exact opposite premise, which contend that the illegal immigrant population commits far fewer crimes by rate than the native populations. Whichever studies one may agree with, however, there remains the undisputed fact that illegal immigrants have been responsible for millions of crimes. From 2003-2009, as estimated by the Government Accountability Office (GAO; *Criminal Alien Statistics*, March 2011; Page 21), the approximately 25,000 murders committed by illegal aliens in the U.S. would not have occurred had those aliens not been in the country illegally. Furthermore, all of the 42,000 robberies, 70,000 sexual crimes, 81,000 auto thefts, 85,000 drug offenses, 95,000 weapons offenses, and 213,000 assaults perpetrated by 'undocumented' aliens in during that period would likewise have been erased with the appropriate rejection of illegal immigration and a respect for the sanctity of our borders. Comparisons of the rates of criminal activity between American citizens and illegal aliens is an argument whose sole purpose is deflection, as the rate of serious offenses by illegal immigrants should be zero.

Drug Interdiction

The illegal drug contagion that has plagued America for decades finds its primary origin at the southern border. If we desire a genuine interdiction of the trafficking of illegal drugs and a solution to the widespread ruin they have catalyzed, then we cannot deny that our disregard for weak borders has only lent itself to the interminable devastation. The amount of drugs seized by the US Border patrol is prodigious. According to the Department of Homeland Security, through its office of U.S. Customs and Border

Protection, patrol agents confiscated, in only one year, the following volume of drugs (*CPB Enforcement Statistics, FY2017*): 9,346 pounds of cocaine; 953 pounds of heroin; 861,231 pounds of marijuana; 10,328 pounds of methamphetamine; and 181 pounds of fentanyl. Considering our willfully thinned and perforated borders, one can only imagine the quantities of drugs that elude detection and consequently destroy countless lives throughout our nation. Those who condone weak borders are complicit in this tragic drug infestation.

Gang Activity

Possibly the most atrocious example of the depredation that illegal immigration has had on the safety and welfare of American citizens is found in the many gangs terrorizing cities and towns throughout the country. According to FBI statistics, there are over 33,000 active gangs with over 1.4 million members operating within the US. While there are no exact numbers, as they would be virtuously impossible to track accurately, the FBI estimates that in some sections of the country up to 80% of gang members are illegal immigrants (FBI: 2013 National Gang Report: *Gangs and the U.S. Border*). The most notorious and dangerous of these gangs is MS-13, which has a presence in nearly every major metropolitan area in the country. In a detailed report in 2020 on the current threat pose by MS-13, the Department of Justice has quantified the number of MS-13 gang members who are illegal immigrants at seventy-four percent (Department of Justice; *Full-Scale Response: A Report on the Department of Justice's Efforts to Combat MS-13 from 2016-*

2020). As evidence of its pervasive presence, MS-13 actually took over a small town (Mendota, California), a base camp within our own country, from where it orchestrated its mafia-like criminal activity. While committing a multitude of violent crimes in America, including "drug-related crimes, weapons proliferation, alien smuggling, human trafficking, murder for hire, prostitution, extortion, robbery, auto theft, assault, homicide, racketeering, and money laundering," MS-13, with an estimated US membership of over ten thousand, has taken advantage of weak borders, DACA, and sanctuary cities, and, supported by the treasonous appeasement of many Progressive leaning government officials, has been afforded safe haven within the borders of our own country for nearly forty years. Some members are now second generation, and by virtue of the legally unsound concept of *'jus soli,'* they are now afforded citizenship simply because they were born on American soil. The fact that this cancer has been allowed to metastasize to the point of a practically impossible eradication lends itself to the blindness of our illegal immigration policies.

Criminal Sanctuary

The practice of offering sanctuary to lawbreakers has become fashionable in our post 'law and order' culture. When elected or appointed officials extend that refuge, however, it is nothing short of subversion. When that subversion aids and abets violent acts against the person and property of the citizenry, it clearly becomes an act of sedition by directly inciting revolt against legitimate federal law, and by presenting a 'clear and present danger' to the safety

and well-being of those the law was meant to protect. 'Sanctuary'
communities, towns, cities, and even states are shielding criminals
with impunity. Astonishingly, the mayor of Oakland, California, has
publicly warned illegal aliens of impending Immigration and
Customs Enforcement raids. Simultaneously brazen, felonious and
irresponsible, the fact that a public servant would so easily break the
law, so insolently betray his or her first obligation to their oath of
office, and not be held accountable, is bearable only by a thoroughly
diminished culture. If government employees and municipalities are
immune to certain federal law, law granted its power by specific
enumeration as proscribed in the Constitution, why are any of us
bound by duly enacted legislation? According to the Center for
Immigration Studies, there are over two hundred sanctuary cities in
the United States. Many now offer illegal immigrants welfare, free
education, subsidized housing, and other benefits that are paid for
with the taxes of legal citizens. Nationwide, Progressives propose
to cover all illegal immigrants for free under the Affordable Care Act,
yet legislated that American citizens be fined for not paying into the
same. In Los Angeles County alone, $1.3 billion in illegal immigrant
welfare was paid out during 2015 and 2016 (LA County Department
of Public Social Services).

Beyond the fiscal irresponsibility, there are many cases where
welcoming illegal entry, ignoring federal detention orders, or actual
deportation/reentry has had disastrous effects:

> Kate Steinle, walking with her father on a pier in San
> Francisco in July, 2015, was shot and killed by Jose Ines
> Garcia Zarate (a.k.a. Francisco Sanchez), an illegal

immigrant who had been deported five times and had seven prior felony convictions.

Jean Jacques, an illegal immigrant who had been previously arrested for attempted murder and was released back into the population after three parole violations, murdered Casey Chadwick, a young Connecticut woman, in 2015.

Also in 2015, Margaret Kostelnik was murdered in her Ohio home by Juan Emanuel Razo, an illegal immigrant picked up by authorities and released only two weeks before. Mr. Razo also confessed to raping a fourteen-year old girl and shooting another woman in front of her two children.

"Johnny" Josue Sanchez murdered five people in 2016. In 2012, Mr.Sanchez was arrested for illegally entering the country…he was released the next day. In January of 2016, Mr. Sanchez was arrested for domestic violence…he was promptly released. In May 2016, Mr. Sanchez was arrested for drug possession…he was promptly released. In June 2016, Mr. Sanchez was again arrested for drug possession…he was released the next day. One week later Mr. Sanchez allegedly set fire to a building in which five people died.

Luis Bracamontes entered the country illegally in the mid-1990s. He was deported in 1997. He reentered the country illegally within two years, and was again deported in 2001. Within a year he was back in the US, and stayed for nearly a decade while committing numerous misdemeanor crimes. In

2014, Mr. Bracamontes killed two police officers in cold blood.

In 2017, Luis Rodrigo Perez was arrested on domestic violence charges in Middlesex County, New Jersey. ICE issued a detainer warrant on Mr. Perez for deportation. Middlesex County, being a sanctuary for illegal immigrants, has a non-compliance policy with ICE, and released Mr. Perez without notifying the feds. Mr. Perez subsequently murdered three innocent American citizens.

Rene Ramos-Hernandez, an illegal alien from Montgomery County, Maryland is accused of raping a seven-year old girl multiple times from 2002-2003. He was finally apprehended in 2020 and charged with two counts of second-degree rape and one count of sexual abuse of a minor. On June 18 he was booked at the Montgomery County Detention Center, and on the following day ICE filed a detainer warrant. Montgomery, a sanctuary county, ignored the detainer and granted bond to Mr. Ramos-Hernandez who subsequently skipped bail and is now a fugitive.

These are not merely infrequent, anecdotal incidents. In 2011, the Government Accountability Office reported that 215,000 criminal aliens in federal, state, and local prisons had been arrested nearly 1.7 million times for close to 3 million criminal offenses (GAO: Criminal Alien Statistics; *Information on Incarcerations, Arrests and Costs;* March 2011). In 2015 alone, nearly 20,000 illegal immigrants were released from prison, and many committed subsequent crimes including murder, sexual assault, domestic violence, arson, human trafficking, child abuse, aggravated assault, fatal hit and run, burglary, forgery, intimidation, identity theft, possession of a dangerous weapon, intimidation, and drug trafficking – each and every crime easily preventable. This goes beyond mere insanity…it is clear negligence in Constitutional duty, not to mention obvious criminal malfeasance, as sanctuary that is extended to illegal aliens by government servants has become sanctuary denied to those they took an oath to serve.

Although there is a debate as to whether or not illegal immigrants have full Constitutional rights under US law, they do unquestionably retain human rights. The extent of these rights, however, is a point of contention between the "open border" segment of Americans and those that subscribe to a stricter adherence with immigration law. The former favor the removal of any obstacle that may prevent a massive inundation of immigrants. They reject any barriers, any laws, any attempts at all to control the nation's borders, with the obvious result (and intent) being cultural erosion and the demise of a nation. The detention of immigrants caught illegally entering the country is considered a human rights atrocity. These 'social justice warriors' claim to favor what they perceive as the more humane practice of allowing illegal aliens to enter society with the only precondition being that they will promise to appear before an immigration judge when there case is adjudicated. The 'Immigration and Customs Enforcement' Agency (ICE), however, has determined that an overwhelming majority of illegal immigrants 'caught and released' never appear before the courts as they have promised. In a 2003 ICE report, *Endgame: Office of Detention and Removal Strategic Plan, 2003-2012,* the agency claims that only 15% of illegal aliens make the mandatory court appearance. With 85 out of 100 aliens breaking the law (for the second time, no less), the common sense response would be to detain them to ensure compliance. Such a response is not a violation of human rights, but a legitimate reaction to their proven widespread disrespect for US law, and yet another in a long list of reasons to secure our nation's borders.

Invasive Asylum

As it relates to US asylum policy, the normalization and acceptance of lawbreaking persists, and is often accompanied with mendacious claims by a significant number of those requesting asylum. From fiscal years 2009 to 2016, the number of potential 'credible fear' asylum cases increased by over 1600% (from 5,523 cases in 2009 to 92,071 cases in 2016: US Citizenship and Immigration Services, *Credible Fear Workload Report Summary*; April 25, 2018). The only evidence presented in nearly all of these cases was the sworn testimony of individual applicants, with no corroboration. The number of cases granted asylum by USCIS in 2016 totaled 20,455 individuals, which represented only 22% of the 92,071 claims (US Department of Homeland Security-Office of Immigration Statistics, *2016 Yearbook of Immigration Statistics: Table 16)*. A full 78% of claims were deemed unworthy of consideration. Asylum requests that were adjudicated by a federal immigration judge in FY2016 totaled 22,186 individuals. Of those, a mere 9,627 were granted, leaving 57% to have been without cause (TRAC Immigration, *Continued Rise in Asylum Denial Rates;* Table

1: Immigration Court Decisions to Grant or Deny Asylum; December 13, 2016). As testament to our largely broken and ineffective refugee/asylum policies, there is very little good faith evidence that a majority of claims are legitimate. The resources required to vet the massive increase in false claims results in burdensome processing delays to the detriment of legitimate claimants. When nearly three-fourths of all asylum requests are determined to be unfounded, there can be no 'compassionate' benefit of the doubt given to persistent lawbreakers and their less than candid testimony.

The resulting convolution has led to serious challenges in the implementation of refugee programs. When asylum requests involve the children of potential refugees, however, the challenges become even more complex. America has always been solicitous to the plight of those legitimately seeking refuge, more so than any other nation, especially in regards to children. Asylum policy, however, must be ordered, not chaotic, and administered effectively with transparent regulation that benefits both refugee and host. The recent wall-to-wall news coverage of the separation of asylum seekers from their children is a drama created and perpetuated by those who would remove any barriers to uncontrolled immigration/asylum. As immigration law now stands, those seeking asylum can enter the country anywhere along the border, not only at official 'points of entry.' They are afforded an entire year to present themselves to government officials. During that time, up until their court hearing, they have typically been released inside the US under their own recognizance, with the aforementioned, and rarely kept, promise of appearing before an immigration judge. More recently, due to their own unwillingness to abide by US law, they have been detained to prevent their widespread defiance. Under this scenario, those entering with children must either be held with those children, or separated, with their children's welfare being secured by the US government. As a response to the placement of minors in detention facilities with their parents, Progressive activists decried the practice with images of young children in 'cages,' and demanded that they be released. When the children were released, the same activists decried that practice as well, with images of babies being 'ripped from their mothers' arms.' Neither situation is acceptable to those espousing unqualified immigration and asylum policy. Children must not be separated from their parents, yet children must not be detained with their parents either. The false narrative that asylum policy is tearing families apart is an emotional ploy too easy to take advantage of by those who feign moral indignation - the same individuals who endorsed the practice to begin with, and the same individuals who only seek unrestrained immigration as a means of maximizing cultural upheaval. What *is* tearing families apart are the calculated decisions made by the parents/legal guardians of their own children, with active encouragement and condonation by domestic enemies of our nation's sovereignty. The outcome is based solely on the choice of the immigrant. It is not the laws that are callous, but a majority of the parents who are willfully breaking the laws and putting their own children in jeopardy of either detention or separation.

Immigrants falsely claiming asylum, in conjunction with open border activists and a collusive media, leverage the moral emotions of Americans and often exploit their own children as mere strategy in the rejection of American sovereignty. Anyone with even a minimal perceptive capacity should be able to clearly see through the smokescreen of incongruous and self-serving moral outrage. A large percentage of the populace, however, those either jaded by ideology or as an accomplice to deceit, refuse to acknowledge the obvious pretension. Those who desire to flee their countries of origin, often with the aid of their own governments and the prompting of some groups within the US, have been emboldened by weak American borders, and have exploited the even weaker commitment of floundering US immigration policy. As such, many have set off en masse to take advantage of a compassionate neighbor. We have an ethical obligation to assist those who seek asylum for legitimate reasons. We have no obligation to assist those who break immigration law and resort to specious claims of asylum just because they happened to be caught crossing the border illegally.

After a rash of immigrants seeking asylum entered the US with their children in 2018, the federal government, bowing to hypocritical tirades and activist judges, attempted to reunite illegal immigrant parents with separated children under the age of five. There were a total of 103 such cases, and nearly half of them (47) involved adults who were not even the parent of an accompanied child, and other illegal immigrants with "serious criminal histories, including charges or convictions for child cruelty, kidnapping, murder, human smuggling and domestic violence" (Joint statement by Health and Human Services Secretary, Homeland Security Secretary and US Attorney General; July 9, 2018). In typical journalistic misrepresentation, the headlines screamed that the government was responsible for a humanitarian crisis by reuniting less than half of all 'migrant parents' with their 'children' under five years of age, while burying the fact that the other half had criminal histories and/or were not even the parents of the children, as claimed. More dangerous than the substantiated perils posed by illegal immigration and asylum abuse are the treasonable lies plotting their progression.

Compassion for the plight of immigrants has rightfully been a national character trait from the earliest days of America's founding. The welfare of American citizens, however, is our government's first responsibility. When disordered immigration policy begins to neglect that commitment, whether by the overwhelming depletion of economic resources, the upheaval caused by cultural disintegration, or the threat to citizen's safety and well-being, the policies need to be brought back into order. When the obvious detriment of mass illegal immigration - accompanied by dubious claims of asylum, gang activity, criminal behavior, human trafficking, and drug infestation - has verifiably imperiled the citizenry, the government's primary commitment is not compassion for immigrants, but compassion for those it is obligated to protect. As disorienting as it is to sound reasoning, it appears that the only parties against a physical barrier at our borders are drug runners, human traffickers, criminals, gang members, freeloaders, and, oddly enough, leftists in our own country.

Nationalism

If there is one facet of our culture that should place the collective ahead of the individual, it is to be found in a shared national pride, or love of country. American nationalism exceeds the mere emotive sentiments of patriotism as it unequivocally exalts the supremacy of originally inspired, American core values. Nationalism is the collective conviction of the empirical, self-evident proof of the objective worth of nations. Throughout the 20th century, the concept of nationalism mutated, then was vilified, largely due to the ideologies of Nazism, Communism and Islam. Nationalism was then recast as a universal pariah, and it is as such, when used as a pretense for global dominion. A nationalism driven by devotion to colonialism, revenge or a brutish desire for imperial conquest is not real nationalism, but global totalitarianism, a tyrannical devotion that leads to nothing but strife, anarchy and demonstrable cultural inferiority. A nationalism forged by devotion to values - eternal, noble and unconditional virtue - and utilized as a force for good throughout the world, is a nationalism that leads to accord, peace, and demonstrable cultural superiority. Indeed, defective nationalism has predicated wars and global chaos. Beneficent nationalism, however, has prevented, and in some cases, ended, the same.

The American chronicle, singular in its foundational acknowledgement of God's intercession in history and the benediction of a people who are faithful to His commands and worthy of His promises, has warranted this very rendering of beneficent nationalism. That story was never written as a narrative of 'America alone,' but as an America that is largely responsible for the ascendency of civilization itself over the past few centuries. Can anyone imagine the state of the world today minus the grand impact of America's emergence and subsequent effect on world affairs? In spite of her faults, America, as conceived, is a nation unrivaled by any other. Any dispassionate observer or unbiased annalist cannot sort through the history of cultures without reaching that very conclusion. The blessings of being born to this heritage, to this 'shining city on a hill,' cannot be refuted except by those willfully ignorant of America's standing when compared to all other nations throughout history. The righteous distinction of America can only be denied by those despising the notion of objective truth and the relative worth of constitutions – the idyllic longing of Progressives. The rejection of nationalism in America has paralleled the advancing repudiation of her very founding, tragically enough, in many cases, by her own citizens. "Take away the heritage of a people and they are easily conquered" (Karl Marx).

American nationalism plateaued decades ago and, more recently, has virtually disappeared, having been rendered a negative cultural trait. For a country to welcome so many from disparate cultures, ethnicities and backgrounds, and yet remain unified in its cultural identity, is historically unprecedented and an astonishing feat, especially over the long-term. The fact that America had accomplished that very goal for over 200 years is a testament to the passion of a unique nationalism once shared by a vast majority of her citizens, both native and immigrant. This was the same passion that inspired patriots to 'pledge their lives, their fortunes, and their sacred honor' against extreme odds; the same passion that ended slavery and healed a divided country; and, the same passion that emboldened soldiers who, in defense of American ideals, freely made the ultimate sacrifice on the beaches and plains of foreign lands. America, unlike most other nations of the world, is, and always has been, a melting pot of ethnicities, and, therefore, has no specific ethnic identity. In its stead, America cultivated a transcendent nationalism that surpasses ethnicity, or any delineation based on place and time. America is much more than a country held fast by boundary or mere custom. America is a promise and a hope, the guardian of 'truths that are self-evident,' and the first nation in history to codify in its founding documents the dignity and integrity of the person. There are times when *Americans* do not live up to such lofty expectations, yet *America* retains this deposit of truth in safekeeping until we, as a people, perceive once again that all of mankind is made in the image and likeness of God. This is the true *American Dream*…our inheritance, our aspiration, and the bedrock of our passions.

Regrettably, however, our current passions seem to be defined more by disgust and shame, actually transforming into an entrenched hatred of America by many of her own sons and daughters. It now takes an act of courage to stand for the American flag. Popularized attacks on many national symbols and social mores has only served to undermine the once respected values of American history and culture. The brunt of the violence has been shouldered by inanimate statues, but has also been directed at religious emblems, holidays, school and college names, and even street designations. Not only is there a propensity to radically manipulate many of our cultural holidays, there is also the outright rejection of others. The recent and unprecedented phenomenon of a revisionist American history has left many of our cultural heroes susceptible to scorn and blatant contempt. The toppling of statues, the desecration of portraits, and the aspersion of personal character has left few of our founding ancestors unscathed. None, however, has been impugned as viciously, and inaccurately, as Christopher Columbus, America's original 'founding' father. In addition, George Washington and Thomas Jefferson, even Abraham Lincoln, as well as many other icons of American history, have all been proclaimed as frauds, possessing neither great character nor any redeeming qualities. As such, all statues, plaques, and memorials must be expunged from the cultural landscape, as their presence creates 'discomfort' and an 'unwelcoming atmosphere,' and a persistence of racism and oppression. These men, as all men, were not perfect, but to hyperbolize their perceived flaws while ignoring the voluminous historical testament to their greatness is evidence of factual ignorance and calculated designs. "A tyrant's first battlefield is to rewrite history" (Walter E. Williams). Much like the false pretenses inherent to the 'separation of church and state,' this forced schism between history and culture is of suspect motivation. Obviously, the goal is to purge all cultural relics that have shaped our heritage, but the final objective is not the repudiation of mere symbols and men, but the actual heritage itself. "Every record has been destroyed or falsified, every book has been rewritten, every picture has been repainted, every statue and street and building has been renamed, every date has been altered. And that process is continuing day by day and minute by minute. . . . Nothing exists except an endless present in which the Party is always right" (George Orwell as Winston Smith; *1984).*

There is dishonor against all who have come before us, and disrespect of the many sacrifices they have made, to trivialize the magnificent impact that America has had on the trajectory of human history. Has America been perfect? Absolutely not. Are there dark chapters in her past, and many blemishes that still exist? Yes, definitely. Our historical treatment of Native Americans and African slaves was largely reprehensible. Does a visible scar remain? Yes, but only as a reminder that we, as a people, retain a peremptory duty to ensure that the crimes of our ancestors are not repeated. As Lord Acton, arguably the foremost historian on the concept of liberty, so wisely declared, "if the Past has been an obstacle and a burden, knowledge of the past is the safest and surest emancipation." In some cases, it is not some remnant scar of history, but an open wound, as in the case of our current malice for the unborn. In spite of these defects, when compared to other cultures throughout history, none has ever surpassed America and her once-honored virtues. There has never existed a nation in the long history of peoples and cultures that has had, for most of its existence, as consistent a moral character as America. When confronted with her failures, she consistently returns to the fountainhead of her distinction as affirmed in her original Declaration. "The greatness of America lies not in being more enlightened than any other nation, but rather in her ability to repair her faults" (Alexis de Tocqueville).

While it is healthy and appropriate to feel some collective shame for our country's former behavior in specific circumstances, any guilt, and therefore, any recompense or debt owed, should rest in history with the actual people who committed the atrocities, not with their descendants. Otherwise, every culture would forever owe a debt to every other culture. Virtually every nation in historical perpetuity, in some way or another, has enslaved or abused every other nation. In varying degrees, all are culpable, but only some are held in contempt. Douglas Murray, founder of the British think tank *Centre for Social Cohesion,* points to an example of this 'tyranny of guilt' as he highlights the cultural disintegration of Western Europe: "I've particularly never heard, for instance, that the country of Turkey should [allow] a large infusion of Yorkshiremen or people from Wales, [or] Dublin, in order to not only diversify that country but to make some kind of reparation for the Ottoman Empire." Why is it only western civilization that must pay for the sins of its forefathers? The same duplicitous guilt that has shamed Western Europe into relinquishing her identity, her borders and her security, has already reached out across an ocean and is intent on submerging America with the same chaos, anarchy and cultural disintegration, all under the façade of 'diversity.' Tragically, there are many in America who have joined the deceitful affair, all for the ambition of a globalist cultural hegemony. Irving Kristol, a political journalist and the 'godfather' of neo-conservatism, defined, without apology, the perfidy of those instigating this revolution of diversity, by stating "what these radicals so blandly call multiculturalism is as much a 'war against the West' as Nazism and Stalinism ever were." Hans Sennholz, an economist and author, further describes modern multiculturalism, not as the multi-ethnicity that has so enriched our culture, but as an 'anti'-culturalism that is intent on destroying it: "multiculturalism does not seek the preservation and promotion of many cultures," as its name would imply, but is rather "a counterculturalism which attempts to destroy the moral foundation of American society."

Innate national pride has now been systematically displaced by a forced narrative of national guilt - a guilt fashioned to advance Progressive aspirations. Whether that be race, gender, immigration, or whatever divisive issue is the latest chosen outrage at any given moment, this guilt is not an emotion that we have come to on our own. Our culture has been of late deliberately programmed to wallow in a national reproach for our sins, whether real or not, all to further the advent of globalism. Now embedded in our culture, this repentant value system resides in a darkness that has furthered our youth's affinity for socialism and communism, and has given rise to the social activists, politicians, even leaders of our own country, who now regularly embark on world tours to fervently apologize, repeatedly, for the perception of American transgression. For many, this constant diatribe is not aimed at distinct instances of American injustice, but to a wholesale denigration of her founding and culture, all under the admitted goal of a 'fundamental transformation' of America, which is apparently evolving into the 'fundamental destruction' of America.

We are even blamed, by Progressive zealots in some quarters, for the recent surge of worldwide refugees, with the implication being that we must somehow pay recompense for an unnamed transgression by opening our borders to all, without qualification. We should never ignore or deny our national offenses, but we should also never stand by and allow them to be contrived and then used as ransom for insurgent cultural change. More than any other nation, America has offered, and should continue to wisely extend, quarter to the refugee, aid to the oppressed, and generosity to the underprivileged, but always with pure intentions and not as an artifice for political benefit or cultural manipulation. As such, this is not really about guilt, responsibility, compassion or reparations…it is all by design to further the multiculturalism of the globalist agenda, also known as the complete rejection, and concomitant annihilation, of American nationalism. Granting safe haven to refugees who are fleeing persecution at the hands of abusive governments is commendable, and, within certain constraints, should be the policy of every able, moral culture. Accepting an endless flow of refugees for diversity's sake, or as compensation for the perceived mistreatment of other cultures, with no regard to the host's safety and sovereignty, however, will soon collapse any culture. Under the affectations of a perpetual national guilt, this is exactly the outcome being sought. We are slowly, yet deliberately, being cultivated away from the deep and abiding roots of American nationalism.

Purposely planting a seed of relentless contrition, and fertilizing that seed with a history rewritten, or at least exaggerated and constantly demoralized, is reaping a culture choked by the weeds of an aggressive yet desolate globalism, smothering the once-flourishing heritage of our national goodwill. The current depreciation of our culture's moral stock, accompanied by the premeditated slander of our largely distinguished founding and history, has opened a culture war on two fronts, both instigated and advanced by domestic enemies who promote utter contempt for the passion of American nationalism.

Radical Islam

Our society's perplexed views on racism, immigration, and nationalism, each borne of the diversity promulgated by Progressivism, have fused perfectly into our fatuous embrace of other cultures whose values, in some cases, are antithetical to our own. For an open and free society to welcome cultural ideologies that are anathema to its founding principles is anthropological suicide. When we allow hospitality to also open the door to a radical faction of this same ideology that openly professes a desire to destroy, not only our way of life but also our lives themselves, then, as a people, as a civilization, as a culture, we have either all gone mad or there is an underlying sinister and treacherous intent.

Radical Islam has perverted nearly every culture it has infiltrated, deliberately and with malice. All religions have some shadows of a dark history that have been an enemy to human dignity, but a majority of those were left behind centuries ago. Radical Islam is trapped in a medieval and plundering barbarism, and, as an ideologically invasive species, has as its main tenet the forced conversion of all infidels. The warped precepts of this 'religion of peace' hold violence, slavery, mutilation and brutal murder as its most hallowed rituals. Misogynistic law, honor killings, cruel and unusual punishment, religious persecution, and the exploitation of God Himself as a mere political tool are only a few examples of radical Islam's utter incompatibility with our Constitution. Its 'holy book,' the Qur'an, has no less than fourteen passages that call for the annihilation of all peoples who do not follow Islam. Such directives as "punish the unbelievers with garments of fire, hooked iron rods, boiling water; melt their skin and bellies" (22:19) and "terrorize and behead those who believe in scriptures other than the Qur'an" (8:12), portray a religion that is anything but peaceful. It is one thing to hold ancient manuscripts and practices in religious reverence even though their current context has been denounced by civilized minds; it is quite another to continue fealty to such an unspeakable sadism. Other savage tenets such as rape being defined, not as a crime by men, but as an appropriate response to lust caused by women, as well as the inhumane practice of female genital mutilation, and that possession of a Bible in some Islamic countries is a justified cause for beheading, are just a small sampling of an ideology hostile to American cultural values and incompatible with immigration policy. Throughout American history, from the Barbary pirates to 9/11, there has been no substantive change in the wanton philosophy of radical Islam.

Many communities across America, in weak-kneed appeasement to political correctness, have made many accommodations to Muslims that would not be made to any other alien culture or religious faith. Many incidents are based on religious considerations, which have been at the foundation of America's allegiance to freedom of religion since its founding. Some of these 'welcoming' gestures, however, are at best incongruous, and, at worst, in direct opposition to, our revered sentiments, and actually give distinction to Muslim culture over American values. A few have crossed the lines of religious accommodation and become dictates to which whole segments of society must conform - from rewriting standard mortgage contract laws to specific penta-prayer times in public schools and the workplace…to altering uniforms and dress codes to appease Muslim sensibilities…to banning pork from school menus but adding other specific Muslim diet requirements…to women-only classes and swim times at tax-payer funded universities and public swimming pools…to the demands that special sinks and footbaths be installed in many businesses. The most egregious examples lie in the growing preeminence of 'Sharia' law as it slowly infiltrates American jurisprudence, especially in the area of civil law. What were once mere requests for religious tolerance and accommodation are, in many cases, becoming demands that expect, then mandate, even non-Muslims to observe specific doctrines of a foreign culture and legal system, both of which rely on oppression and violence.

The dominion of Sharia law among radicalized Muslims is reason enough to decline citizenship to its adherents. Since the horrors of 9/11, there have been 28,957 individual acts of deadly Islamic terror worldwide, forty-eight of them within the US (religionofpeace.com; July 2016). These are not murderous acts committed by people who just happen to be of the Islamic faith, but are murderous acts committed by people *because of* their self-proclaimed commitment to the jihad of radical Islam enshrined in Sharia law. At least in theory, our nation rightfully takes pride in the long-held belief that the individual is not guilty based solely on group association (the internment of Japanese-Americans during World War II being one notable exception). As such, no one of sound mind is espousing that we round up all Muslims within the US on suspicion of an affinity for radical Islam. However, ignoring the real and not infrequent occurrences of actual terrorism within the borders of our country, simply based on the mentally deficient concept of 'racial' correctness, is the definition of cultural insanity. Having experienced San Bernardino, Fort Hood, Orlando, World Trade Center1, 9/11, the Boston Marathon, and dozens of other lesser known jihad-inspired attacks on US soil, and with radicals broadcasting their intentions to continue such attacks and to take advantage of porous American borders, common sense would dictate that there is a legitimate cause to deny entry to any Muslim, even if only to prevent entry of those radicalized. There should at least be a strict examination and a thorough vetting of anyone claiming Muslim heritage or practicing the Islamic religion. The radicalized come, not as refugees or immigrants, but as a self-described, invading army. Their emigration from Muslim countries is calculated, not only for purposes of proselytizing and conversion, but primarily for Qur'an-dictated conquest. Our government is charged with protecting its citizens, not with being a tolerant and welcoming host to the culturally subversive designs of a sickening ideology. An immigration policy of heightened attention is sensible and necessary, and non-radicalized Muslims desiring entry should not cast any blame on America but instead on the clear and present danger of their compatriots' murderous zealotry.

Civilization: An Epilogue

There are widely varied meanings of the word 'civilized.' The contemporary definition is synonymous with the terms modern, urban, sophisticated, technological, and advanced. To be 'civilized' is generally considered a positive trait, whether attached to an individual or, more broadly, to a culture. Much like the word 'diverse,' however, this definition is entirely value neutral. There is no inherent goodness in being 'modern', or 'advanced.' Communist China has quickly become 'civilized' and can rightly claim nearly every one of those descriptive adjectives, yet it remains only a softer master of tyranny and oppression. Prior definitions of "civilized" were more closely aligned with the principles of wisdom, morality, virtue, and truth, not as mere abstractions but as the existential prerequisites of a truly enlightened and perfected culture.

   A Conservative civilization is a plexus of these principles. It is built with the integral components of marriage, family, work, education, responsibility, charity, a respect for law, and a passion for self-order – all held fast by a fixed constitution and a manifest, universal moral code. 'One Nation, under God, Indivisible,' marks a civilization in which each member thrives with the purpose, conviction and certitude of comprehensive personal character and organic thought. God is the origin of this apodictic being and, widespread, a civilized people. The absence of God is the origin of a relativistic being and, widespread, a disordered people…leaving us all susceptible to demonic tendencies that are no longer rare and isolated but instead are now decimating our culture with regularity and normality. We all see the symptoms, and the symptoms we fruitlessly attack. We also see the causes, yet the causes we willfully ignore. After each incident of mass murder, government malfeasance, school shooting, opioid death, child abuse, domestic violence, sexual assault, financial crime, youth suicide…we feign incredulity, pass yet more laws, and blame everyone and everything save the one obvious reality that now so thoroughly defiles our culture – the veneration of our immorality and the conscious rejection of our God. How odd it is that the 'enlightenment' of our culture has bastardized our consciousness, our conduit to God, our gift from God. We now use the *gift* to reject the *Giver*. We have become an enemy to that which is good and an ally to that which is evil. America is degenerating into nothing, if not a modern 'Tower of Babel.' Immorality is the drug that has left our culture in a state of denial with a growing immunity to sound judgment and a decaying mental capacity to perceive our own woeful state.

Such is the darkest folly of modern civilization as we contort that which establishes God's existence into that which denies it - the radical rejection of human consciousness and its surety - objective truth. At the core of Conservative ideology, the individual and, by projection, civilization itself, is consummated, not constrained, by objective truth. When one commends the whole of his integrity to the legions, however, he becomes a slave to collective relativism and mere chattel to the master of his affirmed immorality – and he chaperones his culture's descent.

A Progressive civilization will suborn perjury to become the executor of the individual's estate by supplanting 'the laws of nature, and of nature's God,' with a Progressive humanism; by exchanging enduring 'self-evident truths' for the seduction of moral relativism; by surrendering the 'just powers from the consent of the governed' to the soft totalitarianism of aristocratic overlords; by replacing resolute cultural convictions with the ever-evolving whims of time and populism; and by sacrificing morality to beguile the shame of our disavowed conscience. Summarily, Progressivism must dictate the minutiae of life; it alone must define liberty and administrate the pursuit of happiness. Individuals must be arranged, managed and regulated, for the stated claim of their own benefit, by the gods of Progressivism.

The quest for a sophisticated civilization based on Progressive utopianism must subdue, or at least deform, the moral truths. Progressives apprehend the primacy of morality, for it is eternally written on the minds and hearts of every human being engaged with reason. They choose, however, in diabolical rationalization, to deny the universal transcendence of objective morality. Why? *"Our constitution was made only for a moral and religious people. It is wholly inadequate to the government of any other"* (John Adams). Therein lies the answer. Since morality and the Constitution are inseparable, and since the Progressive movement abhors Constitutional principles, by substitution, its denial of morality becomes an imperative. *"Liberty does not exist in the absence of morality"* (Edmund Burke). As morality is *the* prerequisite of individual liberty, and as individual liberty is an anathema to collective philosophy, Progressives will seek to diminish the supremacy of that moral virtue…at a minimum, rendering it relative, and, at a maximum, displacing it with the absolution of vice. They must create chaos, a contrived cultural discord, and a disordered intellection of good and evil - a dystopia where drugs replace religion; where real marriages are cast aside and fake marriages are heralded; where self-sufficiency is greedy, and indefinite welfare for the able-bodied is just; where property rights are racist and oppressive, while politically correct looting and rioting are an expression of social justice; where lust is freedom of expression and modesty is body shaming; where education is not based on a desire to enrich young minds but on a passion to control them; where being a wife and mother is enslaving and abortion is liberating; where police are castigated as inherently evil and criminality is largely a valid response to racism; where the Pledge of Allegiance is xenophobic and protesting the national anthem is brave; where Michael Brown is a martyr but Franklin Graham, Jr. is a pariah; where Christianity is a Medieval relic, oppressive and barbaric, while abortion and euthanasia are Progressive advancements, dignified and compassionate.

With persistence and patience, therefore, Progressivism must continue to promote, sow, construct, distort and redefine; it must promote racism, sexism and unqualified immigration; it must sow anxiety, confusion and turmoil; it must construct an endless list of rights to exonerate personal irresponsibility; it must distort the basic principles of biology and psychology; it must redefine sexuality, gender and marriage. Progressivism must also command, control, disparage, subvert and appropriate; it must command property, capital and labor; it must control education and health; it must disparage law enforcement; it must subvert the economy and science; it must appropriate the media, charity and religion. Progressivism must finally neuter, demonize, confound, debase and sever; it must neuter the cultural potency of parents and family; it must demonize once-honored tradition and history; it must confound independent thought; it must debase entertainment and the arts; it must sever the soul from the body, morality from the conscience, and the Church from the public square. Again, knowing that morality, natural law, and absolute truth are the linchpins of individual sovereignty, it becomes apparent that Progressivism must tirelessly attempt to corrode these connections so as to fracture their bond and to realize, at first, the attenuation of our culture as founded, and, at last, the culmination of its ultimate demise. Progressivism must strike at liberty, autonomy and self-determination - it must strike at God Himself. These are the works, either active or passive, by which one may know Progressivism - the works that threaten liberty and, by calculation, enervate the integrity of the cultural, political and economic pillars of our nation.

In timid response to Progressive activism, based more on cowardice than conviction, a majority of Conservatives treads the ground ever so lightly amidst the cultural landmines that are strategically strewn in every direction, intentionally paralyzing rational mobility. The fear of igniting offense is so purposely engrained in our cultural psyche that we begin to reject common sense and equivocate truth; the ridicule so palpable and widespread that we shrink from confrontation in diffidence; the derision so automatic and contemptuous that we begin to doubt the veracity of our own certitude. Meanwhile, our society rots from within and slides further and further into moral anarchism as the cultural hegemony of America is timidly retreating into the annals of history. "From whence shall we expect the approach of danger? Shall some trans-Atlantic military giant step the earth and crush us at a blow? Never. All the armies of Europe and Asia … could not by force take a drink from the Ohio River or make a track on the Blue Ridge in the trial of a thousand years. No, if destruction be our lot, we must ourselves be its author and finisher. As a nation of free men, we will live forever or die by suicide." (Abraham Lincoln)

In order to salvage the promise of America, a new and unyielding Conservatism must rise from the cultural ash and gird itself with the ties of morality, religious convictions and faith in God, admitting before all else the ultimate futility of any human endeavor without such reliance. All "adjective" Conservatisms must first denounce the tribal and sectarian divisions that have pervaded American Conservatism over the past century and then form a united front under one banner; namely, the flag of self-determination conjoined with objective virtue. Gone must be the schismatic fragmentations of 'post liberal' conservatism, 'social' conservatism, 'free market' conservatism, 'paleo' conservatism, 'reaganite' or 'trumpian' conservatism, 'integralist' conservatism, 'common good' conservatism, and the myriad other disparate 'conservatisms' whose infightings do nothing but ensure our cultural defeat. Neutralizing the pathologies of Progressivism will require organic reactions at all levels of society to catalyze the grand alliance of an overarching 'Aggregate Conservatism.' This phoenix of our Constitutional Republic must not surrender in its fight against Progressivism at the highest levels of our society, yet, in order to wholly prevail and persist, this new Aggregate Conservatism must once again respect the wisdom of subsidiarity by replanting the first seeds of our culture – individuals, families, schools, churches, businesses, communities, and institutions of all kinds – a manifest and resolute defense of our founding covenants which will reclaim our culture and rebuild our beloved country. An Aggregate Constitutional Revolution, echoing from person to person, school board to school board, township to township, city to city, county to county, parish to parish, and state to state, is the only remedy to thwart the tyrannical aspirations of those who despise our birthright of self-governance.

This is a philosophical call to arms, a trumpeting of ideological warfare, and must be bound by courage, for "courage is the ladder on which all the other virtues mount" (Clare Boothe Luce). Far from an overreaction, a conspiracy theory, or Conservative paranoia, there can be no question that now is the time for America to draft yet another Declaration to proclaim, not her independence, but her resolve to return to Providence through the resurrection of her first principles. No more ground can be conceded. Anger is justified, and action is incumbent. *"He who is not angry when there is just cause for anger is immoral, for anger looks to the good of justice. And if you can live amid injustice without anger, you are immoral as well as unjust* (Thomas Aquinas). There can be no compromise, as compromise is neither possible nor propitious. Compromise is simply tantamount to the advancing capitulation of our human freedoms, and our individual destiny. Conservatism and Progressivism are not cultural philosophies of which one is more advantageous than the other by degree, nor are they comprised simply of policy disagreements, civil debate, or deeply held convictions argued in good faith. No, they are on different spectrums. They are diametrically opposed. Progressivism is an insurrection, a violent coup against America's founding, and the latest variation of Communist hegemony. Know thine enemies. *"If ye love wealth better than liberty, the tranquility of servitude better than the animating contest of freedom, go home from us in peace.*

We ask not your counsels or arms. Crouch down and lick the hands which feed you. May your chains set lightly upon you, and may posterity forget that ye were our countrymen" (Samuel Adams). The fate of America, and, in turn, the fate of all mankind, will be determined by the cultural war being waged. America is the ultimate hope, the final frontier of freedom, and the last dying ember of what was once the blazing glory of Western Civilization. *"If we lose freedom here, there is no place to escape to. This is the last stand on earth"* (Ronald Reagan).

Of Hope and Reality

*On the first day was Hope
Akin to the primal waters of creation
A vacuum of perfection, a vastness without space
The precursor of purpose...the ideal of life*

*On the second day was Reality
Symmetrical to the properties of barren sands
A wealth of wantonness, impoverished by ignorance
The cradle of complacency...the futility of life*

*On the third day was a Commingling
As the waters shall disperse, cleanse and propagate
As the sands shall be enriched, hopeful and perceptive
The whole of humanity...the meaning of life*

"I believe that unarmed truth and unconditional love will have the final word in reality. This is why right, temporarily defeated, is stronger than evil triumphant."

~ Martin Luther King, JR ~

"If my people, which are called by my name, shall humble themselves, and pray, and seek my face, and turn from their wicked ways; then will I hear from heaven, and will forgive their sin, and will heal their land."

~ 2 Chronicles 7:14 ~